LANDSCAPES OF BRITAIN

THE WEST MIDLANDS

Other LANDSCAPES OF BRITAIN

THE SOUTH-WEST PENINSULA
SOUTH-EAST ENGLAND
THE WELSH MARCHES

LANDSCAPES OF BRITAIN

THE WEST MIDLANDS

Roy Millward and Adrian Robinson

MACMILLAN

First published by Macmillan and Co. Ltd. 1971

Published by
MACMILLAN AND CO LTD
London and Basingstoke
Associated companies in New York, Toronto, Dublin, Melbourne, Johannesburg and Madras

Printed in Great Britain by
FLETCHER AND SON LTD
Norwich

To H. P. R. FINBERG

Contents

Acknowledgments

THE authors wish to thank the following for permission to reproduce the photographs listed below: Aerofilms Limited, Plates 1, 5, 7, 8, 9, 10, 11, 13, 14, 15, 16, 17, 1a, 2e, 3b, 3g, 4b, 4d, 5e, 6b, 6d, 7e, 8a, 11b, 11e, 11f, 12d; Dr J. K. St Joseph, Plates 2c, 5c, 7d, 9a, 9c and 11c. They are also indebted to Mr Roger Richards, who prepared prints from the author's own photographs, and to his wife, Suzanne, who typed the manuscript.

Introduction

The West Midlands is one of a series of volumes that tries to make a fresh approach to the study of the regional landscapes of the British Isles. The main part of the book consists of a dozen individual studies taken from the country that lies between the Cotswolds and the south-western fringe of the Pennines. Each study takes as its theme the analysis of the present landscape and arises out of investigations carried out in the field supplemented by information contained in the relevant literature. As an appendix to each essay, with its photographs and sketch-maps, we have made suggestions for field excursions and further work. It is hoped that by the pursuit of these methods a depth of understanding will be achieved in regional studies that will reveal the Midland landscapes as a product both of natural forces and the work of man during the past five thousand years. Taken together the individual studies epitomize the chief features of this major region of the West Midlands.

In order to fit the details of local history and geography into the wider framework of the West Midland region, the book begins with a long introductory essay that treats some of the basic ideas in the landscape-history of the area. Here many places and topics that have been left out of the sample studies are touched upon, and it is hoped that the reader will be able to use these paragraphs for the planning of further field excursions and investigations. The book demands an extensive use of the one-inch and $2\frac{1}{2}$-inch maps of the Ordnance Survey, but we have added sketch-maps and diagrams to aid in the understanding of the text when these are not available. Almost all the places and objects mentioned in the book are located by Ordnance Survey grid-references to allow their easy discovery in the field. By adopting this approach we hope that readers will be led to an understanding of the present environment in terms of a complex set of inter-related factors stemming from several disciplines. Perhaps, too, it will be appreciated that the drab often squalid scenes that characterize parts of the Black Country are no less interesting in their own way than the smooth elegance of a Cotswold parish.

R. M.;A. R.

Part One The Physical and Human Setting of the West Midlands

A Transect across the Region

The landscape of the West Midlands is one of abrupt contrasts. From the Cotswold edge in the south-east to the Pennine foothills in the north, or from the Severn Plain in the west to the less well-defined boundary of Watling Street in the north-east, the pleasant lowland country of green fields and trimmed hedgerows is punctured in places by upstanding masses where older and harder rocks break through the cover of red marls. These may vary from the flat-topped plateau of Cannock Chase to the almost knife-edge ridge of limestone around Dudley in the Black Country. Not only has each of these isolated blocks of country its own characteristic scenery and land-use but in many cases it can look back on a distinctive history which finds expression in the individuality and independence of the people living there. Until quite recently many of these small regions retained their own customs and way of life. Although this is fast disappearing, their physical identity still remains even though man is now changing the natural landscape at a quicker rate than at any time in the past.

Nowhere is the role of different rock types in creating individual elements in the landscape more apparent than in a south-to-north transect across the region from the Cotswolds to the Potteries (Fig. 1). A convenient starting-point in the south is where Cleeve Hill (SO 9826), close to Cheltenham, thrusts out from the main line of the Cotswolds scarp. Here, at a height of over a thousand feet, the flat plateau top falls away sharply to give good views over the Severn Lowlands (Pl. 1). During the Ice Age the oolitic rocks of the top of the scarp were shattered by frost action and moved bodily downhill as a wet sludge. Extensive accumulations of this angular debris (head) occur at many points along the foot of the Cotswolds where it often forms a broad shelf, like that south of Bishop's Cleeve (SO 9627) and around Gotherington (SO 9629).

From the ramparts of the Iron Age hill-fort on Nottingham Hill (SO 9828) there are extensive views northwards across the Avon Valley and Vale of Evesham. Close by are the small outliers of the Cotswolds like Oxenton Hill (SO 9731) and Dumbleton Hill (SP 0035), each with their capping of resistant rock. On a larger scale is Bredon Hill (SO 9640) whose western face is familiar to every rail traveller between Birmingham and Bristol. The capping of Inferior Oolite is sufficiently thick to form a broad plateau surface on top. Rising as it does almost a thousand feet out of

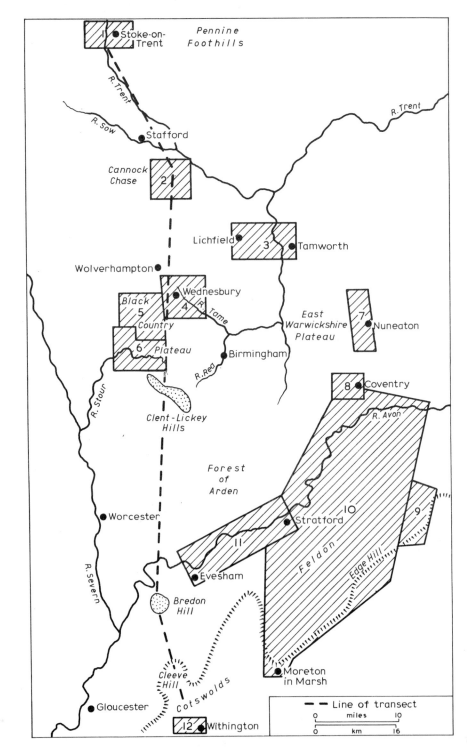

Fig. 1   The West Midlands, showing the location of the sample studies

the Avon Valley, it has steep slopes on every side. Mass movements of rock debris still occur from time to time. Both in 1930 and 1951 localised mud-flows occurred when water percolated through the oolite capping and then lubricated the underlying clay. As a result great patches of hummocky ground cover the upper slopes around the northern and western sides of the hill. Like the adjacent Cotswold scarp, Bredon Hill also has its extensive spreads of gravel around its foot, formed by downwash during the Ice Age. They are most extensive to the south of the hill near the village of Overbury (SO 9537). On the west and north sides of the hill the corresponding spreads of solifluction deposits are more fragmentary and soon give way to the river terraces of the Avon Valley (Fig. 2). The terrace remnants are particularly well preserved in this section and like their counterparts farther upstream (Study 11) they form an ascending staircase with marked breaks of slope between the individual treads. Not all the five terraces which occur in the Avon Valley are present in any one cross-section, and here near Pershore (SO 9445) it is the two lowest terraces which are best developed, with number 4 terrace also prominent on the north side of the valley. In addition to providing excellent land for market gardening, the terraces close to the river make favourable dry sites for settlements like Pershore and Fladbury (SO 9946).

Continuing the transect northward of the Avon Valley, the countryside has the appearance which many regard as typical of the English Midlands. Although close to the main English watershed, the land is usually below 500 feet. The Keuper Marl and Lias Clays everywhere give rise to a landscape of subdued relief – pleasant though not exciting country. Only where the Arden Sandstone outcrops, as around Inkberrow (SP 0157), is there any break in the general monotony of the scenery, and even this formation only gives rise to minor scarps. This type of

Plate 1

*Cleeve Hill:
a northward-projecting
spur from the main
mass of the Cotswolds,
now considerably scarred
by stone quarries*
(SO 9826)

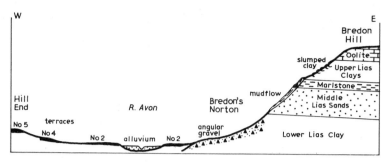

Fig. 2   A cross-profile from Bredon Hill northwards across the terraces of the Avon Valley

country extends for a considerable distance to the east and north-east, a 'land gently creased and dimpled like a ruffled sheet of troubled water'. The clays once carried extensive oak-woods, and names like 'Forest of Arden' and 'The Weldon' (wooded country) are variously applied to the area. Where the narrow thread of the Arden Sandstone intervenes, between Alcester (SP 0857) and Knowle (SP 1876), the low scarps once again add diversity to the scenery and land-use.

Beyond the Avon Valley to the south-east lies the Feldon or open country, a land of richer and more varied soils which was cleared for cultivation at a much earlier date than the Forest of Arden. The country is more undulating, with harder rock beds adding diversity to the scenery. The White Lias limestone, in particular, gives rise to an outer rim of low hills in front of the more impressive marlstone scarp of the Cotswolds beyond. The limestone belt was favoured for early settlement because of the drier sites it afforded and the base-rich soils which were more easily cultivated than the heavy Lias Clays around. Since the last century the limestone has been extensively quarried for cement-making at a number of places like Bishop's Itchington (SP 3958). The outer edge of the Feldon is clearly marked by the marlstone scarp which reaches its greatest development at Edge Hill (SP 3747) where it is over 700 feet high (Pl. 2). Elsewhere the marlstone forms isolated hills like Napton (SP 4661) which rise sharply from the lowland of the Lower Lias Clays

Plate 2   Edge Hill: the Marlstone escarpment from the Lias Clay vale. In the foreground ridge-and-furrow indicates the site of a former open field of Radway. Immediately under the scarp is a remnant of the shoreline beach of glacial Lake Harrison (SP 377488).

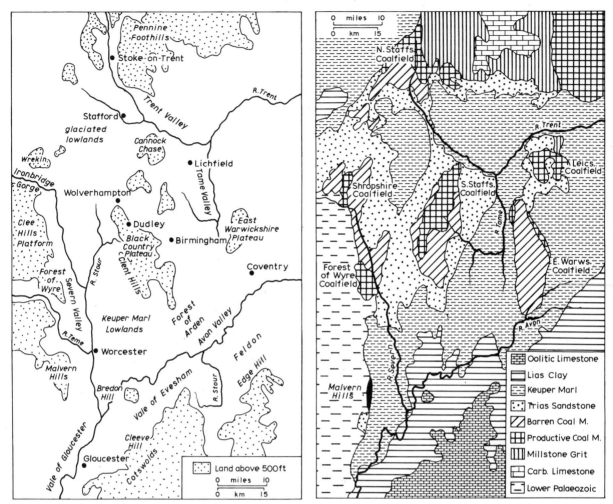

Fig. 3   *The main relief features and sub-regions of the West Midlands*

Fig. 4   *A simplified geological map of the West Midlands*

and add variety to what otherwise would be a very dull landscape. Villages like Priors Hardwick (SP 4756) with their warm, almost orange-coloured, stone houses also contribute to the richness of the Feldon landscape. The whole area of the Feldon and Forest of Arden was once part of the floor of glacial Lake Harrison (Study 10). Minor breaks in the line of the marlstone scarp as near Daventry, Fenny Compton and Avon Dassett were used at various times by the overflow waters from the lake and today they form wide, open valleys with tiny misfit streams running through them.

Resuming the line of our south-to-north transect which has been chosen to bring out the diversity of the Midland landscape, one of the more distinctive small regions, that of the Clent and Lickey Hills, is crossed. Rising to over a thousand feet at Walton Hill (SO 9479), the ridge owes its prominence to the hard beds of Clent Breccia and Cambrian Quartzite. The breccia outcrops mainly in the Clent Hills (SO 9379) where it forms a prominent scarp overlooking the Birmingham Plateau to the north. The hills are greatly dissected by dry valleys which have eaten deeply into the margins. The valleys were probably formed under periglacial conditions when there was much more surface water available for erosion. In addition partially frozen masses of sludge would move slowly downhill. Spreads of angular solifluction debris occur at the lower ends of many of the Clent valleys and this would seem to confirm that periglacial processes have played an important part in etching the present details of the hills. The breccia gives rise to a thin and impoverished soil, and much of the country is covered with heath. Its closeness to Birmingham and the Black Country has meant that it acts as a lung for the conurbation. The same is true on a smaller scale for the near-by Lickey Hills where the quartzite forms a narrow ridge running almost north and south (SO 9975). At its lower, southern end the ridge is crossed by the main Birmingham-to-Bristol railway line which had to overcome steep gradients on the famous Lickey incline.

The upstanding country of the Clent and Lickey Hills is more than simply a topographic break between the red marl lowlands to the south and the Birmingham Plateau to the north. It also marks the boundary between the rural south with its green fields, thorn hedgerows and occasional trees of ash and elm, and the man-made desolation of the industrial Black Country to the north. The break is everywhere abrupt as it coincides with the faulted edge of the South Staffordshire Coalfield on which the industrial prosperity of the 'heartland' of the West Midlands was once based. Topographically the Black Country forms a plateau 500–700 feet high. On its south-west side it is bounded by the Stour Valley around Halesowen (SO 9582) and Amblecote (SO 8985), while the Tame Valley around Wednesbury (SO 9895) and Darlaston (SO 9897) forms its north-eastern margin. Running across the centre of the plateau is the broken ridge formed by the basalt of Rowley Regis with Turner's Hill (SO 9688) rising to 876 feet, the Silurian limestone of Castle Hill at Dudley (9490), Wren's Nest Hill (9391) and Sedgley Beacon (9193) (Study 5). The inliers of limestone projecting through the cover of more recent rocks do not form a continuous outcrop but are staggered in a general north-west to south-east direction. Because of their hardness and faulted boundaries, each of these limestone outcrops forms a distinct ridge towering above the surrounding plateau. No more abrupt boundary occurs in the whole of the West Midlands than at Dudley where the wooded slopes around the castle look down over the tormented landscape of the industrial past at Tipton and Dudley Port (9591) – a green oasis in a man-made desert.

The Black Country Plateau, with its backbone ridge formed by the Silurian limestone and the Rowley Regis basalt, has its counterpart in east Warwickshire. Beyond the Tame Valley lies a plateau at about 500–600 feet which is largely co-

*Plate 3 Satnall Hills: a through-valley cuts across the northern edge of Cannock
Chase and is used by the main road from Rugeley to Stafford. Self-seeded birch
in the foreground contrasts with planted woodland on the opposite slope.*

incident with the syncline of the east Warwickshire Coalfield. On its eastern margin
an anticline brings much older rocks than the Coal Measures to the surface, and
between Bedworth (SP 3687) and Oldbury (SP 3194) both diorite and quartzite
occur. The hard Cambrian Quartzite – the equivalent of the rock of the Lickey
Hills – makes a marked impression on the landscape, especially north-west of
Nuneaton where it forms a hog's back ridge between the coalfield to the west and
the subdued and rather monotonous marl country of Leicestershire to the east
(Study 7).

One of the more distinctive small regions within the West Midlands is Cannock
Chase. It rises quite sharply from the Black Country Plateau to the south, and at
Castle Ring (SK 0412), its highest point, it reaches almost 800 feet. Apart from a
small segment in the south-east where the Coal Measures outcrop, the whole of
the Chase is formed of the Bunter Pebble Beds. These give rise to thin, infertile,
stony soils which until the extensive plantings by the Forestry Commission during
the past forty years were largely under heath (Study 2). The whole area is threaded
with deep valleys, most of which are now dry. These developed during the Ice Age
either as overflow channels, like that between Hednesford (SK 0013) and Rugeley
(SK 0417) from an impounded lake, or as ice-marginal channels cut by escaping

waters flowing parallel to the ice margin like those around Milford (SJ 9721) at the northern end of the Chase (Pl. 3). Many of the short valleys which run into the steep edge of the plateau, especially along the Trent Valley, are the result of periglacial erosion with the Bunter Pebble Beds rapidly succumbing to the freeze–thaw processes and massive flows of sludge towards lower levels. The short, blind valleys with their ribbed slopes covered with bracken, heather and shivering grass add greatly to the scenic attraction of the area. Like the Clent and Lickey Hills to the south of the Black Country, Cannock Chase acts as a week-end playground for many thousands of people from the industrial conurbations. Again it is a case of the fortunate co-incidence of two very different rock types in close proximity, one with thick beds of coal forming the basis of industrial growth and the other consisting of barren beds left as open country, now such a valuable asset to the region.

Much of the West Midlands is close to the main watershed of England and as a result there are few major river valleys. The exceptions are the Severn Valley which forms the western boundary and the Trent Valley which runs across the north-east corner of the region. On our south-to-north transect it is the latter valley which is now entered north of Cannock Chase. Here the river is running through typically undulating country which is often associated with the Keuper Marl. Although the valley-side bluffs are fairly steep, especially where harder sand-stone beds are met, the Trent Valley is quite unlike the deep and often gorge-like valley of the Severn. This distinction reflects the different history of the two river-systems in recent geological times, especially during the Ice Age. Whereas the Severn and its tributaries were rejuvenated following the diversion of a vast flow of water through the Ironbridge gorge – water which formerly flowed north to the Dee – there is no comparable episode in the history of the Trent. The terrace features of the Trent are usually narrow in this section of its course and the present flood plain is seldom more than a quarter of a mile in width. This reflects the fairly rapid flow of the river, whose bed drops on average ten feet a mile between Stoke and Shugborough (SJ 9922), where the tributary River Sow enters the Trent. Down-stream from this junction the river becomes more sluggish, wending its way across an increasingly widening flood plain, often flooded after heavy rain.

The transect of the length of the West Midlands ends in the Potteries. Here, as in many other parts of the region, the presence of the North Staffordshire Coalfield has completely transformed the natural landscape. Spoil-heaps and deep clay-pits intermingle with the pottery kilns and steel-works, and now dominate what before the Industrial Revolution must have been a pleasant section of the upper Trent Valley. In this headwater sector the valley is more deeply intrenched than elsewhere, partly due to the presence of more resistant rocks associated with the coalfield formations. Its closeness to the Pennines is emphasised by the presence of Millstone Grit which outcrops in an inverted V around the margins of the coal-field syncline. The hard grit bands are especially prominent where an anticline

16

brings them to the surface. Here they form pronounced, west-facing scarps like Brown Edge (SJ 9054), rising to 888 feet, and Baddeley Edge (9150), which reaches 787 feet at its highest point. Valleys like that used by the headstreams of the Trent (8953) are cut in the softer shales below the grit escarpments. On the western side of the triangular coalfield, Mow Cop (8557), rising to well over a thousand feet, is another of the gritstone ridges. The view from the sham eighteenth century castle ruins westwards across the Cheshire Plain is very different from that south and west across the Potteries, and serves as a reminder that here the West Midlands end just as abruptly as they begin at the Cotswolds scarp, the beginning of our transect.

Glaciation

Although the main features of the West Midlands landscape, particularly the islands of old, hard rock, had emerged long before the onset of the Ice Age, glaciation acted as both chisel and plane in putting the final impress on the scenery as we see it today. Only in the case of drainage development was there a fundamental change during the Ice Age leading to the creation of whole new drainage basins as a result of ice interference. During the various glacial phases, the West Midlands formed a cockpit hotly contested by different ice masses coming into the region from many points of the compass. From the east and north-east, the ice sheet from the North Sea encroached on the area bringing with it easily recognisable rock erratics like limestone, chalk, marlstone and the distinctive Mountsorrel granite to betray its place of origin. This eastern drift is characteristic of most of east Warwickshire where it forms rather featureless boulder-clay country for the most part. Around Coventry, however, at places like Baginton (SP 3474) and Ryton (3874), are vast spreads of glacial gravels and sands which have been extensively worked in shallow pits. These deposits represent the outwash of an ice sheet which lay only a short distance away to the north-east. This Eastern Ice, after laying down a succession of glacial and glacio-fluvial deposits, moved farther south and ultimately came to rest just north of Moreton in Marsh where its limits are marked by a fairly distinct end-moraine and associated outwash fan (Study 10).

The other main invasion of ice into the West Midlands came from a westerly and north-westerly direction. That from the west was mainly local ice from the Welsh Mountains which moved into the low-lying ground of the Severn Valley and across into the Black Country. The drift deposits it laid down contain many local rocks which it incorporated on passage, as well as the Welsh igneous rocks from its source region. In addition to this Welsh ice many of the western parts of the region were also affected by Irish Sea ice moving into the area from the north-west across the Cheshire Plain. At times the fronts of these two competing ice masses were in contact and even coalesced. The Irish Sea ice laid down a distinctive suite of drifts, including local rocks like Triassic pebbles and sandstones together with erratics clearly derived from Lake District and Scottish rocks. In the foothill country of the south-west Pennines, close to the Potteries, marine shells scooped from the bed of the Irish Sea are found in the drift deposits at heights over a thousand feet. This gives some indication of the strength and thickness of the Irish Sea ice as it moved into the Midlands through the Cheshire Gate. Like the Eastern ice, it too left its mark in the scenery of the area, particularly in the country between Wolverhampton and Shrewsbury. The boulder clay ground-moraine has been shaped into low swells with damp, open hollows in between. This type of 'basket-of-eggs' topography is not common in the Midlands but can be seen on either side of the A5 road (Watling Street) between Wellington and Shrewsbury. Farther east, close to Weston under Lizard (SJ 8010), end-moraines marking temporary stillstands of the ice front as it retreated northwards can be seen as isolated hills. No continuous morainic ridge exists, for subsequent erosion has probably destroyed much of the original topography. This is in spite of the fact that the deposits of this area belong to the Last Glaciation in contrast to those around Coventry, mentioned above, which belong to the Penultimate (Gipping or Chalky Boulder Clay) glaciation. In this same area of Shropshire there are isolated mounds of sand and gravel which have been interpreted as the remnants of eskers or kames left behind at right-angles to the retreating ice sheet. These sand and gravel mounds are prominent in the country around Boscobel (SJ 8307) and Blym-hill (8012), and there is a broken line along the side of the valley of the Back Brook towards Newport (7419). A similar 'esker' train exists near Penkridge (9214) close to the western edge of Cannock Chase. The gravel spreads give poor, infertile soils and in many parts their outcrops are marked by plantations of conifers.

Plate 4 The glacial landscape near Stafford with isolated knolls capped by gravel rising out of a plain of boulder clay. The defensive qualities of one of these hillocks were appreciated by the builders of Stafford Castle (SJ 9022).

At certain stages in the Ice Age, when the various competing ice masses were marginal to the region, temporary glacial lakes occupied the lower, ice-free ground. Lake Harrison developed in this way during the main glacial period (Gipping or Chalky Boulder Clay) in the open valley of a once more-extensive Soar drainage system (Study 10). Its shoreline was formed by the Cotswold scarp in the south-east, the ice front of the Eastern Ice in the north-east and that of the Western Ice in the north-west and the Severn Valley. A similar pro-glacial lake, Lake Lapworth, also existed for a time in the extreme north of the region beyond Shrewsbury and New-port in Shropshire. The two large lakes were not contemporaneous, however, for Lake Lapworth developed during the Last Glacial Phase (Hunstanton or Würm) whereas Lake Harrison belonged to the previous glacial episode (Gipping or Riss). Recent studies have shown that the extent of the lake and the level of its shoreline varied considerably in the time it dominated the landscape of north Shropshire. At its maximum extent it covered an area from Wigan in the north to Newport in the south, with its shoreline at a height of about 330 feet. Later, due to the changes which were constantly taking place in the ice fronts forming part of its margins, the lake level fell to 305 feet and there was a corresponding decrease in size. At the time of the 330-foot lake the main overflow was taking place across the low col at Ironbridge, although an outflow was also occurring at Gnosall, east of Newport, for a time. Ultimately the Ironbridge outflow led to the creation of the spectacular gorge and the permanent diversion of the waters of the upper Severn southwards in preference to their pre-glacial route northwards into the Dee Estuary (see volume on the *Welsh Marches* for a more detailed account and accompanying field study).

At an earlier date, glacial Lake Harrison also varied in height and size. When at its maximum extent, its shoreline lay at a height of about 410 feet, and a prominent lake bench was formed at this level at the foot of the marlstone scarp. At another stage in its history its level lay at a height of almost 430 feet. This variation in height and extent, as well as the differing positions assumed by the containing ice fronts, led to at least three different exits being used at various times by the over-flow waters. Each carried the waters of Lake Harrison away through the Cotswold scarp into the headwater drainage of the Thames. The most impressive of the three gaps is at Fenny Compton (SP 435 2) where the present flat floor of the now dry valley is used by the main road, the London-to-Birmingham railway via Oxford and the once flourishing Oxford Canal. Unlike the Ironbridge overflow, none of the Cots-wolds gaps associated with Lake Harrison subsequently became permanent drain-age channels.

The existence of glacial Lake Harrison, however, had a profound effect on the drainage basins of the West Midlands river systems. Prior to the Ice Age, the main watershed of England, separating rivers flowing to the Irish Sea and Bristol Channel on the one hand and the North Sea on the other, ran approximately north

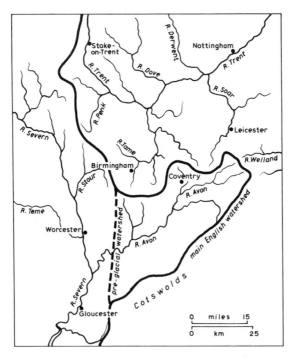

Fig. 5

Changes in the drainage basins of the West Midlands as a result of ice interference

to south across the West Midlands (see Fig. 5). The watershed began just west of the Potteries and then ran southwards through the Black Country to Bredon Hill and thence close to the crest of the Cotswold scarp through Gloucestershire. Although the northern section of this drainage divide still remains, that to the south of the Black Country now makes a big swing to the east, and at the most extreme tip of the bulge it reaches a point south-east of Leicester. This significant change has been caused by the extension of the Avon drainage basin at the expense of the Soar. In pre-glacial times the Soar rose near Bredon Hill and flowed north-eastwards through Stratford, Coventry and Leicester to join the Trent just west of Nottingham. With the development of glacial Lake Harrison this drainage system was completely disrupted, because the lake occupied the old valley floor for the most part. When the ice began to retreat and cause the lake to disappear, it did so first at its south-western end in the Severn Valley. This enabled the Avon to start cutting back into the soft, unconsolidated, glacial and lake deposits long before the Soar could re-establish itself. As a result, the Avon was able to claim a good slice of what had once been Soar territory and create the remarkable eastward bulge in the main English watershed. At the present divide between the Avon and Soar drainage basins at Hinckley no less than 200 feet of glacial and lake deposits occur, resting on what was the original valley floor of the middle section of the pre-glacial Soar.

During the Last Glaciation, when the Irish Sea ice was pushing into the northern part of the West Midlands and temporary lakes like Lapworth were in being, the southern part of the region was ice-free. As a result of a lack of direct ice interference, rivers like the Severn and its tributary the Avon were able to develop unimpeded. Sea level did not remain constant throughout this time and consequently rivers underwent periods of alternate aggrading and downcutting. These changes are reflected in the development of river terraces which, as we have already seen, are prominently developed in the lower Severn and Avon valleys (Pl .5). In the Severn, downstream from Bridgnorth, and in its left-bank tributary of the Stour, several terraces are cut into the margins of the valley (Fig. 6). The highest, consisting of coarse sands and gravels, forms an extensive flat at Hallow Heath, south of Grimley (SO 8360), at a height of about 150 feet. In the tributary River Stour the terrace is very well developed along its eastern bank around Kidderminster (8376) where the higher part of the town is built on it, hence the name Kidderminster terrace often applied to it. Below it lies the Main terrace, perhaps the best developed and most widespread of all the Severn terraces. In the neighbourhood of Kidderminster and Stourport-on-Severn it lies between 40 and 60 feet below the Kidderminster terrace and is separated from it by a pronounced step. In the main Severn Valley, this same terrace fringes both sides of the river from Ripple to Severn Stones, being particularly well developed south of Kempsey (SO 8549), where it is used for market gardening. The terrace was formed about 42,000 years ago at a time when Irish Sea ice occupied the Cheshire Plain and was impounding Lake Lapworth. The next lowest terrace in the sequence, the Worcester, cuts into the Main terrace in places and forms a wide shelf between Holt (8262) and Grimley (8360) where it offers a dry site for the latter village. The Worcester terrace is the highest one which has its equivalent upstream of the Severn Gorge at Ironbridge and therefore must have come into being after the formation of the gorge. The lowest terrace of all, dating from post-glacial times, lies close to the present flood plain of the river. In the Stour Valley between Kidderminster and Stourport-on-Severn it forms the broad, flat bottom to the valley with the river meandering across its flood plain only a few feet below it.

The River Avon, the biggest of the left-bank tributaries of the Severn, has a corresponding sequence of terraces which can be correlated with those of the main valley. This is to be expected, as the tributary would naturally respond to changes of level in the main valley. From oldest to youngest (highest to lowest) the Avon terraces have been numbered from 5 to 1. The Kidderminster terrace of the Severn is the equivalent of number 4 Avon terrace while the Main terrace is probably represented in the Avon sequence by terraces 3 and 2 which are only separated by about ten feet. The lowest terrace of the Avon, number 1, is the equivalent of the Worcester terrace of the Severn Valley and is only found in the section of the valley from Fladbury (SO 9946) to the confluence with the Severn. A fairly full sequence is preserved between Evesham and Stratford (Study 11, Pl. 11b) and as they are cut into the soft, unconsolidated beds of the former Lake Harrison, the surviving terrace fragments are usually broader than the corresponding Severn terraces. For the same reason the Avon Valley as a whole has a more open appearance than the more deeply incised Severn. In both valleys, the terrace sites are much sought after for market gardening, especially in the Vale of Evesham.

Climate

Although the West Midlands covers such a relatively small area, it displays considerable differences of weather and climate within itself. Broadly speaking the climate is transitional between the wet and mild oceanic type characteristic of western Britain and the more extreme but drier semi-continental type such as occurs in East Anglia. In any particular year, depending on the percentage frequency of the various air masses which affect the region, the West Midlands can exhibit either type. A preponderance of tropical maritime air will give a mild winter which leads to a relatively small annual temperature-range. In another year the region might be more subject to polar maritime and tropical air masses with a consequent cold winter followed by a warm, dry summer. This variability in the weather from year to year can have a considerable bearing on the agriculture of the area and has led to crop failures in unfavourable seasons. Fluctuations in rainfall amount can be considerable; at Edgbaston, the annual rainfall can vary from 23 inches in one year to as much as 36 inches in a very wet year. Taking average conditions over a number of years, however, there is no doubt that the West Midlands as a whole has a tendency towards semi-continental rather than oceanic conditions. At Edgbaston the annual temperature-range is 23°F which compares with 22°F at Great Yarmouth but only 16°F at Holyhead. Cold winters rather than warm summers are mainly responsible for this greater range. Birmingham, for example, has 102 days a year when ground frost occurs compared with 69 at Sheffield.

In addition to this continentality which the West Midlands shares with the rest of central England and the interior of East Anglia, there are some important features of the climate peculiar to the region. Sunshine figures are very low considering the low altitude and southerly position of much of the region in relation to the British Isles as a whole. Birmingham has just over 1300 hours of sunshine a year and Droitwich, well outside the industrial conurbation and therefore largely free from industrial smog, has only 1379 hours on average. These sunshine figures compare with 1550 hours at Holyhead and 1650 at Falmouth. Excessive cloudiness is often accompanied by high humidity, and even during the summer months of June, July and August the relative humidity at a station like Coventry Hospital exceeds 73 per cent. In part, it seems that the muggy, heavy weather is associated with the claylands where excessive transpiration losses occur from the permanent grasslands. In the industrial areas of the Black Country and Birmingham, smoke fogs are common and often cause a general gloom to persist for days on end. In

Plate 5 The Avon Valley with its terrace features
at Fladbury (on right of photograph). The view is
looking northward across one of the meander loops of
the river and shows the pasture land of the flood
plain, the prominent development of number 2 terrace
with its market gardening and orchards and a small
river cliff (bottom right) where the number 2
terrace is being cut into by the meandering river.

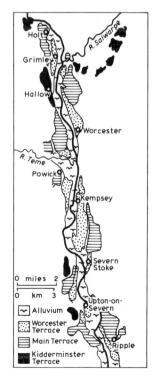

Fig. 6
The terraces of part
of the Severn Valley
around Worcester

contrast, in the adjacent countryside smog is much rarer and even places like Edg-baston and Bournville, so close to the centre of Birmingham, register higher sun-shine-totals than the heart of the city. Although the country districts might escape the worst effects of the industrial air-pollution, they tend to suffer more from advec-tion fog. In the Avon Valley the daily average of sunshine is reduced considerably in winter due to mists and fogs persisting in the area of cold clay soils in the valley bottom. Fortunately the effect is most marked in the winter months when it is not of any great significance in relation to market gardening, and is in any case compen-sated by the earlier spring which the Avon Valley experiences. The latter is due to the fact that there is a tongue of winter warmth which runs in up the Severn and Avon valleys from the Bristol Channel. Even places like Leamington in the middle reaches of the Avon Valley appear to benefit from the slight amelioration of temperature. The early spring is of special importance to the market gardeners and fruit-growers in the Vale of Evesham. Here the date of blossoming of fruit trees is 14–20 days earlier than in the Black Country. Vegetable-growers exploit the earlier season by sowing and planting well in advance of other parts of the West Midlands or the Fenlands, the other great producing-area which supplies the Midland market. Outdoor crops of runner beans and early summer cauliflower are often planted up to a month earlier here than in other parts of Worcestershire. The only risk is late frosts, and if these occur in early May replanting may be necessary. The late frosts are also a hazard to the fruit-grower. The floor of the Avon Valley is very susceptible to the downslope flow of air which often takes place at night under anticyclonic conditions; hence the desirability of siting orchards on the valley sides. The orchards themselves can considerably impede the free flow of air and therefore increase the likelihood of damaging frosts.

The distinctive character of the climate of the Avon Valley is but one example of the local variations which can occur throughout the West Midlands. Relief is another factor which can affect not only precipitation amounts but also windiness and degree of exposure. The close relationship existing between height and rain-fall can be clearly illustrated from a section across the heart of the region from the Clent Hills to Cannock Chase. In the south-west on the Clent Hills the rainfall exceeds 30 inches during most years but this amount drops to about 26 inches at Wednesbury, only to rise again to 29 inches on the southern fringes of Cannock Chase. Farther north the Potteries, in direct line of the prevailing South-Westerlies as they approach the Pennines, receive up to 20 per cent more precipitation than the Black Country Plateau. The higher susceptibility to windiness is another prob-lem to be faced in the upland areas. On the plateau top of the Cotswolds, for ex-ample, wind speeds are estimated to be one-third greater than in the surrounding lowlands. Even the valleys do not offer the shelter that might be expected because they tend to funnel the winds and create quite local wind directions. In a north–south valley, there is always a higher percentage of northerly winds than on the adjacent plateau top only a few miles away. The degree of exposure is considerably reduced in upland areas where afforestation has taken place. Although the main reason for the extensive planting of conifers on Cannock Chase has been the poor, stony soils, an additional benefit has been a marked reduction in windiness and exposure which has done much to remove some of the bleakness of the area. The same is true to a lesser extent on those parts of the plateau top of the Cotswolds where long lines of trees have been planted as shelter belts. Again, they not only serve a useful purpose but add variety to what might otherwise be a dull landscape.

Soils and Agriculture

In a region with so diversified a landscape as the West Midlands it is natural to expect a multiplicity of soil types (Fig. 7). Both the underlying rock type and the character of the superficial deposits, mainly glacial drifts, play a major part in determining soil type. Most of the region, apart from a small area in the extreme south, is covered with drift deposits. In the central area of the Black Country Plateau soils based on boulder clay predominate. Where this has been derived from the Triassic rocks it is mainly red in colour but elsewhere it forms a brown, heavy and often ill-drained soil. The latter occurs especially on the flat plateau tops

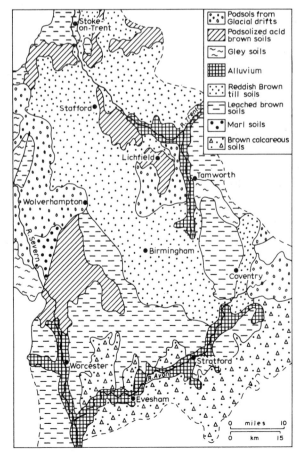

Fig. 7
A generalized soil-map
of the West Midlands

where it may even become a gley soil under waterlogged conditions. In their natural state these boulder clay soils are mainly under permanent pasture with patches of rushes in the damper hollows. Where the glacial drift is mainly sand or gravel, as in the country to the north and west of Wolverhampton, acid brown soils and podsols are more typical. Many of the more sterile soils are given over to heath in their natural state or are now planted with conifers. Similar poor, acid soils occur on the glacial deposits around Coventry, especially the outwash gravels and sands associated with the former glacial Lake Harrison. Again the area once contained extensive heaths, but reclamation in the nineteenth century, with widespread marling, changed their original appearance and now only names like Dunsmore Heath, east of Coventry, survive to indicate their former presence. In parts of Shropshire the Ice Age left behind ill-drained hollows, many of which are still occupied by meres, especially around Ellesmere. Where the water has drained away, organic accumulations of the remains of aquatic vegetation like the reed and sedge have taken place. Later sphagnum moss and cotton-grass have become established, and even the purple moor-grass and heather have colonized the drier parts. In time black, peaty soils have formed, and where these can be adequately drained the former mosslands make excellent arable land. Where drainage is not possible the land is allowed to remain under grass and in time may become covered with thorn and hazel scrub. Ill-drained hollows like Whixall Moss (SJ 5038) have been worked for their peat, at first valued as a local fuel but more recently for horticultural purposes.

Akin to this varied assemblage of glacial drifts with their associated soils types are the river terrace deposits which occur particularly in the Severn, Avon, Trent and Tame valleys. Those bordering the Severn and Avon have an importance out of all proportion to the area they cover in view of the intensive agriculture practised there. The two lowest terraces of both valleys carry a sandy, well-drained, acid soil with a large content of Bunter Pebbles originally brought by the meltwater of the ice sheet when it lay to the north near Shrewsbury. The soil profile of reddish brown, sandy loam, with irregular bands of pebbles, usually extends to a considerable depth. It is these soils which are extremely suitable for market garden crops, although they require frequent applications of fertiliser. In the Vale of Evesham, in particular, all available terrace land bordering the Avon is intensively cultivated to provide both the London and Midland markets with fresh vegetables (Study 10). In addition many acres are planted with orchards of plum, apple and pear. Horticulture in the West Midlands is not exclusive to the Vale of Evesham for there is a considerable area given over to fruit-growing and vegetable crops in the district between Kidderminster and Worcester, and in the Kempsey–Severn Stoke (SO 8546) section of the Severn Valley south of Worcester. Here climatic conditions similar to those found in the Vale of Evesham occur with the tongue of warmth extending from the Bristol Channel giving earlier springs.

Plate 6   A field of brussels sprouts on the top of the Cotswolds; in the background is the long barrow of Belas Knap and typical drystone wall (SP 0225)

In both the terrace lands of the Severn and Avon valleys, the traditional crops grown are those which not only are suited to the local soil and climatic conditions but also can be fitted into a close rotation which makes the maximum use of the land and spreads the work evenly throughout the year. Spring cabbage, with a season lasting from December until May, often fetching more than £200 an acre, is a popular and well-tried crop. This is often followed by salad onions, the Vale of Evesham producing over a quarter of the entire crop marketed in this country. Early summer cauliflowers are often grown as an alternative and on the better land can be cut in early June. Leeks also grow well in the district and, except for harvesting, their labour-demands are low. They often follow spring cabbage, and after a severe winter the crop can be highly profitable. Two crops which have increased in importance in recent years have been runner beans and brussels sprouts. The former are grown mainly on sticks in the Kidderminster–Worcester area but in the Vale of Evesham the greater part of the crop is allowed to trail unsupported. The value of the crop often exceeds £400 an acre but against this figure must be offset the high growing and harvesting costs. The growing of brussels sprouts has changed considerably in recent years. Formerly the Vale of Evesham specialised in early varieties which gave large, pale green sprouts, but as these proved less popular with the consumer than the dark green, button type many growers have abandoned the crop on their terrace lands. Instead some of the larger growers rent land in the nearby Cotswolds where they are responsible for planting, applying fertiliser and picking the crop. Some of these rented sites are between 10 and 15 miles away from the main holding and therefore the extra cost

27

of harvesting and general cultivation has to be met from increased yields or a higher price for the desired type of sprout.

Although the same basic pattern of horticulture is practised in the Severn Valley as in the Vale of Evesham, there are one or two distinctive features. Potatoes are much more common on the lighter soils of the Kempsey area south of Worcester. The varieties grown are usually main-crop potatoes such as King Edward or Majestic and are sold direct to local merchants, including those from the Black Country who take most of the potatoes straight from the farms. The presence of the British Sugar Corporation beet factory at Kidderminster has led to an increase in the growing of sugar-beet in the vicinity, although most of the 500 acres planted are on the heavier claylands between Kidderminster and Droitwich, and not in the Severn Valley. On specialised fruit-farms, blackcurrants are a popular crop, especially since it is possible to mechanize all operations except pruning and picking, and hence reduce labour-costs. Much of the crop goes to the syrup-making factories rather than being sold as fresh fruit.

In contrast to the terrace lands, the flood plains of the Severn, Avon and Trent are floored with imperfectly drained gley soils free from stones. In both the Trent and Severn valleys winter flooding of the alluvial flood plain is a common occurrence. Under these conditions arable cultivation is impossible, though the land may still be of considerable value as summer pasture or for hay. Improved drainage and embanking is likely to minimise the risk of periodic flooding in the future, but it is unlikely that the flood plains of the Midland rivers will be used for anything but the traditional pastoral farming with the emphasis on dairy cattle.

In areas away from the river valleys and where the glacial drift cover is thin or absent, the soils reflect more closely the underlying solid rock formations. Poor, stony, podsol soils are commonly associated with rock formations like the breccia of the Clent Hills or the Hopwas Breccia which occurs in a belt of country around Tamworth in the extreme east of the region. The thick Bunter Pebble Beds which underlie the greater part of Cannock Chase also gives rise to infertile though well-drained soils. In areas such as these, the growing of arable crops is unprofitable if not impossible, and the planting of conifers, particularly the Corsican pine, seems the best solution (Study 2).

In contrast to the poor country associated with the breccias and pebble beds, the lowlands developed on the Keuper Marl form rich agricultural land. As might be expected the acid brown soils tend to be heavy but are ideal for grassland because of their subsoil water reserve. A surprisingly high percentage of the land is under permanent pasture, Worcestershire having over 160,000 acres, a figure three times the temporary-grass acreage. Where grass is part of a crop rotation short leys lasting only 2–3 years are common. Dairy farmers make considerable use of Italian rye-grass to obtain an early spring bite, with perennial rye-grass pastures to follow. For dairying purposes, the British Friesian is by far the most popular breed, accounting for well over half the dairy herds. The size of herd has risen steadily over the years and now averages about twenty-six cows. On farms where there is an emphasis on beef cattle the Hereford is the most popular breed, followed by the Aberdeen Angus.

South of the Avon Valley there is an extensive outcrop of the Lower Lias Clay extending up to the Cotswold scarp. The soils for the most part are calcareous, brown clays which are inherently fertile and when well managed break down into a fine tilth, especially if autumn ploughing is practised to allow the winter frosts to break down the topsoil. Wheat and grass, the latter in relatively long leys, are the dominant crops over the greater part of the area. Barley has recently made considerable headway at the expense of oats. On the whole the soil is not suitable for root crops, although potatoes are often grown as a first crop on newly ploughed up pasture. The Vale of Evesham falls partly within this area, and there has been a considerable extension of the horticulture and fruit-growing of the Avon terraces on to the Lias Clays. Plums do exceptionally well, as do the more vigorous growing varieties of apple like Bramley's Seedling. Soft fruits like red- and black-currants are also grown, but soil conditions are unfavourable for raspberries and strawberries. As in the area close to the Avon around Evesham, more and more glasshouses are being erected, and combined with cloche cultivation, enable the vegetable-grower to produce earlier crops, particularly of the salad vegetables. Although elsewhere in England asparagus is associated with sandy soils, here in the Vale of Evesham it is customary for the crop to be grown on the heavy Lias Clays. The usual life of the asparagus beds is about ten years but some last much shorter than this, especially where the grower has developed his own strains with higher-quality shoots.

Human Geography

The paucity of finds in the Midlands dating from the main periods of prehistory before the Iron Age has given rise to the belief that the triangle of country between the valleys of the Severn, Avon and Trent remained unused and almost unpopulated until the second century B.C. Stray discoveries of bronze tools or weapons were thought to be accidental droppings on the trade routes across the region between the mining and metal-working centres of Wales and Ireland and their markets in south-eastern England. It was believed that the West Midland countryside in prehistoric times was covered with a dense and impenetrable forest. Few ideas stand unchallenged for long. Already new facts are coming to light that will change this view of the role of the Midlands in prehistory. Since 1955 a thorough air-survey of the Avon Valley has revealed prehistoric features which are too faint to be noticed from the ground. They show as dark lines and patches among the growing crops on the fertile terraces of the Avon. Some of the marks suggest huge rectangular enclosures that may be of Neolithic date. Dark rings are interpreted as the sites of huts, and thick, concentric circles are probably the last remaining evidence of 'henge' monuments of Bronze Age date. Altogether 141 sites have been discovered in the Avon Valley by this aerial survey. They abound between Warwick and Stratford on Avon, and the proximity of these symbols of prehistoric occupation to the villages and hamlets of today suggests that the plan of settlement in this valley was first sketched out in the Neolithic and Bronze Ages between 3000 and 1000 B.C. At Hampton Lucy (SP 2556), for instance, two fields adjoining the village to the south-west are filled with the marks of hut circles, enclosures and narrow lanes. This evidence, all but obliterated from the eyes of man, points to the beginning of settlement on the river terrace at Hampton Lucy deep in prehistoric time, perhaps 4000 years ago. The valleys of the Avon and Trent probably formed wide corridors of settlement from Neolithic times onwards. Sir Cyril Fox's sentence, written almost forty years ago in his book *The Personality of Britain*, no longer summarizes the state of the Midlands in the centuries before the Romans. He described central England as 'the heavily wooded Midlands where pre-Roman occupation of any kind is likely to have been scanty or transient or both'.

The Iron Age and Romano-British Period

The first coherent picture of the human geography of the West Midlands can be drawn about the third century B.C., when ramparted enclosures were built on prominent hills and spurs. In every part of the region one does not have to travel many miles to come across an Iron Age hill-fort. Usually these hill-top earthworks are explained as military features, strong-points in tribal warfare or part of a defensive system thrown up in the middle of the first century A.D. to stem the Roman occupation of the West Midlands. They may have served this purpose for a short time, but at the few sites investigated there is little sign of serious military engagements. Instead, the most recent work outside this region—at Croft Ambrey in Herefordshire and on hill-top forts in Somerset and North Wales – shows that they were dwelling-places. Clusters of hut circles and the foundation-post holes of larger buildings point to settlements of the size of villages and in some places as big as a medieval town (see Pl. 7). Also many of them were inhabited over a long span of time, covering the centuries between 200 B.C. and the end of Roman power in Britain. The Iron Age forts are probably the symbols and only surviving relics of a social and political order in the West Midlands that preceded the imposition of a Roman political system upon the Celtic-speaking British. The Romans seem to have taken note of the structure of society which they found in the Midlands in the location of their own towns. For instance, Viroconium (SJ 5608) was founded on the banks of the Severn under the shadow of the Wrekin and its gigantic hill-fort. Perhaps an even more striking relationship between a Roman settlement and a

British hill-fort may be found at Wall (SK 0906). Here an important Roman town stands within the territory overshadowed by Castle Ring (SK 0412), a large Iron Age camp on a southern spur of Cannock Chase. Curiously enough the link between the two features, the Roman settlement and the hill-top fort, is completed in the realm of place-names. The old name for Castle Ring is *Caer Luydcoed*, a Welsh name meaning 'the fortification by the grey wood'. The Roman name for Wall was *Letocetum* and it is derived from the old name of Castle Ring.

In several parts of the Midlands British social and economic groups probably remained intact and distinctive into the Saxon period. The forests of Kinver and Morfe, the hills of Cannock Chase, and the country of the Staffordshire–Shropshire border around Penkridge and Eccleshall seem to have survived as islands of a pre-Roman culture. The evidence lies in the abundance of place-names with British elements and also the presence of estates made up of several scattered hamlets instead of the compact unit of land that was typical of the Roman villa and the later Anglo-Saxon manor. To take only one example from Staffordshire, Eccleshall (SJ 8329) had twenty outlying hamlets. Its possessions were scattered like little islands amid the properties of other estates. The place-name, too, contains the British element, *eglysyg*, a church. The same kind of dispersed manor is very common in Worcestershire and again in the western parts of Gloucestershire. Here there seem to survive traces of the system of land-holding that belonged to the society that built the Iron Age forts, a system that dates back before the Roman Conquest.

The West Midlands contain Iron Age forts in an astonishing variety of sites. Along the crest of the Cotswold escarpment near Cheltenham their grassy ramparts occur on almost every spur, each within sight of its neighbour (Fig. 8). The

Fig. 8

Iron Age hill-forts on the Cotswold escarpment near Cheltenham

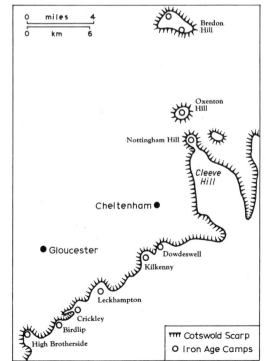

*Plate 7   Bredon Hill: site of an Iron Age hill-fort on a spur in the middle
foreground. Note the ramparts and within the enclosure the dark rings of hut
circles, suggesting that this was an inhabited place. In the distance on the
flat hill-top the faint, broad ridges point to arable cultivation in the Iron Age.
The steep face of the hill (right) shows evidence of slumping (SO 9540).*

huge mass of Bredon Hill carries the remains of two hill-forts (see Pl. 7). Excavation
at the southern site, Conderton Camp (SO 972384), has revealed the circular foundation of huts that tell of a village within the ramparts. In the region of the northern
Cotswolds almost every parish contains an Iron Age fort; and the deep coombes
between the projecting spurs of the escarpment often contain the site of a Roman
villa. Hill-top enclosures and Roman villas are the last faint symbols on the ground
of a British society and political order that accepted and absorbed a Roman way of
life. The framework of the modern settlement pattern was sketched in those
distant centuries.

Iron Age hill-forts abound in the West Midlands beyond the Cotswolds. The
Wrekin lifts itself magnificently over the plain of the Severn, and its huge hill-top
camp seems to symbolise a powerful regional capital. Berry Ring (SJ 8821), near
Stafford, surveys a landscape that on clear days stretches from the foothills of the
Pennines to the south Shropshire Hills. Another powerful hill-fort crowns a
northern spur of the Clent Hills above Hagley (SO 9281). Its name, Wychbury,
reminds us of a place-name element, *bury*, that so often belongs to these ancient
sites of pre-Roman Britain. And so we could go on listing the last surviving features of a vanished British society in the West Midlands. We have already noticed
that the military terms 'fort' and 'camp' probably give a false impression of the

purpose of these Iron Age constructions. Likewise, they were not invariably built on hill-tops, spurs and commanding places. The Warwickshire Avon and its tributaries contain Iron Age camps in valley floors and on lowland sites that lack any features of strategic worth. Wappenbury for instance, occupies a terrace on the north bank of the River Leam (SP 3769) overshadowed by higher ground on almost every hand (Fig. 9). As you explore the site today there is not much left of the Iron Age fort – little more than a feeling of a grassy ridge in the fields to the west of the church. But a tiny strip of Wappenbury's half-erased rampart and ditch was carefully excavated in 1958. The results suggest a long period of settlement. A group of Iron Age farmers seems to have settled on the bank of the Leam in the first century B.C. Pottery found at the site helps to date the rampart to the years just before the Roman conquest. Towards the end of the fourth century A.D. Wappenbury had its own pot-kilns close to the river. Wappenbury has now been recognised as the source of pots found on other Roman sites in the neighbourhood – eastwards at High Cross and Mancetter on Watling Street, at Kenilworth and at Stratford on Avon. Finds of even later date, a grey dish and a black cooking-pot, show that the site was inhabited in late Saxon times. Wappenbury is a place over which the imagination can roam. Its church and two farms – the core of the settlement – all stand within the enclosure of the Iron Age camp. Already a very limited dig has displayed the continuity of settlement at this place on the bank of the Leam.

The Roman occupation of the West Midlands in A.D. 47 added many fresh features to the landscape. Chief among these was a network of roads and many new settlements – forts, villas and small towns. Two of the most important roads in the Midlands had been built by A.D. 50. The Fosse Way, part of a long cross-country route between Exeter and Lincoln, skirts the southern edge of the region. Watling Street pursues a north-westward line across the Midlands from its junction with the Fosse Way at High Cross (SP 4788) by Wall and on to the important Roman city of Virconium on the Severn. Another road, Ryknield Street, can still be traced

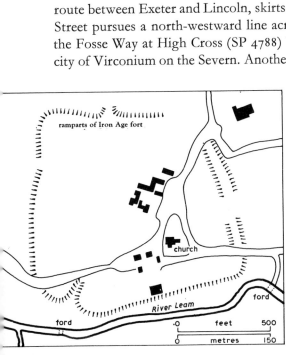

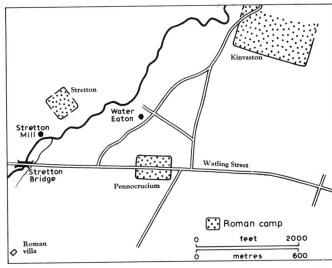

Fig. 9 *Wappenbury: a village within the rampart of an Iron Age fort*

Fig. 10 *Roman sites around Stretton*

in long stretches by Alcester and the heart of Birmingham to its crossing with the Watling Street at Wall. The network of Roman roads in the West Midlands was completed with several minor roads and branches. Greensforge (SO 8688), where a Roman fort stood on the bank of the Stour, gathered tracks from Stretton, Droitwich and the hilly, wooded country of the Welsh Marches to the west. Stretches of Roman road still form important elements in the Midland landscape. To the north of Birmingham, in Sutton Park (SP 0897), Ryknield Street survives as a narrow ribbon of Roman paving cutting through the pale sand and clumps of dark heather. Again, the modern trunk road to the north-west, A5, still follows for many miles the line of Watling Street, and there is no doubt that for much of its course a foundation of Roman paving and gravel lies beneath the tarmac.

The most important Roman settlements in the Midlands were spaced out along the main roads. Every few miles along Watling Street a village or military station was built and enclosed by an earthwork. Research in the past fifteen years has uncovered a lot of fresh facts about the Roman stations along Watling Street. For instance, the exact site of Pennocrucium (SJ 9010) was only discovered in 1946 as the result of an air survey made by J. K. St Joseph. Photographs showed the marks of a rectangular enclosure astride the Watling Street on the rising ground to the east of the Penk (Fig. 10). Centuries of ploughing had made these features invisible from the ground. The existence of Pennocrucium was known from a Roman road-book, the Antonine Itinerary, which lists the settlements along the Roman roads of Britain. Camden and other early topographers and historians had placed Pennocrucium at Penkridge, a large, clustered village more than two miles to the north of Watling Street. At the end of the seventeenth century, Dr Plot argued in his *Natural History of Staffordshire* that Penkridge lay too far from Watling Street and decided that the Roman posting-station was sited at Stretton (SJ 8811). Air photography and archaeology have now revealed an outline of the geography and history of Pennocrucium. There was a small settlement astride Watling Street with buildings made of clay daub and timber. Three cobbled lanes ran from north to south at right-angles to the main road and the whole settlement was enclosed by an earth rampart. Pennocrucium was inhabited for a long time, probably for most of the Roman period. The Penk Valley in the neighbourhood of its crossing by Watling Street has been proved by recent investigations, with the aid of air photography, to be a complex of Roman settlement. Besides the village of Pennocrucium on Watling Street, two forts stood on either side of the valley less than a mile to the north (8911 and 9111). Again, on the bank of the Penk, half a mile south of the Roman road, stands the site of a Roman villa (8910). This complex of Roman forts, a villa estate and a roadside village stood at the junction of several minor routes. Perhaps this group of Roman settlements was established in a tract of country which had already been opened up by the British and whose centre lay at Penkridge – a place with a Celtic name.

Plate 8　Gloucester: the gridiron plan of a Roman and medieval town. The cathedral is built across the north-west corner of the former wall. In the distance beyond the cathedral is the suburb of Kingsholm, site of the Roman legionary fortress which preceded the colonial town (date of photo 1962).

Apart from the Roman sites along Watling Street other important settlements of this period lie mainly in the southern part of the region, in the valleys of the Avon and Severn. Chesterton (SP 3459) was a small town or village on the Fosse Way. The salt springs at Droitwich attracted the Romans and a town grew alongside a fort. The Roman military station stood on the north bank of the Salwarpe and the civil settlement arose on the other side of the river on the site of modern Droitwich. Gloucester and Worcester were even more important places, regional capitals in the truest sense. Gloucester began its long history in A.D. 47 with the founding of a legionary fortress at Kingsholm (SO 8319), now swallowed up in the northern suburbs of the cathedral city (see Pl. 8). As the frontier against the Silures was pushed westward from the Severn to the Wye so Gloucester abandoned its role as a military centre, and in A.D. 75 the Second Legion moved from Kingsholm to a new fortress at Caerleon-on-Usk. Already a settlement had grown up outside the Kingsholm fortress on the eastern channel of the Severn where there was a landing-stage. The ground plan of Gloucester was firmly drawn out between A.D. 96 and 98 when a chartered town or *colonia* was founded to settle retired soldiers from the Second Legion. On slightly higher ground behind the port a rectangle of

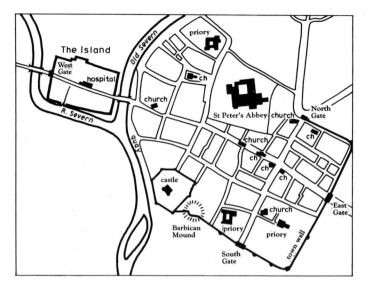

Fig. 11
Gloucester,
where the medieval
town took over the
street-plan of the
Roman colonia

forty-five acres was marked off by a stone wall guarded by towers at its four corners. This Roman town was to form the heart of medieval Gloucester (Fig. 11).

The Anglo-Saxon Settlement and Medieval Colonization

The chief clues to the first stage of the Saxon settlement of the Midlands are found in place-names that have survived from the sixth and seventh centuries and in cemeteries which show pagan practices of burial and cremation. The conversion of the Saxon state of Mercia to Christianity began in A.D. 653, so the middle of the seventh century is the last possible date for the making of the pagan burial grounds. The Avon Valley has the richest collection of pagan cemeteries. Sixty cremations were unearthed from the Saxon cemetery at Baginton near Coventry (SP 3474). There are others at Bidford, Brinklow, Marton, Tiddington, Compton Verney and Milcote. All these burial grounds of the pre-Christian period point to the Fosse Way as an important line of entry for the Anglo-Saxons from the east into the heart of the Midlands.

The Severn Plain between Worcester and Tewkesbury has no pagan burial grounds and lacks the evidence of early place-names. This suggests a settlement of the westernmost parts of the Midlands after the middle of the seventh century when the Saxons were already converted to Christianity. But the separateness of the Severn region in the Saxon period probably has a more complex origin. Here the settlers probably approached from the south across the Cotswolds, and not by the rivers of the East Midlands. Their settlement began only at the end of the sixth century after the Battle of Dyrham in A.D. 577 allowed the penetration of the Cotswolds and Gloucestershire. It seems most likely that the Saxons who filtered into the area around Worcester and Tewkesbury were absorbed into a state that was an active remnant of the Romano-British order in this part of the South-West Midlands. Some believe that Christianity never died in this district and that the Saxons who settled the Severn Plain accepted Christianity with much else of the culture and society surviving from earlier centuries.

Mercia was the name of the Saxon kingdom that emerged in the Midlands. Its core lay in the early settlements of the Trent Valley and its tributary the Tame. In the first half of the seventh century, when Penda was king of the still-pagan Mercia, this Saxon state expanded westward towards the Severn and Dee, absorbing several large tracts of country that were probably still inhabited by Celtic-speaking peoples. Bede, in his *Ecclesiastical History*, names some of the tribal groups within Mercia and shows that it was a large and complex kingdom. The Hwicce were the most important tribe absorbed by Mercia. Their regional centre lay at Worcester and in the Severn and lower Avon valleys. The meaning and origin of the name Hwicce is still unknown, but it seems likely that it may be Celtic and that the tribal area of the Hwicce was, in reality, a British kingdom absorbed by the advance of Mercia. The diocese of Worcester was sketched out in the year 680 and its frontiers seem to coincide with the sub-kingdom of the Hwicce. The Magonsaetan, another tribal group, lived beyond the Malvern Hills in the plain of the middle Wye. The boundaries of the Hereford diocese came to define their territory. By the middle of the eighth century King Offa drew the western frontier of Mercia through the hills and deep valleys of the Welsh Marches and raised one of the greatest earthworks of the British Isles in Offa's Dyke. Mercia had reached its greatest extent. One suspects that it contained large tracts of Celtic-speaking people whose economy and modes of life had been handed down with little change from Iron Age times. The conversion of Cannock Chase, Kinver and Morfe forests, the Malvern country and the plain of Hereford to English ways remains one of the great problems of history.

The colonizing of tracts of country beyond the primary zones of Saxon settlement brought about an even greater change in the human geography of the West Midlands. This secondary colonisation began in the middle of the eighth century and continued in fits and starts until the close of the thirteenth century, adding a collection of new and distinctive place-name elements to the Midland landscape. Names that describe woods and forest clearance are abundant. Of most frequent occurrence are *ley*, *worth*, *field* and *hurst*. The effects of this secondary colonisation are clearly written on the large-scale maps and the landscapes of the region. For instance, country to the west of the River Arrow contains many examples of settlements from this period such as Weethley (SP 0555), Bradley (SO 9860) and Bentley (SO 9966). In addition, there are many 'greens' among the place-names of this district once known as Feckenham Forest. Another feature in this landscape of late settlement is the moated farmstead. Even so, Feckenham Forest was not a total wilderness when the long, silent colonisation of the Middle Ages began. Across it runs the Roman road from Alcester to Droitwich and this route gave rise to a tract of earlier settlement with cores at Feckenham (SP 0061) and Hanbury (SO 9564).

37

Both are centres of large parishes each covering about twelve square miles, a first clue to the great age of these settlements. Already in the eighth century Hanbury was one of the scattered manors that belonged to Worcester Cathedral and there was a small monastery there before the year 800. The place-name speaks, too, of Hanbury's role as a primary centre of settlement. The *bury* element suggests an Iron Age fort that has long disappeared from the landscape, though one might guess that the site is now occupied by the parish church, isolated on the summit of a hill away from the main settlement and with wide views across the surrounding country. By contrast, Hanbury's neighbour, Bradley, occupies a small, narrow parish confined largely to the eastern flank of the Seeley Brook (SO 9860). The site of the core of the hamlet, on the very edge of the parish, suggests that Bradley was carved out of the larger unit of Hanbury and that the parish boundary which follows the lane through the settlement once formed the divide between the older settlements of Feckenham and Hanbury. Similar landscapes of late settlement and colonisation occur in the Forest of Arden to the south of Birmingham. North-east Warwickshire is another area of secondary colonisation where Baddesley, Baxterley, Hurley, Fillongley, Arley and Bentley are only a few of the names that point to the time and mode of evolution of this piece of the Midland countryside.

By the ninth century the territories of the former great Saxon power, Mercia, were hemmed in by two dangerous marchlands – the border zone of Wales defined by Offa's gigantic earthwork and the new eastern frontier with the Danes in the Trent and Tame valleys. The unsettled decades of the Danish raids caused the

Plate 9   Stafford: a pre-Domesday walled town with an axial street leading to the crossing of the Sow. Two parishes existed in Stafford before Domesday times represented by St Mary's to the left of the main street and St Chad's to the right.

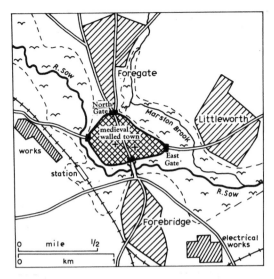

Fig. 12

The site of Stafford

building of forts in the West Midlands. Some were thrown up in established centres of population to give them greater security. For instance, sometime between the years 889 and 899 the *ealdormann* of Mercia, Aethelred, and his wife Ethelfleda made an agreement with Bishop Werferth for the fortifying of Worcester. Tamworth, at one of the most exposed sites on the eastern frontier, was rebuilt under the same Ethelfleda in 913 (see Study 3). Stafford, also on the eastern march of the Danelaw, came into existence in the same period (Pl. 9 and Fig 12). Warwick, too, began its urban life in this same period of political crisis. The Anglo-Saxon Chronicle says that a Danish army was making raids in the Midlands in the year 914 and it was then that Ethelfleda built the *burh* at Warwick 'in the early autumn'. Both Stafford and Warwick were new towns born of the Danish crisis at the beginning of the tenth century. At Stafford the castle that formed the core of the town in the marshy loop of the River Sow was erased from the landscape centuries ago.

Domesday Book gives some hint of the importance of towns in the West Midlands. In the whole area between the Cotswolds and the southern foothills of the Pennines only ten places are recorded with burgesses; six of these towns lay in the richest and most densely populated area of the south-west. Gloucester, living within the bounds of the former Roman wall, was probably the biggest and most prosperous of the urban settlements. Pershore, Winchcombe and Tewkesbury lived under the shadow of their great monasteries. An abbey had been founded at Pershore about A.D. 690 and a small town had come into being at the abbey gate, occupying a long street that led down to the crossing of the Avon. Domesday Book's laconic account mentions only the twenty-eight burgesses at Pershore and the toll of twelve shillings taken from the market, but behind these medieval statistics one can sense a prosperous Saxon town. The most interesting town in the region was undoubtedly Droitwich. By the time of the Norman Conquest Droitwich possessed at least 150 burgesses, and it is likely that salt-making had con-

39

tinued from the time of its first exploitation by the Romans. Only four Domesday boroughs are named in the survey for the remaining counties of the West Midlands – Warwick, Tamworth, Stafford and Tutbury. The last of these may be excluded from our list of Saxon towns, because it was a new settlement created soon after the Norman Conquest. These facts speak of the poorly developed, thinly populated country to the north of the Avon Valley.

Domesday Book's list of boroughs in the Midlands probably provides an incomplete picture of the settlements that were engaging in trade and beginning to acquire the functions of towns in the eleventh century. Tamworth is known as a Domesday borough only because twelve of its burgesses are recorded in the entries that deal with the neighbouring royal manors of Wiggington and Drayton Bassett. Otherwise this former capital of Mercia would have passed without mention in the great survey. Evesham's great abbey was founded in the first year of the eighth century. Its inhabitants did not achieve a charter of incorporation as a borough until 1604, almost a century after the dissolution of the monasteries, but it is more than likely that Evesham was as much a town as Pershore by the tenth century (see Study 11).

Another event of major importance for the later history of the Midlands was the creation of the shires about the beginning of the eleventh century. Mercia and its sub-kingdoms had vanished completely, but the new pattern of shires reveals the role of the river valleys in the medieval economy of the Midlands. Staffordshire was based on the Trent and the new shire town of Stafford. Warwickshire finds its axis along the Avon and its core in the Saxon town of Warwick. Worcestershire is focused on the middle Severn Basin. The three medieval shires met among the hills, broad valleys and forests of the Birmingham Plateau, then among the least populated parts of the Midlands.

In the twelfth century large areas of the Midlands were thinly populated. The Norman kings placed them under the forest laws which gave priority to the huntsman and the preservation of deer, wild boars, hares and other animals of the chase. A belt of great 'forests' stretched across the West Midlands from south-west to north-east. Feckenham Forest and Kinver Forest lay close to the Severn. The wooded tract of Arden occupied north Warwickshire and it was continued beyond Walsall by the vast wilderness of Cannock Chase. On the northern border of the region another medieval 'forest', the Lyme, stretched across the headwaters of the Trent. Towards the end of the twelfth century the new town of Newcastle-under-Lyme was growing on its edge. In 1167 its inhabitants were fined seven marks or £4 13s 4d for breaking the forest laws.

The medieval forests of the West Midlands were not total wildernesses. Although they were composed of many square miles of woodland and heath, there were also clearings with villages and hamlets. The Crown, in the years after the Norman Conquest, tried to halt the advance of settlement into the royal hunting-preserves. The forest laws forbade the process of 'assarting', the clearing of patches of land for cottages, new farmsteads and hamlets. In some places at the time of the Norman Conquest efforts were made to roll back the settlements that were already encroaching on the royal forests. For instance, Domesday Book reports that at Ashwood (SO 8688), in the Forest of Kinver, land had gone out of cultivation – 'now it is waste for the sake of the King's forest'.

The efforts to preserve large tracts of country for hunting were doomed to failure in the two centuries after the Norman Conquest because of far-reaching changes in the population and economy of medieval England. The most striking feature of the period was an impressive growth in population. It is calculated that between the Norman Conquest and the outbreak of the plague in 1348 the population of Warwickshire had tripled, rising from about 25,000 at the time of the Domesday Survey to more than 70,000. The impact of this population explosion has left its marks on the landscape of Warwickshire. The well-settled southern part of the country, the Feldon, was probably already suffering from overpopulation at the time of the Domesday Survey. With a shortage of land and the inflexible society of the manorial village, the problems of rising population in south Warwickshire were solved by the migration of people to the forested and undeveloped country of Arden to the north of the Avon. The Forest of Arden has been described as 'a countryside in an early colonial phase of exploitation' at the time of the Norman Conquest. The succeeding three centuries saw the creation of a distinctive landscape of late settlement marked by hamlets, winding lanes, irregular patchworks of small fields, tiny holdings and larger manor farms enclosed by the still waters of a moat (Pl. 10). Fifty new parishes came into existence in Warwickshire between the time of the Domesday Survey and the middle of the fourteenth century.

Plate 10   The Forest of Arden: a view across a landscape of late colonization with irregular fields and tree-lined hedges. In the foreground the long street of Henley-in-Arden, a thirteenth-century town (SP 1566).

Beside the poor squatters and the wealthier freeholders who attacked the woodlands of Arden, the great monasteries were among the pioneers of the wilderness in the twelfth and thirteenth centuries. The place-name element 'grange' still provides a clue to their activities even though the monasteries were destroyed four centuries ago. In the country to the south of Coventry we find the granges, the outlying farms, of Stoneleigh Abbey (SP 3171). Cryfield Grange (3074), Stivichall Grange (3276), Stoneleigh Grange (3373) and Bockendon Grange (2775) all lie within a short distance of each other.

The same story of forest clearance and piecemeal settlement is true for many other parts of the West Midlands in the two-and-half centuries that followed the Norman Conquest. Medieval documents contain two terms which are especially characteristic of this time and descriptive of the newly settled lands. They frequently mention *assarts* or else use the even more telling phrase of *novae terrae*, new lands. Both were new terms introduced by Norman landlords and lawyers into the English language. The Red Book of Worcester, a detailed fourteenth-century survey of the estates of Worcester Cathedral, mentions fifty-seven assarts in the district of Alvechurch and another forty clearances are named in the midst of the Forest of Feckenham around Hanbury.

Population pressure in the old, settled tracts along the main river valleys of the Midlands encouraged the colonisation of the belt of forests that stretched across the heart of the region. Although the most dramatic changes in the twelfth century were taking place in these new areas of settlement, the cores of older settlement such as Warwickshire's Feldon were not completely static. For example, a new hamlet called Northend grew in the parish of Burton Dassett (SP 3951) that overlooks the clay plain of the Feldon from the steep slopes of a marlstone hill. Today the post-Domesday hamlet of Northend (3952) has taken over completely from the parent village because Burton Dassett was destroyed in 1499 when Sir Edward Belknap enclosed 360 acres in the open fields for sheep-farming. This single south Warwickshire parish displays two of the great themes of English medieval history, the rise of population and the spawning-off of new settlements before the fourteenth century and the desertion of villages that accompanied the development of specialised sheep-farming in the fifteenth and sixteenth centuries (see Study 9).

West Midland Towns after the Norman Conquest

The twelfth and thirteenth centuries were particularly favourable for the creation of new towns. The pattern of development is the same nearly everywhere. The story almost always began with the granting of a weekly market and the right to hold an annual fair to a community that was largely rural in its outlook and occupations. This first stimulus to the growth of trade and industry usually came from the lord of the manor. The final stage in the political evolution of the town was the

Plate 11   Newcastle-under-Lyme: a new town of the twelfth century whose core can still be traced in the 'market street' to the right of the parish church. No trace of the castle remains, but the site of the 'castle pool' is represented by the public car park on the extreme middle left of the picture (date of photo 1962).

granting of a full borough charter by which the burgesses were freed from the control of their manorial lord. Only a few places in the Midlands such as Coventry ran through the whole cycle of urban development before the sixteenth century.

Newcastle-under-Lyme (SJ 8446) is first mentioned in a document of 1149 as 'the New Castle of Staffordshire'. A few years earlier, most likely between 1142 and 1146, Ranulf Gernons, Earl of Chester, had built a castle mound and cast around it the wide water-defences of the Castle Pool by damming the Lyme Brook. This uninviting site in the valley floor of a tiny stream was chosen to strengthen the defence of the territories of the earls of Chester whose manors stretched across the North Midlands between the Welsh border and Lincolnshire. It seems to have been called the New Castle to distinguish it from the older Roman site at Chesterton, three miles to the north (SJ 8248). The town came into existence soon after the building of the castle. In Norman England, and especially in the wilder parts of the country, castles gave security. They encouraged the settlement of merchants and tradesmen, and the garrison stationed at this outpost of the earls of Chester no doubt provided work for craftsmen and a small, steady market. An entry in the Pipe Rolls shows that an urban community of some size had come into existence at Newcastle by 1156. It says, 'Newcastle is a member of Trentham but on account of the eminence of its castle and market received the prerogative of the name'.

43

Already the new town is beginning to overshadow the parish of Trentham where it had sprung up only a decade earlier. In 1171 another document records some expensive improvements to the big pool of the new town, *de Novo Oppido*. And then two years later, in 1173, a Pipe Roll mentions for the first time the *borough* of Newcastle. It is assessed for tax at £23 6s 8d. In the same document the much older borough of Stafford is taxed at only £10. Within a quarter of a century Newcastle-under-Lyme seems to have come to the front rank among the towns of Staffordshire, outstripping the older borough of Stafford (Pl. 11).

Why was Newcastle so successful? Perhaps the most important factor in Newcastle's rapid evolution to the full status of a borough was its acquisition by Henry II in 1154. Royal towns usually fared better than places under the control of a local lord. Distant royal authority was more likely to grant to the inhabitants of a town the full management of their own affairs under a borough charter, though often at a heavy price in cash. Newcastle seems to have been favoured by medieval kings at the expense of Stafford and this probably helped to ensure the successful growth of a town on the bleak fringe of the Pennines. Later, the nearby coal field, the growth of the pottery industries, and Newcastle's important role in the eighteenth century as a road centre all ensured the active growth of Newcastle as the first coherent regional centre of north Staffordshire.

Coventry certainly has the most spectacular town history of the post-Domesday epoch of expansion (see Study 8). In 1086 Coventry had a population of between three and four hundred; it was a village and no different from many other rural manors in south Warwickshire enumerated in Domesday Book. By the end of the fourteenth century Coventry ranked among the leading towns of England, not far behind London, Bristol and Norwich, and with a population of more than 7000.

Many towns came into being in the West Midlands during the two centuries of Coventry's first spectacular stage of development. None of them was as successful in putting down its economic roots and in acquiring the political institutions of a powerful borough. Several of the urban foundations of the twelfth and thirteenth centuries turned out to be total failures; some progressed slowly towards borough status. Dudley, for instance, prospered as a market-town, but under the shadow of its castle and a powerful overlord it failed to make any headway towards a borough charter until the nineteenth century (see Study 5). Wolverhampton, too, has had a long history of trade and industry, but it received a borough charter only in 1848. Wolverhampton's first steps towards urban status were probably taken in the middle of the thirteenth century when it gained the right to hold a weekly market in 1238. The Avon Valley contains an astonishing variety of urban histories (see Study 11). Warwick never freed itself completely from the dominance of its huge castle. It was one of the proudest possessions of the earls of Warwick, foremost among the powerful aristocratic families of medieval England. Consequently the burgesses of this shire-town only achieved incorporation at a late date in 1546, at a time when the earldom was vacant. For centuries Warwick was unable to free itself from the strategic role that loomed so large at the time of its creation in the first years of the tenth century, while Coventry strode ahead as the chief centre of trade and industry in the Midlands.

Among the most fascinating places in the West Midlands are those settlements that began the evolutionary process towards urban status but which failed to pass beyond the first stage of holding a weekly market. The 'failed' towns were usually founded by ambitious landlords who were anxious to stimulate trade and industry in rural manors and thereby to enlarge their own revenues. Aston Cantlow (SP 1359) aspired to become a town in the thirteenth century (Pl.12). It stands on the River Alne where it winds out of the Forest of Arden to join the Avon. With the Norman Conquest Aston became the property of the Cantilupe family who gave the place the second part of its name. The Cantilupes have left their mark on several pieces of the topography of Aston Cantlow. The faint earthwork of their castle stands in a field between the church and the river. In 1227 William de Cantilupe began the most ambitious attempt to transform the economy and landscape of Aston Cantlow when he obtained a grant to hold a weekly market and an annual fair in his manor. History makes no further mention of trade at Aston Cantlow. The attempt to create a town was a total failure. If we try to find the explanation for the collapse of William de Cantilupe's urban experiment, no clear reasons are forthcoming. Its site was no worse than Henley-in-Arden's; they stand on the same river. Aston Cantlow, too, is crossed by one of the medieval salt-roads from Droitwich. It is likely that competition within this district was too severe. By the end of the thirteenth century there were four markets within five miles of the Cantilupe manor, at Stratford, Bidford, Alcester and Henley-in-Arden.

Aston Cantlow's failure to become a centre of trade is matched by the history of Bretford (SP 4377). Here all the forces of geography seemed to be in favour of the development of a town, for Bretford stands on the north bank of the Avon where the Fosse Way crosses the river. Today there is only a cross-road settlement of red-brick cottages, and a narrow hump-backed stone bridge spans the Avon. In the thirteenth century the de Verdon family, owners of the nearby castle at Brandon (4075), tried to found a town on their property. What better site than a place

Plate 12

Aston Cantlow:
the medieval guildhall
in a 'failed' town (SP 1460)

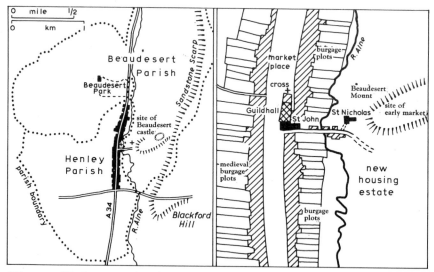

Fig. 13   Henley-in-Arden: The core of the town

on the oldest road through the South Midlands, the Fosse Way, which happened
to form the eastern boundary of Brandon parish? The effort to make a town at
Bretford was a total failure, and yet the value of its site in geographical terms was
far higher than that of the prosperous, expansive Coventry. The failure to make a
town at Bretford probably lay with the de Verdons, a failure that is matched by the
tumbled grassy mound of their former castle in the flood plain of the Avon.

Several towns took off successfully in the period of medieval expansion but lost
their positions as boroughs in later centuries. Henley-in-Arden (SP 1566) ranks
among the most impressive of these. The modern topographical map bears several
clues to the development of Henley-in-Arden. For instance, the town is contained
within a tiny parish that seems to have been carved out of a larger unit. The parish
church of Henley stands only a few yards from the village church of Beaudesert,
separated by the wriggling course of the River Alne. An examination of the two
churches gives the most important clue to the history of the two settlements. St
Nicholas, at Beaudesert, has a completely Norman chancel. At Henley-in-Arden
the parish church of St John the Baptist stands in the centre of the mile-long High
Street; the whole building dates from the fifteenth century. The two churches, in the
dates of their building, suggest that Henley was a later insertion into the landscape
of Beaudesert; but only through the documents can one trace the exact course of
events.

The upper Alne Valley is almost a perfect example of the effects of the Norman
Conquest on the English landscape. Here the de Montfort family acquired an
estate which they called Beaudesert, the 'beautiful wilderness'. By the twelfth
century a castle, surrounded by a deep ditch, had been built on a steep spur projecting into the flood-plain of the Alne. The first record of the castle appears in the
documents in 1140 when Thurstan de Montfort obtained a charter to hold 'a

46

market in his castle of Beldesert'. Here is the first attempt to stimulate trade at this place in the wilds of Arden. The castle-crowned spur must have proved an unsatisfactory place for the gathering of merchants, so a century later we find another de Montfort engaged in a more ambitious effort to stimulate trade at Beaudesert. In 1220 Peter de Montfort obtained a charter for a weekly market on Mondays and the right to hold an annual fair on the eve and day of St Giles's Feast. This is the beginning of Henley-in-Arden; the site of the market has been moved from the castle spur to the valley floor (Fig. 13). One might guess that Peter de Montfort was a successful creator of towns, if one remembers that William de Cantilupe attempted a similar development at Aston Cantlow seven years later. Was this an imitation of a prosperous enterprise at Henley? History is silent about such speculations, but the real success of Henley-in-Arden is measured in 1296 when a survey of John de Montfort's lands shows that the place contained sixty-nine burgesses who paid an annual rent of £7. 18s. 10d. The long High Street, still so sudden and unexpected in the wooded countryside of Arden, was the work of ambitious speculators in the thirteenth century. We shall never know why the de Montforts succeeded at Henley and the de Verdons failed at the much more propitious site of Bretford on the Fosse Way, but their family histories illustrate clearly the part played by the Norman invaders and their descendants in the making of medieval towns.

Plate 13   Part of the former open-field system at Napton on the Hill shows up in ridge-and-furrow. Note the blocks of strips lying in different directions. The Oxford Canal and the boundaries of the present fields show a considerable disregard for the older pattern of strips (SP 4560).

After the end of the fourteenth century one theme dominates the history of the Midland landscape, the conversion of open arable fields and common pastures to hedged and fenced enclosures (Pl. 13). The transformations cover at least four centuries and the Parliamentary Enclosure Acts represent only the closing stages of a long process of change in the countryside. The first Parliamentary Enclosure Act in Warwickshire dealt with the village of Lighthorne (SP 3355) in 1720. The details of Lighthorne's enclosure award show that the great changes of the eighteenth century were not just a sudden destruction of the classic three-field system at the stroke of a pen. This first Warwickshire Act allowed the enclosure of one open field and a tract of common. It was the end of a long process of change in a single parish, where open fields had already undergone quiet enclosure at some unknown date. Everywhere in the Midlands a detailed study of the landscape, on the scale of the parish, teaches that the enclosure movement was a long process and itself only a symptom of deeper changes in the economy and society of England.

The West Midlands display many examples of villages with two and three open fields in the Middle Ages, but local studies reveal many departures from the classic norm. A two-field system of farming seems to have been common on the light and stony soils of the Cotswolds, but it was also to be found in some manors of the Lias Clay vale to the north. Tysoe (SP 3444) and Kenilworth both had two large open fields, and the deserted site of Upper Radbourn (SP 4558; see Study 9) was a two-field village. The three-field system occurred widely along the valley of the Avon and Severn, and again in the Trent Valley and its tributaries. Alcester (SP 0957), for instance, still had a three-field economy in the middle of the eighteenth century. But the agrarian history of parishes up and down the West Midlands shows that field systems did not remain static down the centuries until their final enclosure. Where land was available, and in times of population pressure, new open fields were added to the older arable lands of the community. Elford (SK 1810), in the Tame Valley, shows an evolution from a two-field system to one that worked four

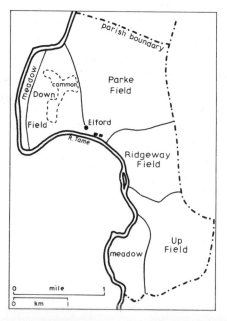

Fig. 14

The four-field system at Elford

fields (Fig. 14). The oldest fields were Parke Field and Ridgeway Field lying close to the village. A later addition was carved out of the woodland that adjoined Ridgeway Field to form Up Field. Elford's role as a classic three-field village was short-lived when another field, with scattered arable strips, was shaped out of the meadows and common land in the arm of the river. Aston Cantlow (SP 1359) perhaps presents a truer picture of the medieval field-systems of the Midlands. This large parish is composed of a main village and several outlying hamlets. In 1273 Aston Cantlow, the chief settlement, had two large open fields, but by the middle of the fourteenth century, on the eve of the Black Death, it had evolved into a three-field community. The creation of a third field perhaps indicates the pressure of rising population, which had been slow but continuous since the beginning of the twelfth century. But a glance at the hamlets around Aston Cantlow shows that each of them possessed open fields, and of varying numbers. Newnham (1560) had four common fields at the beginning of the seventeenth century: a hundred years later, still another open field had been added. Wilmcote (1658) had four fields and there were seven common fields at Little Alne (1361). It is likely that the number of fields in the hamlets was determined by the amount of land available for clearing. Little Alne is particularly suggestive because the hamlet stands on the edge of the deer park enclosed by the Cantilupes early in the thirteenth century. Some of the fields of Little Alne were carved out of the land of the former deer preserve, as the name Park Field indicates.

From the late Middle Ages until the economic transformations at the end of the eighteenth century the Midland landscapes were changing and evolving on a local scale. In some places land was cleared and laid down to common farming in strips as late as the close of the seventeenth century. Elsewhere, wholesale enclosures of common arable land were in progress by the end of the fifteenth century. The total destruction of scores of villages in the South Midlands has left scars on the countryside that have lasted into the twentieth century. The evidence of deserted villages is not very striking in the field until the imagination has been stirred by the documentary history of particular parishes and the knowledge that Warwickshire alone contains 110 abandoned sites. It is only when one crosses such a tract of country as the Lias Clay plain at the foot of the Marlstone escarpment between Southam (SP 4161) and Fenny Compton (4152) that one becomes aware of the great changes shaping the English economy and landscape in the fifteenth century. There seven deserted parishes lie side by side (see Study 9). Even today there is a great emptiness about this countryside with its sites of ruined chapels, grass-grown hollows that once were fishponds, and the faint patterns of former village streets clearly outlined on the bleached January pastures. Once you have walked over the ground at Wormleighton, Lower Radbourn, Hodnell and Chapel Ascote you begin to realise that the settlement pattern of parts of the South Midlands is a mere skeleton of the hamlets and villages that existed in Domesday times.

The earliest deserted villages in the West Midlands are at Upper and Lower Smite on the eastern outskirts of Coventry. They vanished about A.D. 1150 as a result of the foundation of Combe Abbey (SP 4079). The remains of Upper Smite have been completely erased from the ground and the village site was rediscovered only a few years ago with the help of aerial photography. It lies a few hundred yards to the south-east of Mobbs Wood Farm (425828) close to the junction of several bridle roads and field paths (430825). Total destruction did not overtake Lower Smite, for the remains of its church, St Peter's, form part of the farm Peter Hall (412808). The conversion of the Smites to pasture and the destruction of the hamlets happened so long ago that the parish name itself has gone out of use. It is known today as Combe Fields, though the Smite brook that flows westward through the green hollows of former monastic fish-ponds (407805) commemorates the vanished settlements. Stoneleigh Abbey (SP 3171), like Combe an important centre of the Cistercians, was the cause of the destruction of seven neighbouring hamlets during the fifteenth century. Not all of the late-medieval enclosures were for sheep-farming. For instance, Fulbrook (SP 2460) makes a gap in the settlement pattern of the right bank of the Avon between Warwick and Stratford on Avon. The village once stood in the valley between Court Farm and Lower Fulbrook Farm (2560), and it was deserted when the Duke of Bedford made a deer park there in 1421. Another deserted site, Compton Wynyates (SP 3341), stands in a coombe at the foot of the Marlstone escarpment. In 1510 Sir William Compton secured a patent from the Crown which allowed him to enclose 2000 acres in the parish. Two years later the transformation of Compton Wynyates began with the expulsion of twenty families from the village. In 1520 work started on the magnificent house set in a park that occupied the acres of the former open fields (Pl. 14).

Warwickshire illustrates to perfection the making of deer parks, grand Tudor estates and huge sheep-farms in the fifteenth and sixteenth centuries, but the same social and economic changes affected parts of Worcestershire and the Trent Valley in Staffordshire. Deserted sites are harder to detect in Worcestershire because dispersed settlement patterns are common in that county. Nevertheless, a pointer to important changes in Worcestershire's settlement geography in the fifteenth century is given by the Lay Subsidy Roll of 1427–8. It includes a list of parishes that were freed from taxation 'since they have not ten inhabitants'.

Pendock (SO 8133), to the west of the Severn and three miles from Tewkesbury, has a fascinating history that joins together several important strands in the historical geography of the West Midlands. Its Norman church stands lonely on a hilltop close to the weathered, grassy rampart of an Iron Age fort. A large field beside the church contains the ridge-and-furrow that suggests the strips of a medieval open field. And the grass-grown ridge-and-furrow gives way to the faint rectangles and squares that denote the foundations of houses along a one-time village street. Pendock, too, is named in the Lay Subsidy Roll as a place with less than ten inhabi-

Plate 14   Compton Wynyates: a Tudor park on the site of a deserted village. The ridge-and-furrow of the former open fields may be seen beyond the park on the right of the picture.

tants. Here is a medieval desertion characteristic of the southern and eastern parts of the Midlands. But at Pendock we are on the very edge of the Welsh Marches where Celtic themes begin to take over in the landscape-history, and the place itself has a Celtic name.

The Parliamentary Enclosure Acts are the last phase in a centuries-long history of changing land-use and ownership in the Midlands. In all, 175 Parliamentary Acts dealt with the landscape of Warwickshire, and 124 of these were concerned with the enclosure of open fields. Staffordshire's first Enclosure Act, in 1719, began the transformation of the landscape of Gratwood Heath (SJ 7731), an extensive tract of common near Eccleshall. There followed 112 enclosure awards for the county, but among these only 20 included any reference to open fields. Much of Staffordshire was a land of heaths and commons on the hungry soils of the Bunter Sandstones or the raw heights of the Coal Measures Sandstones and the Millstone Grit. Patches of open field had been widespread in the county, but they quietly disappeared in many places through the seventeenth century. For instance, in 1614, the open fields of Tunstall (SJ 8651) were enclosed by agreement among nine owners.

The enclosure of the common lands after 1700 left a great impression on the landscapes of the West Midlands. One Staffordshire example must suffice for this large topic. A late enclosure award dealt with the heath at Salt (SJ 9527) in 1817. The small rectangular fields of this hilly country above the Trent Valley speak of late enclosure (Fig. 15). In the mind's eye one can reconstruct the former open heath, and there is a crude freshness about the man-made features of this landscape. But a detailed examination of Salt Heath shows that beside the rectangular enclosures there are two blocks of tiny fields, long, narrow strips enclosed by stone walls or tall hedges and each entered by a separate gate (at 950271 and 950266). Here the

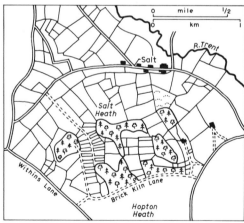

Fig. 15 *Salt Heath: a nineteenth-century enclosure preserves the shape of former strips of arable land amid the heath*

enclosure award has fossilised, for all time as it seems, a fragment of the earlier landscape. The collection of narrow strip-like pastures, represent a former tiny rectangle of open-field arable amid the heath. They represent a system of farming in small outfields that was once common in the upland districts of north Staffordshire.

The newly enclosed commons and heaths provided land for much second-rate farming at the time of the Napoleonic Wars and in the first half of the nineteenth century, when high corn-prices brought profits from the most marginal of land, but they also gave ground for urban expansion in Birmingham, the Black Country and the Potteries. For instance, Handsworth Heath (SP 0490) remained untouched until an enclosure award of 1793. Soon afterwards, as Pitt describes in his *History of Staffordshire*, it became submerged in the urban growth of Birmingham. West Bromwich grew on another tract of enclosed common and the new settlement was aligned along the turnpike road to Holyhead.

The Industrial Revolution

The quickening pace of industry in the eighteenth century created new landscapes in the Midlands. The belt of greatest change stretches from the south-western fringe of the Black Country across the ridges and former heaths of the Birmingham Plateau to Cannock Chase. The Trent Valley intrudes between Rugeley and Stone with scenes of great pastoral beauty – red soils, suave parks at Shugborough and Sandon, and the Trent winding through water meadows that could well belong to Sussex. But the theme of industry is taken up again as one reaches the Potteries. Here the Trent and Mersey Canal, one of the most important monuments of the Industrial Revolution in western Europe, threads through landscapes of utter despoliation. At many places in the Black Country, around the industrialised heart of Birmingham or in the streets of Coventry there are buildings, canals, place-names and patches of derelict land to record the effects of industry on the English landscape. The process has certainly not finished. New buildings and rebuilding are transforming the topography of whole quarters in Midland towns and cities, testifying to a pace of change that must equal that of the most active years of Victorian economic growth. The Industrial Revolution is far from ended; likewise it is hard to know exactly when it began.

The roots of Midland industries lie deep in time. For instance, the mining of coal and iron ore near Wednesbury is recorded in the fourteenth century. The pottery industry in north Staffordshire seems to date back to the same period. Proof is found in the Court Rolls of the manor of Tunstall which tell us that in 1348 'William le Potter gives the lord 6d. to have license to make earthen pots'. The beginning of the potteries of the Burslem district has been attributed to the Cistercian abbey at Hulton, but there is nothing to prove that the craft of pot-making did not first develop among the medieval farmers of this bleak countryside where coal and fire-clay were always so accessible (see Study 1). Coventry, too, has a continuous industrial history from the late twelfth century (see Study 8).

The most important phase of growth in the embryonic medieval industries belongs to the seventeenth and eighteenth centuries. Robert Plot's *Natural History of Staffordshire*, published in 1686, shows that Burslem already had a leading position in the Potteries in the seventeenth century (see Study 1). He says, 'but the greatest pottery they have in this county is carried on at Burslem near Newcastle-under-Lyme where for making their several sorts of pots they have as many different sorts of clays which they dig around about the towne all within half a mile distante, the best being found near the coal. . . .' Likewise in the Black Country it was said that in 1620 there were 20,000 smiths at work within ten miles of Dudley Castle (see Study 5). Already the shape of an evolving industrial conurbation may be faintly discerned behind this figure. In 1758, John Wilkinson, perhaps the greatest inventive genius of the iron trade, built his first blast-furnace at Bradley (SO 9595) just outside Bilston. It is interesting to remember that one of the last active steel-plants of the Black Country stands not far from this site today. A whole cycle of industrial growth and decline has unrolled in this region in less than two centuries. Perhaps the greatest change in the economic geography of the West Midland Plateau in the eighteenth century was the extension of coal-mining along all the accessible outcrops of the Thick Coal in the Tame and Stour valleys. By 1750 mining had reached all the districts where the Thick Coal was lying at or near the surface.

The canal system made at the end of the eighteenth century is one of the most striking features of Midland geography. The growing centres of Birmingham, the Black Country and north Staffordshire were served indirectly by a number of river ports on the fringes of the West Midlands (Fig. 16). Bewdley and Bridgnorth

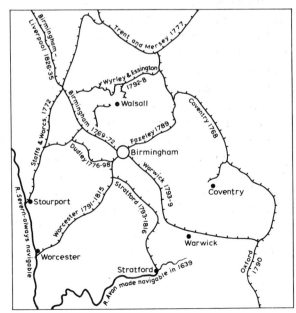

Fig. 16

The canals of the West Midlands

ranked among the greatest inland ports of eighteenth-century England. The Potteries were at the greatest disadvantage in the communications of England before the canal age. Pots were carried out by wagon and pack-horse for export. What was worse, some of the heavy raw materials for the making of fine china – clay from Cornwall and flint stones – had to be brought in by inadequate roads that were rutted and filled with mud in the late autumn and winter. When the agitations for the building of a canal between the Mersey and Trent were at their height in the 1760s, Richard Whitworth wrote in his *Advantages of Inland Navigation* about the organisation of transport from the Potteries. 'Three pot waggons go from Newcastle to Bridgnorth weekly . . . and carry about eight tons of pot ware every week at £3 per ton. The same waggons load back with ten tons of close goods, consisting of white clay, grocery, and iron.' Little wonder that Josiah Wedgwood and his colleagues were in the forefront of demands for a waterway through the North Staffordshire Coalfield.

The main line of the Trent and Mersey Canal, the Grand Trunk, was completed in 1777. During the ten years of its construction other waterways were transforming the economic geography of the heart of the Midlands. James Brindley, the most imaginative mind of the first years of the canal era, who was dead before the completion of the Trent and Mersey waterway, surveyed the routes of all the Midland canals that were in the making about 1770. He left his mark on the West Midland landscape perhaps more sharply than anyone since the nameless surveyors of the Roman roads. By the end of the eighteenth century long and important waterways served the eastern and southern flanks of the Birmingham Plateau. The Coventry Canal and the Oxford Canal gave a water route from the Trent to the Thames, from the industries of north Staffordshire and Birmingham to London. The triangle of canal communications in the Midland Plateau was completed with the scheme for a line between Birmingham and Worcester which was allowed by Act of Parliament in 1791. But this thirty-mile-long canal was opened only after a quarter of a century of money-raising, of smouldering opposition from the Birmingham Canal Company, of severe technical problems, particularly of securing an adequate supply of water in the long summit-level across the Keuper Sandstone Plateau. The Midland canals stretched out to the Severn and Trent and further afield to the Mersey and Thames, but the most intricate network arose in the coal basins of the Black Country. Coal-carrying was the chief task of the new waterways and their main contribution to the progress of the Industrial Revolution.

Canals made an enormous impact upon the places which they touched. The Trent and Mersey Canal created new settlements at Longport and Middleport (see Study 1). New life was given to established market-towns such as Stone (SJ 9034), already an important place on the turnpike roads from London to Carlisle and Chester. A traveller through Staffordshire in the 1780s has left a clear impression of the effect of the canal upon the Trent Valley.

In a few years after it was finished, I saw. . . . the value of manufactures arise in the most unthought of places; new buildings and streets spring up in many parts of Staffordshire, where it passes; the poor are no longer starving . . . and the rich grow steadily richer. The market town of Stone from a poor insignificant place is now grown neat and handsome in its buildings, and from its wharfs and busy traffic wears the lively aspect of a little seaport.

Canal junctions brought into existence busy little settlements with dock basins, and neat terraces of red-brick cottages. Great Haywood (SJ 9922), Autherley (SJ 9001), Fazeley (SK 2001) where Peel built his cotton mills in the 1780s, and Braunston (SP 5366) at the junction of the Oxford and Grand Union canals were some of the key places in the Midland system of waterways. Far more dramatic were the ports that came into being at the great canal terminals. Birmingham became a great inland port with its numerous coal-wharves, barge basins and warehouses in the quarter of Broad Street (SP 0686). The elegance and beauty of much of the building in this first phase of the Industrial Revolution is summed up by Stourport where the Staffordshire and Worcestershire Canal joined the Severn. The simplicity of Georgian warehouses and cottages, quiet reflecting pools, and the soft trickle of water through closed lock-gates sum up this vanished age of busy water-transport (Pl. 15). In 1775 this new Severn port which had eclipsed Bewdley was the show-piece of the West Midlands. Stourport still attracts its day trippers, but now the place is a museum-piece rather than the herald of a new age.

Canals have contributed some monumental features to the Midland landscape. The tunnels at Harecastle (SJ 8452) lead the Trent and Mersey Canal from the North Staffordshire Coalfield into the Cheshire Plain. Telford's new tunnel of 1827

Plate 15   Stourport: a new town and port on the Severn created by the completion of the Staffordshire and Worcestershire Canal. The wide canal-basins, warehouses and Georgian terraces make it the most elegant of the towns of the Industrial Revolution (SO 7282).

runs beside the original work of James Brindley. The Harecastle tunnel communicated with underground coal workings and could be traversed by pleasure-boat. One eighteenth-century account says, 'the view back upon the mouth was like the glimmering of a star, very beautiful; the various voices of the workmen from the mines were rude and awful'. For the rest, the imprint of the canal-builders remains in countless smaller features of the landscape, the toll offices, bridges and aqueducts. In the Birmingham district the constant problem of the canal engineer was water-supply (see Study 4). Several small reservoirs mark the crossing of the Keuper Sandstone Plateau by the Birmingham and Worcester Canal (SP 0174), and Telford added a feature to the Birmingham landscape when he made the Rotton Park reservoir in 1826 (SP 0486). He also surveyed the huge cutting at Smethwick, which is more than seventy feet deep; it is one of the most monumental objects of the canal age to be found anywhere (SP 0189).

The Growth of Towns and Conurbations in the Nineteenth-Century

The evolution of the urban and industrial landscapes of the nineteenth century was an extremely complex process. Beside the powerful forces that were acting for change – the railways and the major technological developments – one has to remember the frequent persistent links with the past. For instance, the sites of the former open fields of Wednesbury have had an important effect on the distribution of industries in the town (see Study 4). The sum total of the process of change since 1850 has been the creation of large tracts of industrial and urban landscapes in the heart of the Midlands. The pattern of population of all previous periods of history has been reversed. The former centres of population in the Avon, Trent and Severn valleys have been eclipsed by the Birmingham Plateau, the coalfields around the Dudley ridge and the five towns that have loosely grown together around the pot-kilns and pit-heads in the headwaters of the Trent.

Birmingham epitomises the processes that have shaped England since the middle of the eighteenth century. Today it is the second largest city in the British Isles with a population of 1,105,651 at the 1961 census. At the first national census in 1801, Birmingham had a population of 70,000, which reflects a considerable period of growth in the eighteenth century. The town's population had quadrupled since 1700, an expansion which can still be traced in the topography of the inner parts of the city despite all the changes that have happened since. Between 1700 and 1730 Birmingham grew across the high land to the north-west of the Bull Ring. Today the most notable landmark of this phase of expansion is the cathedral church of St Philip, completed in 1715. Towards the end of the eighteenth century the chief centre of growth in Birmingham turned to the west of St Philip's where land came on to the market for building development, and the canal wharves and basins around Broad Street gave a new economic focus to the town.

Between 1801 and 1831 the population of Birmingham almost doubled, rising from 70,000 to 130,000. The town grew with the laying out of new streets at Deritend, and on the heath to the north; but much of the growth in the first quarter of the nineteenth century was taken up in the building over of gardens and allotments and waste patches of ground inside the town. The densely built cores of our larger towns are the result of this kind of process before the railway age.

Railways brought a revolution in communications that had deep effects on urban topography. In the space of five years, between 1837 and 1842, four railways reached Birmingham and each followed the corridor of the Rea Valley. The canals focused the industrial development of the late eighteenth century around their wharves on the western edge of the town; now the railways turned industrial growth towards the eastern fringe of Birmingham. Birmingham's first railways, like the canals, came only to the edge of the built-up town. Consequently, the stations lay a mile and more away from the town centre. Curzon Street (SP 079871), the terminus of the London and Birmingham Railway, was inconveniently placed in the squalid suburb of Duddeston. In 1846 the London and Birmingham Railway had been absorbed into the newly formed company of the London and North Western. It was decided to move the terminus from Curzon Street closer to the centre of the city. The problems of taking railways into the centre of Birmingham were immense for the time. The site, on the lip of the Keuper Sandstone Plateau overlooking the Rea, involved the making of elaborate tunnels and cuttings. Land had to be bought at a high price and a densely built quarter of slum streets was cleared to make way for New Street Station.

The railways started a revolutionary series of transformations in the topography of the town centre and its suburbs. They opened up the possibility of the rapid growth of the city. The shift of population to the encircling ring of suburbs started drastic changes in the topography of the heart between the Bull Ring and St Philip's Church. From 1860 onwards shops and offices replaced houses in the central streets. The climax of this process was the making of Corporation Street between 1878 and 1882. This main thoroughfare was cut through a district of narrow streets, of dark and congested courts. The making of Corporation Street was one sympton of Birmingham's emergence as a regional capital, as a centre that was to serve a wide area of the West Midlands.

Between 1920 and the sixties Birmingham has added a huge ring of outer residential suburbs, broken here and there with industries. Railways are no longer a factor in the growth of the city, and their role has been taken over by road transport. Styles of building and layout changed drastically after the First World War. The ideas of the 'garden city movement' swept away the Victorian concepts of urban development, the chessboard street-pattern and the terrace. One of the earliest experiments with new ideas in town-planning was the 'model village' at Bournville. In the thirties the same ideal of the semi-detached house in its own garden beside a winding, tree-lined boulevard became the dominant theme in corporation housing-estates. Highter's Heath (SP 0879) is typical of this phase of Birmingham's development. Around King's Norton the inter-war housing-estates merge into the building of the fifties and early sixties. Tower-block flats, shopping-centres, and more varied, cellular layouts in street-plans characterise this age. Compared with the inter-war period of building there is more variety of height, function and pattern. For instance, the Hawkesley Farm housing-estate at King's Norton preserves a moated farm-house in its make-up, a memory of the lost landscape of Arden. Only the attempts to preserve a green belt around the western and southern flanks of the city prevent Birmingham from eating more deeply into the countryside.

Birmingham displays more clearly than many places the themes of urban growth over the past century and a half (Fig. 17). City cores tend to be rebuilt and their street patterns reshaped several times as the conurbation swamps the surrounding countryside (Pl. 16). We have seen that the railways ushered in a half-century of reconstruction and changing functions. Now, in the mid-sixties, the process of rebuilding is once more powerfully at work, sweeping away many of the landmarks of the railway age. The motor car has caused severe congestion in the streets of central Birmingham and the key to the redevelopment of the centre is the four-mile long Inner Ring Road. This scheme that tries to solve the problem of traffic movement at the city centre will probably be imitated in several British cities before the 1980s. Whether it is the right solution still remains a matter of hot debate. The making of the Inner Ring Road is related to three zones of new building. To the north-west of Birmingham's heart lies the Civic Centre, where an elaborate scheme of development was started before the Second World War. Another pole of urban renewal is centred at the Bull Ring, the village green of medieval Birmingham and the place where the Victorian markets were built. Today, the Bull Ring is the site of a shopping-centre that is without parallel in the British

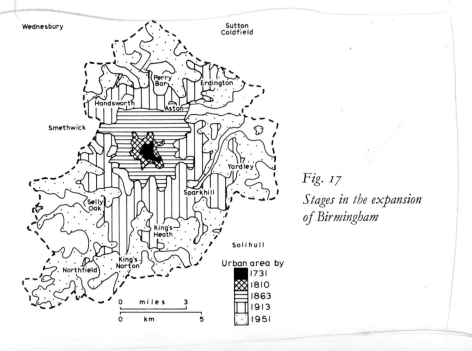

Fig. 17

Stages in the expansion of Birmingham

Urban area by
- 1731
- 1810
- 1863
- 1913
- 1951

Plate 16 Birmingham: the large-scale replanning of a city centre. In the middle distance we see the Rotunda and the Bull Ring Centre, and further away the tower-blocks in the redevelopment quarter of Ladywood. Note, top right, the site of the eighteenth-century canal terminus (date of photo 1964).

Isles in its layout and design. The third zone of active rebuilding at the centre of Birmingham fringes the new Inner Ring Road. Here the small metal-working and jewellery industries that occupied single storeys and sometimes single rooms in the long-established industrial quarter to the north of St Philip's Cathedral are taking up space in 'flatted factories', eight- and ten-storey buildings with high glass curtain-walls which house a host of firms. The industrial structure of central Birmingham that evolved in the eighteenth century still governs the architectural reshaping of the city today.

The remaking of Birmingham in the 1960s concerns not only the core – the site of the medieval village and the eighteenth-century town – but also a circle of densely built inner suburbs in Duddeston (SP 0887), Ladywood (0586) and Nechells (0989). They took shape in the first half of the nineteenth century. Their depressingly grey streets of terraced houses were entangled with forges, metal-working

59

shops, coal-wharves and canals. At the outbreak of the Second World War large tracts of these inner suburbs were slum property in need of clearance. As in Coventry (see Study 8) German bombs prepared the way for redevelopment. In 1945, at the end of the war, Birmingham had 12,000 destroyed or severely damaged houses. The city corporation bought five tracts of land in the run-down inner suburbs and set about their clearance and rebuilding between 1948 and 1953. Now, in the mid-sixties, the schemes are coming to completion. The transformation of an early Victorian urban landscape could hardly be more radical. Each of the five areas has been treated as a 'new town' and the aim is to house between 6000 and 15,000 people in each unit. Even so, they will contain only half the number of their former residents. The Nechells Green redevelopment was the first to be started, and there the population has been reduced from 19,000 to 12,500. Even more striking is the housing of the people in tall tower-blocks which have given a new skyline to Birmingham.

The transformations in the topography of central Birmingham in the middle of the twentieth century are matched by equally radical changes in the style of its architecture. Just as Corporation Street, the triumphant piece of replanning in the 1880s, expressed itself so clearly in the fashionable styles of the age, so the Bull Ring, the rebuilt New Street Station and the tower-blocks of the 'new towns' bring Birmingham to the fore as a centre of twentieth-century architecture. Birmingham possesses some compelling buildings from every stage of its evolution. We have discussed St Philip's Church as representative of the stage of growth at the beginning of the eighteenth century. As one walks through the streets of the city it is hard to take one's eyes off the classical lines of the Town Hall. It has been described as 'aloof and awe-inspiring'. In another part of the city Curzon Street Goods Station was the original terminus of the London and Birmingham Railway when it opened in 1838. Its four gigantic Ionic columns form a marvellous monument to the start of the railway age, especially now that its counterpart at Euston has been destroyed. Perhaps the styles of Corporation Street are even more dramatically expressed on the university campus at Edgbaston where the Chamberlain Tower, modelled on a campanile at Siena, overpowers the buildings at its feet. The same dramatic qualities of soaring height belong to one of the newest buildings of central Birmingham, the Rotunda, completed in 1965. It crowns the top of the hill above the Bull Ring and rises to almost 300 feet above the Inner Ring Road. The Rotunda is the most compelling feature of central Birmingham, particularly when seen as part of the skyline across the Rea Valley from the east – a view gained to perfection from the front windows of a diesel train as it crosses the Rea viaduct before plunging into the tunnel that leads to New Street Station. The striking qualities of Birmingham are expressed not only in a few of its individual buildings but also through the juxtaposition of styles of architecture from different periods of the city's history. And what better than the placing side by side of the new Bull Ring complex and the original parish church of St Martin's. St Martin's, albeit a church heavily restored by the Victorians, shelters the four-teenth-century tombs of the de Birmingham family, lords of the medieval manor. There, in St Martin's, one may start a field excursion to trace out the story of the development of Birmingham, and sufficient pieces of visual evidence survive to sketch the main stages in the city's evolution ending in the Rotunda and the tower-blocks of Ladywood.

The Potteries stand aloof from the heart of the West Midlands, closer to Man-chester than Birmingham. In the evolution of their six scattered industrial cores, Burslem, Fenton, Hanley, Longton, Stoke-on-Trent and Tunstall, the functions of a regional capital have remained dispersed. Stoke-on-Trent became a city in 1925, but a city lacking in a concentration of the functions and activities of the true regional capital and devoid of city architecture. In the 1950s one discerns an effort to overcome some of these severe disabilities. For instance, a modern city museum and art gallery was opened at Hanley on the site of a former pottery in 1956. Formerly, Burslem, Tunstall, Hanley and Stoke had their own museums. Topo-graphy helps to explain the failure of the Potteries to achieve cohesion. The towns stand apart from each other on their ridges above the headstreams of the Trent, while the communications of the canal and railway age lie below the urban centres, narrowly focused in the trough of the Fowlea Brook. But behind the divisive character of the landscape lie the social outlooks and attitudes of the inhabitants of the pottery towns. Perhaps the real answer to this problem of the development of the conurbation may be found in the pages of Arnold Bennett where the 'five towns' are drawn with sharply different characters, miniature nations living out their spiteful enmities (see Study I). Proud and ancient Newcastle is cut off from the pot-kilns and coal pits of Burslem by a far greater barrier than that imposed by the trench of the Fowlea Brook, the barrier of class and occupation.

Along the eastern flank of the Black Country, town-growth was extremely sluggish despite the good communications that have served the region in the turn-pike road following the line of Watling Street, a canal system that joined the Trent to the Thames and Birmingham, and one of Britain's busiest trunk railways. The London and North Western Railway left its mark on the landscape of Rugby. The railway added a new quarter to the town, north of the old nucleus of the mar-ket-village. It is unmistakable in the present topography of Rugby where the narrow, crooked streets of the town-centre give way to a rectangular gridiron pattern with monotonous terraced housing. This could be a piece of the townscape of Crewe and for the very good reason that both places developed under the shadow of the same railway company. Rugby's period of growth and pros-perity lay between 1850 and 1880. The London and North Western Railway and the high reputation of Dr Arnold among the Victorian middle class have between them left an indelible mark on the topography of the town. Railways and a great public school shaped Rugby so that today it is a compact museum of buildings from the High Victorian period. All is summed up in the parish church of St Andrew where a village church of the late fourteenth century was enlarged between 1877 and 1885 to meet the needs of the growing town. Butterfield was the architect of much of Rugby School and we meet his aggressive, colourful style in the large additions to the parish church. Here the medieval and Butterfield's High Victorian polychrome are present in one building, just as Rugby still presents two topographical faces – market-village and railway-town. Now in the twentieth century large new industries devoted to electrical engineering have grown in the flood plain of the Avon across the railway tracks that hem in the Victorian town.

It is curious that the long strip of country between Stafford and Rugby should remain poverty-stricken in the urban developments of the past century and a half. The story is different on the south-western flank of the Birmingham Plateau. Worcester and Gloucester have both flourished as regional capitals in a way that has been denied to Lichfield and Tamworth. Gloucester's steady prosperity in the nineteenth century added large, dull suburbs outside the medieval town on the road to Bristol and around the railway lines. The burgage plots of the former medieval town were rebuilt so that a contemporary writer could say, 'Gloucester resigned itself to becoming the blotch on the face of a fair county that it is today, a place of which it has been truly said that no royal and ancient town in England has murdered its past more thoroughly, and none is meaner in its present aspect'. But if the late nineteenth century ruined Gloucester, the beginning of the period saw the making of a new town at Cheltenham that is one of the finest in western Europe (Pl. 17). There was nothing at Cheltenham before the middle of the eighteenth century. In 1748 a mineral spring there was first exploited and by the 1780s a single street of houses, the High Street, had come into existence. In 1788 George III took the waters at Cheltenham and by that act set the town on a course of explosive expansion. Between 1801 and 1821 the population rose from 3000 to 13,000. New suburbs of elegant Georgian terraces were laid out at Montpellier and Pittville, and each had its own pump-room.

Today spas are out of fashion. Cheltenham and Leamington survive on their other merits – as regional shopping-centres, tourist resorts for day-trippers, for their private schools and colleges, and as places for retirement. But one can discern a new function that might become predominant in the life of the Midland spa towns long before the end of the century. Since 1940 the outskirts of Leamington and Warwick have been chosen by new industries – particularly by firms engaged in the making of the many accessories for the car factories of Coventry and Birmingham. New industries, too, have been attracted to the six-mile belt of country between Cheltenham and Gloucester. Before the end of the century it seems likely that two fresh Midland conurbations will appear – one in the Avon Valley between Coventry, Kenilworth and Leamington, the other at the foot of the Cotswolds

Plate 17   Cheltenham: the magnificent terraces and crescents of a Georgian spa town

linking Cheltenham and Gloucester. These are the West Midland's natural growth-areas in the middle of the twentieth century, but in other parts of the region the shapes of new towns can be discerned that may well form potent features of the landscape and the economy by the year 2000. The huge planned town of Telford is already beginning to obliterate the fields and derelict land around Dawley on the historic coalfield of east Shropshire. And at Chelmsley Wood (SP 1887) on the out-skirts of Coleshill, Birmingham Corporation has started building a council estate that will house a population as big as one of the ancient regional capitals such as Worcester or Shrewsbury.

The Coventry district is among the most rapidly developing areas of Britain. Today one can sense the expansion of Coventry on the city's north-east margin at Wyken and Sowe Common where new housing-estates are pushing out across the abandoned tips of the East Warwickshire Coalfield. But one can imagine that in the next-half-century a new sort of development will take place to the south of the city. One element of the Warwick–Coventry conurbation is already in being with the site of the new University of Warwick in beautiful rolling parkland between Coventry and Kenilworth (SP 3075). The conurbation of the late twentieth century could be very different from its Victorian forerunners in Birmingham and the Black Country. The astonishing variety of Coventry's present topography (see Study 8) might be combined with the Regency elegance of Leamington and the early eighteenth-century buildings of Warwick's High Street. Kenilworth and Warwick castles might be skilfully juxtaposed with tower-block buildings of the kind that are now arising in Birmingham. Urban beauty lies in a contrast of styles, the placing together of contrasting shapes and colours – a lesson that still has to be consciously learnt in the making of our cities. Today we see in the landscapes of the West Midlands the product of many phases of history, but we also survey a landscape that is changing more rapidly than at any time since the first Neolithic farmers cleared the forests that clothed the dry summits of the Cotswolds.

Select Bibliography

Beaver, S. H. 'The Potteries: a Study in the Evolution of a Cultural Landscape', *Transactions of the Institute of British Geographers*, vol. XXXIV (1964) pp. 1–32.

Buchanan, K. M. *Worcestershire*, pt 68 of the Land of Britain series, ed. L. D. Stamp (1944).

Darby, H. C. and Terrett, I. *The Domesday Geography of the Midlands* (1955).

Dreghorn, W. *Geology Explained in the Severn Vale and Cotswolds* (1967).

Eastwood, T. *et al.* 'Geology of the Country around Birmingham', *Memoirs of the Geological Survey of Great Britain* (1925).

Edmunds, F. H. and Oakley, K. P. 'The Central England District', *British Regional Geology* (1947).

Finberg, H. P. R. *Gloucestershire* (1955).

Hadfield, C. *The Canals of the West Midlands* (1966).

Mackney, D. and Burnham C. P. *The Soils of the West Midlands* (1964).

Macpherson, A. *Warwickshire*, pt 62 of the Land of Britain series, ed. L. D. Stamp (1946).

Myers, J. *Staffordshire*, pt 61 of the Land of Britian series, ed. L. D. Stamp (1945).

Pape, T. *Medieval Newcastle-under-Lyme* (1928).

Pevsner, N. *Warwickshire*, The Buildings of England 30 (1966).

Victoria County History, Warwickshire, vol. VII, *The City of Birmingham*, ed. W. B. Stephens (1964).

Webster G. and Hobley, B. 'Aerial Reconnaissance over the Warwickshire Avon', *Archaeological Journal*, vol. CXXI (1965) pp. 1–22.

Wills, L. J. 'The Pleistocene Development of the Severn from Bridgnorth to the Sea', *Quarterly Journal of the Geological Society*, vol. XCIV (1938) pp. 161–242.

Birmingham and its Regional Setting, a Scientific Survey, ed. M. J. Wise (British Association for the Advancement of Science, 1950).

Part Two Individual Studies

1 Burslem—A Potteries Town

The North Staffordshire Coalfield is one of the most compact industrial regions of England. Its six towns are Tunstall, Burslem, Hanley, Stoke-on-Trent, Fenton and Longton. They make up a straggling conurbation that stretches for almost eight miles at the headwaters of the Trent. Small, isolated moorland settlements at the beginning of the eighteenth century expanded throughout the nineteenth century into a sprawling string of towns. The industries that brought about this urban growth – coal-mining, iron-smelting, brick- and tile-making and, supreme among them, the pottery manufactures – were responsible for the individuality of the landscapes of the North Staffordshire Coalfield. They even gave rise to its regional name – the Potteries.

The chief elements of the Potteries landscape are the blue-grey hills of slag marking the sites of collieries many of which are now abandoned, the deep gashes in the Etruria marls where clay is got for brick- and tile-making, the stubby, square chimneys of brick-works, and formerly the fantastic clusters of bottle-shaped kilns. Today, the bottle-oven is a fast-disappearing feature. In 1936 clouds of smoke billowed over the six towns from more than 2,500 kilns. By 1964 only 200 of these bottle-shaped ovens were left standing and now at the end of the decade less than forty are left. They are relics of the past, cold and disused in the cramped, square yards of potteries. Since 1950 gas-fired and electric kilns have spread rapidly. This fresh stage in the technology of a continuing industrial revolution has changed the very landscape of the North Staffordshire Coalfield. The day is not far off when the bottle-kiln will have gone from the landscape completely, apart from an occasional one preserved as a museum specimen.

The Earliest Features of Burslem

Burslem stands on a bleak, flat-topped ridge at almost 700 feet above sea level. The seams of the Middle Coal Measures outcrop along the eastern flank of this ridge. To the west, the coal-bearing rocks disappear beneath the sandstones and shales

Plate 1a Burslem: St Johns Church stands in the foreground surrounded by potteries with their distinctive bottle-kilns. In the distance is the site of the former green now hemmed in by some of the more important potteries. The main road to the right is Waterloo Road (date of photograph 1961).

of the Upper Coal Measures. Their purple-coloured sandstones have been a favourite building-material in the Potteries and we see them today in churches, town halls and sumptuous Victorian houses. The Upper Coal Measures also contain the Etruria Marl, a deposit that is a thousand feet thick and which provides clay for the brick-and-tile works. The Fowlea Valley runs along the outcrop of the Etruria Marl and separates Burslem from Newcastle. The hill-top settlement of Burslem in the eighteenth century lay close to raw materials, coal and clay, that have played such a part in its industrial development. So close is its site to the out-cropping seams of the Middle Coal Measures that they lie underneath the buildings at the centre of the town.

At the beginning of the eighteenth century Burslem was a collection of moor-land farms gathered in a rather irregular way around a village green. As a part-time occupation most of the farmers made pots and each farm-house had an oven and small sheds for carrying on this work. By about 1750 there were twenty-three small potteries at Burslem. Coal for the kilns was mined in small pits to the east of the village.

66

Despite all the changes in the appearance of Burslem since the end of the eighteenth century, we can still trace the pattern of the former village at the heart of the modern town. Burslem's street plan is based on the lanes of the original moorland settlement. The cluster of open places and short streets at the town centre was already established by the middle of the eighteenth century. They include St John's Square, Market Place, Swan Square, Queen Street, Wedgwood Street and Greenhead Street (Pl. 1a). The age of Burslem's town centre is revealed, too, in the number of buildings that date from before the middle of the nineteenth century. There is more Georgian architecture here than in any other town in the Potteries. The low buildings around Market Place still give a Georgian atmosphere to this part of the town. The best example is now the Midland Bank at the corner of Market Place and Moorland Road. It used to be called the Big House and was built by Thomas and John Wedgwood in 1751. The excellent state in which it is kept today helps to remind us that this was the most palatial house in Burslem in the middle of the eighteenth century.

Another feature of modern Burslem that dates back to the eighteenth century is the location of the pottery and china works close to the centre of the town. Several important firms have developed from the small potteries owned by the farmers of two centuries ago. They stand on their original sites where the farms lay close to the centre of the former village (Pl. 1b). The air photograph (Pl. 1a) shows several potteries close to the centre of Burslem, although the destruction of the bottle-shaped kilns in large numbers since 1950 makes this a far less striking picture than one which might have been taken twenty years earlier. Nevertheless, we can see in the photograph a concentration of potteries to the north of Market Place where bottle-kilns, chimney stacks, and the long, low sheds that house the modern gas-fired kilns jostle each other. Among these is the Overhouse Pottery in Wedgwood Place. It has the longest history of any pottery in Burslem and has worked without a break for at least 250 years. A seventeenth-century legal document, dated 1667, says that a building was leased at Overhouse that was 'used for pothouses', with a pot-oven and a smokehouse, and with the right to dig clay and marl on the site. For most of the eighteenth century Overhouse was owned by the Wedgwood family, and the Thomas Wedgwood who was in charge in the 1780s included among his products 'a china glazed ware painted with blue'.

Plate 1b

The façade of a pottery close to the centre of Burslem. The building has recently been demolished.

Stages in the Growth of Burslem

The cutting of the Trent and Mersey Canal through the valley of the Fowlea Brook started the first great changes in the geography of Burslem. The canal opened in 1777 and within a few years a bunch of potteries and potters' houses had arisen on its banks close to the crossing of the road from Burslem to Newcastle (P. 1*d*). Longport (8549) was the name given to this new industrial suburb on the western fringe of Burslem. Two other industrial clusters, Middleport (8649) and Newport (865488), came into being on the banks of the Trent and Mersey Canal early in the nineteenth century. In 1805 a short branch-canal was cut from Newport and at its head Burslem Wharf was built (865494). From the town-centre Navigation Road ran down the steep slope of Burslem's ridge and it formed the first tentacle of industries and houses joining the hill-top settlement and the valley floor of the Fowlea Brook.

If you look at the map of Burslem in 1832, copied from the survey of Thomas Hargreaves, you can see clearly the layout of the town in the first quarter of the nineteenth century (Fig. 1*c*). The long slopes that led down to the Fowlea Valley and the Trent and Mersey Canal were being developed for industry and housing, but there was still a lot of open agricultural land between Burslem and its separate industrial outliers along the canal at Longport, Middleport and Newport. When Hargreaves made his map St Paul's Church had just been built and it still lay in open country. Like so many churches in the textile towns of south Lancashire, St Paul's was built mainly with a grant from Parliament (Pl. 1*e*). It reflects the concern that was felt over the new centres of population that were beginning to swarm

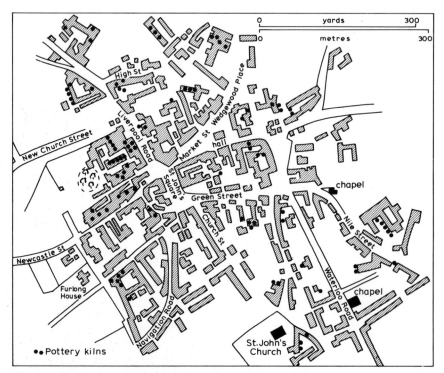

Fig 1c Hargreaves' map of Burslem as it appeared in 1832

Plate 1d
Trent and Mersey Canal
at Longport

Plate 1e

St Paul's Church, Burslem:
typical of the early
nineteenth-century churches
built from parliamentary
grant in growing
industrial towns

Plate 1f

A Victorian terrace in
Newport Lane where the pavement
is made of Staffordshire
blue bricks

69

on the coalfields of England in the first quarter of the nineteenth century. Government in London turned a blind eye to many of the problems in the new industrial regions, but in nineteenth-century England they could not neglect the demands of religion; hence the parliamentary churches built as cheaply and as quickly as possible. St Paul's, huge and dark, is in the Perpendicular style of the kind that Victorian architects were to produce by the hundred from their drawing-boards. A writer of the time described St Paul's about ten years after it had been finished. He notes the box pews 'of good deal, painted to resemble oak' and the front of the gallery 'made of stucco, but painted in oil, in resemblance of pannelled Gothic wainscot'. Here is the Victorian mania for making cheap materials look like something more expensive.

Longport and the canal-side settlements remained separate from the core of Burslem until about 1850 (Fig. 1g). In the third quarter of the nineteenth century the two became joined together by a gridiron pattern of streets with terraced houses and a scattering of industrial development. You can see these blocks of Victorian terraces on either side of Newport Lane where it leads down from St Paul's Church to the Trent and Mersey Canal (864492) (Pl. 1f). The streets have a formal rectangular pattern that was laid out in the fields flanking the Burslem branch-canal. The terraced houses of this quarter are built of a glistening red brick that a century of grime belched from the neighbouring pot-kilns and tile-works has failed to tarnish. The front doors along each strip of houses stand together in pairs as the builder set them out to the same unalterable plan. The pavements of these streets, and of so many others in Burslem, are made of the dark blue bricks, baked out of the clays of the Etruria Marl that outcrops along the valley of the Fowlea Brook. This is the Burslem that Arnold Bennett describes so vividly

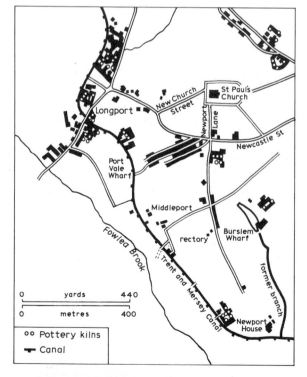

in his novel *Clayhanger*: '. . . on a little hill in the vast valley was spread out the Indian-red architecture of Bursley – tall chimneys and rounded ovens, schools, the new scarlet market, the grey tower of the old church . . . and the crimson chapels and rows of little red houses with amber chimney pots. . . .'

On the ridge top, above the Trent and Mersey Canal, the construction of new roads about the turn of the eighteenth century controlled the later development of Burslem. Josiah Wedgwood

Fig. 1g

Settlements and industries along the Trent and Mersey Canal as shown on Hargreaves' map of 1832

was the force behind the building of two important turnpike roads into Burslem. One road from the north gave access to the Cheshire Plain and Liverpool and was completed in 1763. The second was finished in 1765 and ran through Etruria (8647) to Newcastle. You can follow the line of this second turnpike road southward from Burslem along Nile Street and Elder Road to Cobridge (8748). In 1817 the geography of Burslem was transformed once more by the opening of the Waterloo Road (872493). This long, straight road, so closely dated by its name, summarizes in its buildings the growth of Burslem through the nineteenth century. At the northern end of this drab and busy street, just after leaving the junction with the earlier turnpike at Nile Street (870497), there are low-built terraces that date from the time when Waterloo Road was cut. The names of crossing streets – Pitt Street East, Wellington Street and Adelaide Street – all reveal the period of the making of this suburb of Burslem in the 1820s. Zion Street, with the Bethel Chapel standing at its corner, reminds us of another strand in the social history of the Potteries, of the success of the Nonconformists, of chapel Christianity, in this industrial region. Bethel Chapel was built and opened in 1824. Because of the movement of population from the centre of Burslem in the years since the war and the falling attendance at its services, Bethel Chapel was closed in 1955. Since 1960 it has been used as a warehouse by a firm of china- and earthenware-manufacturers. Here, in a little more than a century, we can see the cycle of events in the history of a chapel that one finds repeated in so many of the industrial towns of England. Changes in population, especially the movement of people from the run-down slums close to town centres to new council estates, and a sharp fall in the membership of the Nonconformist churches has caused the closing of so many chapels. Some have been demolished; many have been turned into small factories and warehouses. The whole of this early nineteenth-century suburb of the Waterlooo Road is on the point of extinction, awaiting the bull-dozers of of the 1970's.

Further along the Waterloo Road we come to the Washington Works and the American Hotel facing each other. Both were built in the 1830s, and the American Hotel has a striking bow-window of three storeys. During the first half of the nine-teenth century this was the limit of the built-up part of Burslem on the Waterloo Road, a fact that is brought home to us when we continue along the way to Co-bridge. After the Washington Works building-styles change completely. The road is now lined by the large houses built by the richer people of Burslem in the second part of the nineteenth century. Potters, solicitors and doctors made this first upper middle-class suburb of Burslem. As one leaves Burslem behind, so these large houses in the varied styles of the late nineteenth century, 'gabled Tudor' and 'Italianate stucco', become later in date. Perhaps this Victorian ribbon develop-ment is best summed up when we come to a palatial brick-terrace in Cobridge. It was built in the 1880s and today it houses the Arnold Bennett Museum. And what more suitable place, for Cobridge is 'Bleakridge' of Bennett's novels *Clayhanger* and *The Card*.

Buildings and the Growth of Burslem

The streets and suburbs of Burslem mark out the main stages in the growth of the town (Fig. 1*k*). As we have already noticed, some buildings commemorate certain epochs and episodes of local and national history. St Paul's Church is typical of the first great period of town growth connected with the Industrial Revolution. The Wedgwood Memorial Institute in Queen Street sums up the third quarter of the nineteenth century when the topography of the English industrial town was changing rapidly with the erection of great public buildings – libraries, museums, art galleries, concert halls and meeting-places. Often they were ornate, pompous and showy, reflecting the wealth and security of Victorian England's upper middle class. The Wedgwood Institute housed a museum, picture gallery, library and lecture rooms. Its strikingly elaborate front in the Venetian Gothic style is designed to display the industry and the industrialists that made nineteenth-century Burslem. Between the two storeys are oblong panels of terracotta that show the different processes of the pottery industry, and above the richly decorated doorway stands a statue of Josiah Wedgwood. This building was put up between 1863 and 1869; it is still a landmark of the urban scene in Burslem and it commemorates an epoch in the town's history. What could be more appropriate than the fact that its foundation stone was laid by Gladstone?

The parish church of St John the Baptist illustrates more than one phase of Burslem's history in its building-stones. The squat sandstone tower, blackened by the smoke of the kilns that still overshadow the churchyard from the north, is the oldest feature of Burslem's townscape. It was built in Henry VIII's reign, probably in 1536, and is late Perpendicular in style. The rest of the building, the nave and chancel, stands in great contrast; they are of brick and belong to the eighteenth century. The nave was built in 1717 and replaced an earlier timber-framed building. Towards the end of the century Burslem parish church was described as 'being too small for the number of inhabitants' and the chancel was added in 1788.

With the rapid growth of the town in the nineteenth century St John's established its 'chapels of ease' in the outlying suburbs of Burslem. First, St Paul's (863497) was built in 1831 and this was followed by Christ Church (876487) at Cobridge ten years later. At the parish church the growth of Burslem is recorded in the extension of the churchyard. New ground had to be added to it in 1804, 1847 and 1878. We can still pick out the old part of the churchyard by the brick walls that date from the end of the eighteenth century. Today St John's churchyard commemorates some of the less pleasant features of Victorian industrialism in the

Plate 1h
The entrance to Wade Heath Pottery near the end of Burslem

Plate 1i
One of the crate works making wooden boxes for the pottery industry

Plate 1j (below)
An abandoned branch of the Trent and Mersey Canal, now an eyesore but once part of the flourishing industrial economy of the Potteries

Potteries. This plain eighteenth-century building is held together by a frame of iron posts and metal straps – proof of the subsidence that has occurred with the mining of the coal-seams beneath Burslem. The medley of black obelisks and tombstones in the vast churchyard is almost lost in a jungle of unkempt grass and the narrow, winding tracks made by dogs and children. The whole scene is a sombre memorial to Victorian industrialism.

Further Reading

Beaver, S. H. 'The Potteries: a Study in the Evolution of a Cultural Landscape', *Transactions of the Institute of British Geographers*, vol. xxxiv (1964) pp. 1–31.
Moisley, H. A. 'The Industrial and Urban Development of the North Staffordshire Conurbation', *Transactions of the Institute of British Geographers*, vol. xvii (1951) pp. 151–65.
Victoria County History, Staffordshire, vol. viii (1963) pp. 105–42.

Maps

O.S. 1-inch sheet 110 (Stoke-on-Trent); O.S. $2\frac{1}{2}$-inch sheet SJ 84

Suggested Itineraries

(*a*) A detailed study may be made of the centre of Burslem noting the pattern of streets and open spaces at the core of the pre-industrial settlement (Fig. 1*k*). The Midland Bank, once the Big House of the Wedgwood family, stands at the junction of Market Place and Wedgwood Street. Note the two town halls that remain standing. The first, on the market place, was built between 1854 and 1857 and is now a public library. Then see the cluster of potteries to the north of the town centre and very close to it – Royal Overhouse Pottery; the Royal Pottery, now

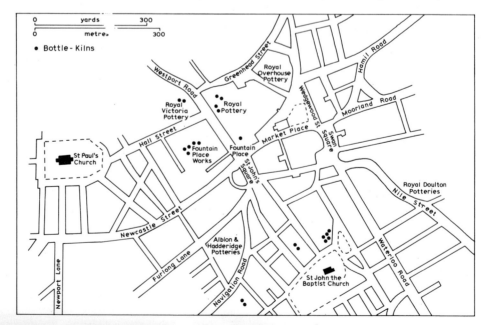

Fig. 1k   The centre of Burslem at the present time

the Royal Works producing electrical porcelain, and the Hill Top Methodist Church and Sunday School (here are gems of architecture belonging to the early Industrial Revolution); the Georgian façade of Enoch Wood's Fountain Place Works still surviving above a group of shops at the corner of Westport Road and Packhorse Lane. Conclude the excursion by looking at the Wedgwood Memorial Institute in Queen Street and follow Bournes Bank, on the line of a country lane in pre-industrial Burslem, to the parish church. On the right, at the foot of Bourne's Bank, a cluster of active bottle kilns still remains, now converted to oil firing.

(*b*) A field study of the southward growth of Burslem along the Waterloo Road may be started with a walk through the three streets to the south of the town centre in the order of their making. Walk from Queen Street along the oldest way, Bournes Bank; cross by Zion Street to Nile Street, the turnpike road cut in 1765; return to Swan Square and the beginning of Waterloo Road, opened in 1817. Follow Waterloo Road to Cobridge, noting details of its buildings *en route*.

(*c*) A long field excursion begins with a study of the centre of Burslem, follows with Longport (858496) and the Trent and Mersey Canal, making an exploration of the tow-path through Middleport (860495) to Newport and Burslem Wharf (865494). Return to Burslem through the streets of the mid-nineteenth-century quarter around St Paul's Church (863497). This may be continued with an exploration of the Waterloo Road (see above) to Cobridge; visit the site of Grange colliery that is today a waste dump above the Fowlea Valley, but an excellent viewpoint for the Shelton Iron and Steel Works, the Trent and Mersey Canal and a general view of Burslem and Tunstall (868487). Return to Burslem through the mining suburb of Sneyd with its marl-pits and brick-and-tile works, whose colliery was closed in 1968.

Field Work

(*a*) With the help of Hargreaves's map of 1832 (Fig. 1*c*) make a list of some of the features marked there that you can still see in the landscape today.

(*b*) Prepare in class a sketch-outline of the course of the Trent and Mersey Canal between Longport and Newport, including the abandoned branch to Burslem Wharf. As you walk along the tow-path, map and name all the industries that you find there at the present time.

Further Work

(*a*) From the air photograph draw a large sketch-diagram of the centre of Burslem marking the main streets and the areas taken up by industry, public buildings and housing.

(*b*) If you are able to visit Burslem for field work, name the following on your diagram – the parish church, the site of the first town hall, the oldest surviving pottery, the oldest buildings in the town centre, the turnpike road built in 1765 and Waterloo Road.

2 Cannock Chase

Cannock Chase is one of those small distinctive regions which occur throughout the West Midlands. In both an historical and a physical sense, this upland tract of infertile country is set apart from the more inviting lowlands around. The name Cannock is probably derived from the Celtic *cnoc* meaning hill, and it is perhaps significant that the earliest Iron Age settlers built their camp on its highest part at Castle Ring (0412). The Saxon colonisers, however, shunned the area and preferred to settle in the rich and varied lands of the Trent Valley to the east. To the Mercian kings, who ruled this part of the Midlands Cannock was set aside as a royal hunting-ground. This was to continue to be its role after the Norman Conquest, for Domesday Book, prepared in 1086, records that it was held by William the Conqueror as a royal 'forest' (forest in this sense meaning a game- and hunting-preserve). In 1290 the king sold his rights over the land to the Bishop of Lichfield and so the 'forest' strictly became a 'chase', a name which it has retained to the present day. With the dissolution of the monasteries by Henry VIII in 1537, Cannock Chase was given to William Paget, one of the king's favourites at court, and it was his heirs who built the fine Elizabethan mansion at Beaudesert and converted much of the surrounding country into a deer park. Although the mansion was demolished in 1933 and much of the original deer park has been planted with conifers, part of the open parkland landscape with its scattered oak trees remains.

It is easy to understand why Cannock Chase remained a game-reserve for so long, fit only for hunting and recreation. The greater part of the area is underlain by thick deposits of the Bunter Pebble Beds. A good exposure of these occurs by the roadside (A513) as it cuts through the Satnall Hills (981207). In this section there are thick beds of white and liver-coloured pebbles with occasional beds of sandstone occurring at intervals in the bare quarry face (Pl. 2a). On top of the pebble beds the soil is seen to be thin, with the ash-grey colouring typical of a leached podsol. Although much of the Chase was thinly wooded at one time, with oak as the dominant tree, the poor soils would be unlikely to grow fine stands of timber. As the trees were cut down for fuel and for making charcoal – once a flourishing industry on Cannock – their place has been taken by heath vegetation which covers large areas of the plateau, particularly on its north-west side. The heather, cross-leaved heath and patches of bilberry are all represented in the vegetation along

with the occasional silver birch. In many places the spread of bracken has almost swamped this heath vegetation, particularly on the better-drained slopes where it seems to flourish. On some of the hill-tops, for example, Oat Hill near Milford (9720), the hair grass, once the herbage of the locally bred and distinctive Cannock sheep, forms a continuous sward. Here also are the isolated clumps of Scots pine planted by the Anson family of nearby Shugborough Hall when they attempted in 1780 to add variety to the open heath country of the northern part of the Chase.

It is the Forestry Commission who have been responsible more than anyone else for changing the open character which the Chase had acquired following the cutting of the original oak forest. In 1920 they acquired large areas of the estate of the Marquis of Anglesey, a descendant of the Paget family of Beaudesert Hall. By 1950 the greater part had been planted with Scots and Corsican pine, trees which are able to withstand the relatively low rainfall (about 30 inches) and the freely draining gravel subsoil. Other trees have been tried, like the Norwegian spruce and Japanese larch, but they have been rather slow-growing compared with the Corsican pine. Some of the plantations are almost mature, and for many years the smaller tree-thinnings have provided pit props for the local collieries.

The geology of the Chase, in particular the presence of the Bunter Pebble Beds, has had a considerable influence on the landforms of the area. Nearly everywhere the plateau top is flat and featureless, and where it has not been planted with conifers extensive views are possible on every side. The heath country around Anson Bank and Brocton Field (9817) in the north-west corner of the Chase portrays this type of landscape to perfection. The margins of the plateau are everywhere abrupt as the Pebble Beds are sufficiently coherent to form steep slopes. It is the sharp edge to the whole Chase which emphasises its regional distinctiveness in relation to the surrounding lowlands. Many of the marginal slopes are deeply cut into by small valleys which head back into the plateau top. Although these are seldom more than 200 yards long, they are so arranged as to give a serrated margin to the plateau edge. This rather distinctive feature of the landscape can be seen to advantage along the roadside between Rugeley and Milford where the A513 road runs close to the north-eastern edge of Cannock overlooking the Trent Valley. The valley slopes on the margins of the Chase are also ribbed, as, for example, the Sherbrook Valley around Coppice Hill (9819). The feature is well brought out in the furrowed contour pattern of the one-inch Ordnance Survey Map. The short valleys must all have been formed relatively recently, probably towards the end of the Ice Age when there was much more surface water running off the plateau top, and their ribbed Appearance suggests active periglaciation.

Many of the longer valleys which cut into the plateau surface must also have developed their deep form at the same time. The picturesque and much visited Sherbrook Valley, although cut 200 feet into the plateau surface, is now occupied by the tiniest of streams, which would be quite incapable of forming such a deep valley. Once again it is necessary to think in terms of the much greater volumes of water available during and following the Ice Age to account for the development of the deeply cut valley.

Some of the most striking scenery of Cannock Chase occurs at its northern end where it overlooks the Sow and Trent Valley. Here near Brocton and Milford

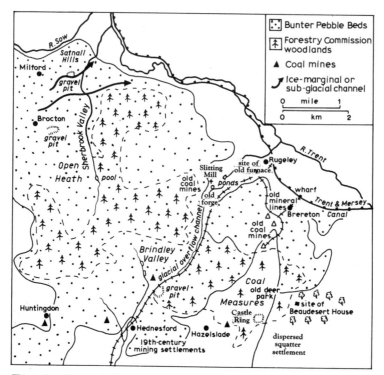

Fig. 2b   Cannock Chase with its glacial features and evidence
of past and present industrial development

Plate 2c   The glacial channels cut in parallel fashion along the northern edge of Cannock Chase in the vicinity of the Satnall Hills (990202)

there are a number of steep-sided valleys which, unlike the Sherbrook Valley, run parallel to the plateau edge. The Mere Valley, for example, starts near Brocton (9719) and then winds its way eastwards for about $2\frac{1}{2}$ miles cutting a gash into the gently sloping plateau surface. Its steep slopes reveal the freshness of youth, while its flat floor with marshy hollows but no proper drainage system suggests that the feature has been formed as a result of glacial action rather than normal river erosion. Steep-sided, dry and twisting valleys of this type are common in upland areas which have been glaciated and are usually looked upon as ice-marginal channels. At a late stage during the Ice Age, a tongue of ice moved eastwards down the Sow Valley and into the Trent. For a time it was banked up against the northern edge of Cannock Chase. The Mere Valley and its continuation eastwards were cut by melt-water streams along the junction of the ice edge and the bare plateau to the south (Pl. 2c). As the ice edge retreated northwards, a second ice-marginal channel system developed and cut the equally impressive gash between the Satnall Hills and Oat Hill (9720), now a dry valley followed by the Rugeley to Milford road An

79

alternative explanation of the origin of these transverse valleys suggests that they were formed by meltwater streams under the ice when the whole of the northern edge of Cannock was overridden by the ice sheet. This sub-glacial origin provides a more satisfactory explanation of many of the features of the channel systems, namely their rather haphazard arrangement and the up-and-down profile of their valley floors.

The long through-valley which runs diagonally across Cannock Chase from Hednesford to Rugeley also dates from the glacial period (Fig. 2b). Ice coming into contact with the western edge of the plateau impounded a small glacial lake around Hednesford (0012). As the level of this lake rose, it later overflowed across a low col and into the valley of the present Rising Brook which runs eastwards to Rugeley. The lake overflow quickly reduced the height of the col so that by the time the western ice sheet had disappeared and the lake was drained, a long through-valley had been formed. The rapid downcutting of the valley, particularly near the original col at Hednesford, has created an almost gorge-like feature with bare rock exposed in places. The products of this erosion, mainly sands and gravels, were spread out as a great fan in the Trent Valley and the town of Rugeley has been built on them to take advantage of the dry site.

On its southern edge, Cannock Chase is very much a landscape of coal-mining. Development on a large scale came rather late to this part of the South Staffordshire Coalfield and it was not until the middle of the nineteenth century that the area was opened up by sinking new pits to tap the coal-seams at no great distance beneath the surface. Villages like Hednesford (0012), Hazelslade (0212) and Heath Hayes (0110), each with their drab rows of terraced houses of red brick and grey Welsh slate, developed within a decade of the opening of their collieries. Coal-mining on a smaller scale had been going on for centuries previously, particularly in the area of Beaudesert and Brereton. Here the Coal Measures make a triangular segment into the Pebble Beds which occupy the greater part of the Chase. In places the outcropping seams had been worked in shallow 'gob' pits since medieval times. Celia Fiennes, who journeyed around the lanes of England towards the end of the seventeenth century, records that at Beaudesert she saw the miners 'draw up the coale in baskets with a little wheele or windlass like a well, it's very good'. Little trace remains of these early workings except for patches of rumpled ground, now grassed over or wooded, in the vicinity of Beaudesert. Farther north nearer Brereton, at the apex of the Coal Measure outcrop, a large mine was opened up at the beginning of the nineteenth century on the slopes of Brereton Hill (048156). With the Trent–Mersey Canal so close, it was decided to build a short incline tramway down to the wharves at Brereton village. The track of the incline has long since been removed but its alignment can still be seen in the pattern of field boundaries on the $2\frac{1}{2}$-inch Ordnance Survey Map.

Along with coal-mining, iron-working was one of the early industries which came to the area. At first the sites were near the available beds of ironstone which occur in the Coal Measure series. Local supplies of charcoal were also available in such quantities that there was no problem in making wrought iron. At a later date, when water-power became of great importance for driving the hammers of the forge and the bellows in the furnace, the iron industry became more localised and tended to concentrate in the deep valleys of the Chase. Ponds were dug in the valley floors to act as storage basins. Usually there were two pools, one supplied water-power for the forge and the other for the furnace. In the Sherbrook Valley, the upper and lower pools are more than a mile apart. In the Brindley Valley they are much closer together. We know that in this valley the pools were not built until 1734. The greatest concentration of the iron industry was in the deeply cut glacial overflow channel of the Rising Brook running down to Rugeley. Here in the vicinity of Slitting Mill (0217) – the name itself is revealing – there were a number of furnaces and forges, each dependent on water-power and local supplies of iron ore. As elsewhere in the Chase, the only real remains of this former industry are the pools built in the valley floor. That by the roadside at Slitting Mill was one of the largest, with a big artificial embankment holding back the water. It was fed by a leat which carried water from the Rising Brook some distance upstream. The main use of the pond was as a storage basin for water so that the slitting-mill, located at the end of the embankment, could carry on in times of drought (see Pl. 2d). At all

Plate 2d Slitting Mill, where the pond is the sole surviving feature of the once active iron industry (0217)

other times, the water for driving the wheel of the mill was derived directly from the leat, which gave a drop of almost twenty feet above the general level of the valley floor. Nothing remains of the mill today; but the leat, cut through an outcrop of Keuper Sandstone, is still working and can be approached by the track which leads down from the Horns Inn at Slitting Mill. A little distance downstream near the site of an old pond in the valley floor (033172) stood a rolling-mill of which no trace now remains. The forge in the valley floor has also disappeared, although the name Forge Farm survives close by (026165). Like the slitting- and rolling-mills, the forge had its own water-storage pond but this is now largely overgrown.

Throughout Cannock Chase evidence of the early industrialisation is fast disappearing. Ponds are being filled in, slag-heaps removed, old coal-workings overgrown and coal-tips levelled. Everywhere the dark green hues of the conifer plantations are blotting out the open landscape which man himself had created through grazing his animals and cutting down the original forest to supply the charcoal for the early industries.

Further Reading

Barrow, G. 'The Geology of the Country around Lichfield', *Memoirs of the Geological Survey of Great Britain* (1919).
Cannock Chase, Staffordshire (H.M.S.O., 1957).
Cockin, G. M. *The Ancient Industries of Cannock Chase* (1905).
Stevenson, P. 'The Geology of the Country around Burton, Tamworth, Rugeley and Uttoxeter', *Memoirs of the Geological Survey of Great Britain* (1955).
Victoria County History, Staffordshire, vol. V (1959) pp. 62–3 vol. II (1967) pp.69–70.
Birmingham and its Regional Setting, a Scientific Survey, ed. M. J. Wise (British Association for the Advancement of Science, 1950) pp. 269–88.

Maps

O.S. $2\frac{1}{2}$-inch sheets SK 01, SJ 91 and SJ 92.

Suggested Itinerary

Any visit to Cannock Chase should attempt to include a study of both its glacial features and its industry, past and present. This can be done by a walk in one of the several parts of the Chase.

(*a*) A relatively short and particularly instructive walk is that along the glacial overflow channel which runs from Hednesford (0012) to Rugeley (0418) all within the $2\frac{1}{2}$-inch sheet SK 01. The layout of a modern coal-mine can be seen at the West Cannock No. 5 colliery (008141) (see Pl. 2*e*), a good viewpoint being the slopes of the

Plate 2e The modern layout of West Cannock colliery on the southern slopes of the glacial through valley which cuts across Cannock Chase between Hednesford and Rugeley (date of photograph 1964)

opposite side of the valley. On these same slopes a large pit working the sands and gravels of the Bunter Beds has been opened up and this gives good sections of the deposits which underlie the greater part of the Chase. Passing farther along the glacial through-valley, evidence of the early iron industry is found in the old ponds (021147) which supplied the water-power for the furnaces and forges. The name Furnace Coppice for the wooded slopes above is a reminder of the dependence of the industry on charcoal in the early stages before the locally won coal could be used. Further evidence of the early iron industry can be seen by taking the minor road which leads from Smarts Buildings (0215) past Slitting Mill (0217) to Rugeley. The site of a former forge occurs in the valley floor near Forge Farm (026165) with its storage pond now largely overgrown. The track which leads off from here in a westerly direction can be followed for a short distance into the wood. About a quarter of a mile from the road, the old spoil banks of the Fair Oak colliery are reached, now largely covered by stands of mature timber. Returning to the road and then continuing as far as Slitting Mill, one of the largest ponds still remaining in this area is reached. The embankment of the pond, the leat and the site of the slitting-mill can be reached by the track which runs down from alongside the Horns Inn (029172).

(*b*) The ice-marginal channels at the northern end of Cannock Chase can form the basis of a short excursion. The track leading into the Chase from the A513 road at Weetman's Bridge (0020) should be followed, bearing right to enter the ice-marginal channel shown Pl. 2*c*. The character of the valley sides whose ribbed appearance is probably due to periglaciation should be noted as well as the vegetation, typical of Cannock Chase as a whole. At the Satnall Hills, the A513 follows a similar ice-marginal channel, with steep, curving sides and a flat floor (982208). A good exposure of the Bunter Pebble Beds can be seen in the old gravel quarry by the roadside (979208). Further ice-marginal channels occur around Milford (979202) and can be approached either directly from this point or by continuing the original excursion from Weetman's Bridge across the Sherbrook Valley (987200).

Field Work

In an area such as Cannock Chase where changes are rapidly taking place the current Ordnance Survey map and even air photographs quickly become out of date. During the course of the above excursions, note and map the changes which have taken place in the character of the landscape (including vegetation changes) since the original survey.

Further Work

(*a*) Using the air photograph (Pl. 2*e*) of the West Cannock No. 5 colliery (008141), list the evidence which suggests that the mine is relatively modern.

(*b*) For the area covered by the air photograph (Pl. 2*c*) across over the north-eastern part of the Chase in the vicinity of Haywood Warren (9920), contrast the landscape associated with the Bunter Pebble Beds in the foreground with that of the flood plain of the Trent beyond.

Why do the sides of the ice-marginal channel have a ribbed appearance?

How do the bracken-covered slopes with isolated silver birch trees reflect man's interference with the original natural vegetation of the area?

3 Tamworth and Lichfield— An Urban History of Two Mercian Towns

Lichfield and Tamworth were both important centres in the long-vanished Saxon kingdom of Mercia. Tamworth was a residence of kings, a place of government and, later, a strong-point in the defences of Anglo-Saxon England against the Danes. Lichfield rose to importance when St Chad named it as the head of the Mercian diocese in A.D. 669. By the beginning of the eighth century there was a church on the site of the present cathedral. The state of Mercia vanished with the Danish invasions at the close of the ninth century, but the different characters of Lichfield and Tamworth, already established in this primitive Anglo-Saxon kingdom, have prevailed until the present day.

The Sites of Tamworth and Lichfield

Tamworth is a river-town standing at the junction of the Anker and the Tame. Its name means 'the clearing by the Tame'. Along the Trent and its tributaries, the Sow, Penk, Tame and Anker, the Saxon settlers based their large manors on forest clearings. The town of Tamworth grew across a broad spur, covered with boulder clay, at thirty feet above the valley floor. The historic focus of the town, the castle, stands on a huge artificial mound that was raised at the time of the Norman Conquest. Today you look out from the castle mound across the lawns and flower beds of a public park to the Castle Pleasure Grounds with their open-air swimming bath, cafés and tennis courts. But it does not need too much imagination to reconstruct something of the Tamworth of the past when the same viewpoint took in a vista of marshes and summer meadows at the junction of the two rivers. For days on end in the wet weeks of late autumn and winter Tamworth must have been half-encircled by a waste of waters. Even now the numerous ditches and channels in the flood plain between the Tame and Anker are reminders of the many attempts to cope with floods in this part of the valley. Only fifty years ago floods were still common, and the making of the Castle Pleasure Grounds in 1929 required the tipping of hundreds of tons of waste material from the slag-heaps of neighbouring collieries to raise the bowling-greens and tennis courts above the river's flood level. Tamworth grew as a river-town, though its chief strategic feature, a girdle of marshes, has now disappeared from the landscape.

Lichfield stands on the rolling plateau of red Keuper Sandstone that forms one of the recurring elements in the scenery of the West Midlands. The town has grown across a shallow valley that is drained by the Curborough Brook. At Tamworth the river and its wide marshes provided a natural defence to the town for many centuries, while at Lichfield the shallow depression where two insignificant brooks join together presented no such obstacle. In fact, men have shaped and changed the landscape of this valley to suit their various purposes over several centuries. Today two lakes, Stowe Pool and Minster Pool, give as much to the character of Lichfield as the dark red sandstone spires and ornate façade of its cathedral. Yet these are far from being remnants of the natural landscape untouched by man and his works.

Until the beginning of the eighteenth century a third pool, Bishop's Fish Pool, existed to the west of the street that now forms the main north–south axis of Lichfield. It disappeared steadily as a result of heavy silting and the tipping of rubbish at the western end of the pool. The two pools that have survived until the present day in Lichfield have undergone some important changes since the eighteenth century. In 1771 Minster Pool was dredged and reshaped, trees were planted and Minster Pool Walk was made along the south bank. It is a typical example of the landscaping popular in the eighteenth century. In 1855 both Stowe Pool and Minster Pool were bought by the South Staffordshire Waterworks Company and Stowe Pool became a reservoir.

History and the Topography of Tamworth

The first clear proof of a settlement at Tamworth dates back to the year A.D. 757 when King Offa of Mercia built a palace close to the meeting-place of the Anker and the Tame (Fig. 3a). This great hall, built of wood, probably disappeared in the Danish invasions of the second half of the ninth century. Certainly, Tamworth was burnt and plundered in A.D. 874. Today even the site of Offa's palace remains a complete mystery. The most recent search for the location of this Mercian palace, through excavations in the castle grounds in 1960, failed to reveal any trace of it. Yet there was such a place because the charters of Mercia, issued by King Offa, are signed from the royal 'Palace at Tamworth'.

After the Danish invasions Tamworth was built again in A.D. 913. By this time Mercia had disappeared as a separate Saxon state and was part of the large kingdom of Wessex. In the year 912 King Alfred's daughter, Ethelfleda, was given the government of Mercia and she ordered the rebuilding of Tamworth. In the second stage of Tamworth's life the political geography of the English Midlands had changed completely. Not only had Mercia disappeared as a state, but Tamworth was now on the very line of a hostile frontier between the Anglo-Saxon and Danish parts of England, between Wessex and the Danelaw. Thus, in the rebuilding under Ethelfleda the dangerous politics of the Midlands were uppermost. Tamworth

86

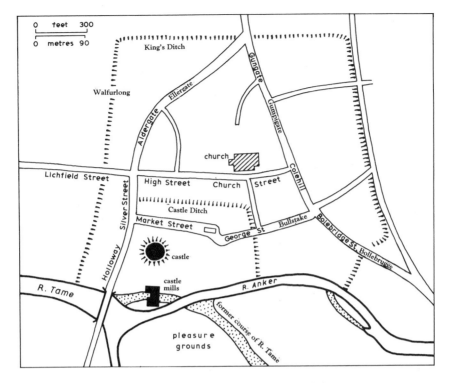

Fig. 3a   The street plan of Tamworth with the medieval features

became a fortress on the banks of the Tame where the river turns north-eastward towards the Trent and the very heart of the Danelaw with its strong-points at Nottingham, Derby and Leicester. The foundation of towns, hedged around by earthen banks or stone walls, began in the reign of Alfred the Great. These *burhs* or fortified townships are the first in the long history of the making of towns in the English countryside that goes on almost unbroken, until the fourteenth century. The Mercian Register, a document of the tenth century that tells something of events in the West Midlands, mentions the creation of ten *burhs* by Ethelfleda. As well as Tamworth, they include Stafford, Bridgnorth and Warwick.

At Tamworth Ethelfleda had an earth rampart built around the outside of the town (Fig. 3*a*). It formed three sides of a square, and the fourth line of defence, on the south, was made by the strip of marshes and the watery ribbons of the Anker and the Tame. Nothing can be seen of this tenth-century defensive work today. The archives of Tamworth contain many references to the letting of parts of the ditch as gardens in the sixteenth century. Since then the digging of trenches for building and the making of sewers has uncovered part of this fortification against the Danes. It is remembered, too, in the names of features that have themselves disappeared from the landscape of Tamworth. For instance, Orchard Street is built along the line of this pre-Norman earthwork and adjoining it there was once a field called the *Walfurlong*. Even though today nothing can be seen of this rampart and ditch on the ground, you can trace parts of its course from the air. On the air photograph (Pl. 3*b*) an axial street runs down the centre from top to bottom of the picture. The lower part of this street, below the cross-road almost at the centre of the photograph, is called Lichfield Street. To the right of this street a long rectangle of gardens and waste land marks the former site of the earthwork. To the left of Lichfield Street you can see a timber-framed building that was built on the line of the ancient ditch. Beyond that a factory obliterates this feature of the pre-Conquest *burh*. The site of the earthwork recurs again at the road junction on the left-hand margin of the picture. Beyond that again begins the *Walfurlong* – part of one of Tamworth's open fields that was crossed by the late Saxon earthwork. A piece of this earthwork, the first town wall of Tamworth, was excavated in 1960 during the search for the foundations of Offa's palace. The date of the earthwork was fixed in the early tenth century by this excavation; here is tangible proof of the foundation of Ethelfleda's *burh*.

The castle mound is the most impressive remnant of medieval Tamworth (Pl. 3*c*). It is almost a hundred feet high and fifty feet wide on top. On its flat, circular summit several styles of military and domestic architecture from widely

Plate 3b   Tamworth: showing the castle and River Tame to the right of the picture with the axis of the High Street and Church in the centre. Note the site of the market place much reduced in size through later encroachments (date of photo 1964).

separated periods of English history are huddled together within the precinct of a precipitous, castellated wall. For a long time local historians believed that this mound, crowned by the keep of a Norman castle, dated from the rebuilding of Tamworth in the first years of the tenth century. There seems to be a suggestion of this in the part of the Anglo-Saxon Chronicle that describes the events of the year 913 when 'Ethelfleda, the Lady of the Mercians, went with all the Mercians to Tamworth, and there built the *burh* early in the summer, and after this, before Lammas, the one at Stafford'. But it is now known that the castle mounds at both Tamworth and Warwick date only from the time of the Norman Conquest.

Along with the castle mound the earliest features of Tamworth are the Norman keep and tower that form the present entrance to the castle. These were built in the time of Robert de Marmion who was given the royal castle at Tamworth as a reward for his help at the Battle of Hastings. Perhaps an even more interesting feature is the curtain wall that crosses the dry moat. It is twenty-five feet high and ten feet in thickness, and its stones are laid in the herring-bone pattern typical of the late Anglo-Saxon and early Norman period (Pl. 3*d*). Here is one of the finest examples of herring-bone masonry in the country and it probably dates from the busy phase of castle-building at Tamworth under Robert de Marmion between 1070 and 1100. Again, like the mound, it is often dated wrongly to the late Saxon times of Ethelfleda almost two centuries earlier.

Proof of Tamworth's importance before the Norman Conquest may be found today in the Castle Museum that contains a collection of Anglo-Saxon coins minted at Tamworth. The royal mint at Tamworth was founded in the reign of Athelstan (A.D. 924–40) and it was not closed down until the reign of Henry II in 1154. There are twenty-eight coins in the museum today that were issued from the royal mint. They belong to the reigns of eight of the late Anglo-Saxon and Norman kings. Here in the tiny, mutilated, silver coins in a museum case is proof of Tamworth's early history as a town, because the possession of a mint may be taken as a sure sign that a place was also a borough in tenth-century Wessex.

The second great period of building in the history of Tamworth Castle is connected with the Ferrers family who lived there from 1423 until the end of the seventeenth century. During the reigns of Henry VIII and James I the Ferrers built a house on the tight summit of the castle mound. It stands out plainly from the medieval military architecture not only in the style of its building but also in the building-materials. The rough stone blocks of the curtain wall and keep, Norman in date, give way to brick. We notice the patterns in red-brown and blue bricks that are typical of Tudor country houses. The finest part of the Ferrers' mansion at Tamworth Castle is the Great Hall built in Henry VIII's reign. A curious moment in the history of the Great Hall was in 1790 when Robert Peel rented it for some months to use as a smithy while he was building his first cotton mill at Tamworth.

Tamworth, like so many English towns, grew under the protection of a castle, but it lacks the simple layout of a planned town such as Ludlow. There is no wide market place stretching between the two focal points of the town – castle and parish church. Instead, the narrow High Street runs gently downhill westward towards the Tame from the parish church. The market place is cramped and clotted with car traffic, a mere widening of the street on the northern boundary of the castle; and over the centuries there have been several changes in its topography. Until the middle of the sixteenth century the market place was built up only on its northern side. A row of houses and shops looked across the open space of the market and Castle Green to the steeply rising hump of Tamworth Castle. After Henry VIII's reign Castle Green disappeared as houses were built on the south side of the market place. The encircling ditch at the foot of the castle mound was filled with soil and rubbish, and buildings grew over it on piles to counteract the sub-sidence of this infirm land. In 1701, the area of the tiny market place was reduced again when Thomas Guy built a new town hall at its centre. This plain building, in pale red brick and raised on arches, is one of the most handsome features of modern Tamworth (Pl. 3e). The Tudor development of Castle Green stands as an early example of a lack of foresight in the shaping of a town of which there are so many instances from the Victorian period and our own times. Squares and open spaces are a necessary element in the beauty of towns. They provide a contrast to narrow and crowded streets; they open up vistas and viewpoints upon grand buildings. At Tamworth a wide market square would have made a fine contrast to the bulky mass of the castle. Instead the castle is cut off completely from the town. As you stand in the narrow, built-up market place there is no hint of its presence. By contrast Lichfield's cathedral may be admired across several open spaces, close up from The Green or through a curtain of trees across Minister Pool (see Pl. 3g).

Until 1899 the borough of Tamworth lay in two counties, Warwickshire and Staffordshire. This division that has existed for almost a thousand years has left its mark on the town in many ways. For instance, Tamworth owned two pieces of common land. The Warwickshire Moor lay to the east of the town in the Anker Valley; to the west was the Staffordshire Moor that is commemorated today in the name of Moor Street. The commons probably came into existence with the first Anglo-Saxon settlement by the Tame. By the fourteenth century the owners of houses in Tamworth had rights to graze animals on one of the two moors. If they lived in the eastern part of the borough, they took their cattle down to the water meadows and marshes in the Anker Valley. From the western part of the town, the Staffordshire piece of Tamworth about Lichfield Street, they went out to the west-ern common. The moors were greatly reduced in the eighteenth century as a result of enclosure and again, in 1847, with the building of the London and North-Western Railway.

Plate 3c
Tamworth Castle,
set on its great
artificial mound
overlooking the
Tame

Plate 3d
The herring-bone masonry of the wall
by the side of Tamworth Castle,
possibly dating from an earlier
Saxon castle on an adjacent site to
the present Norman structure

Plate 3e
The Town Hall built in 1701
at the end of the market place

Many of the English counties were first clearly defined in the reign of Alfred the Great. It is likely that this was the time when the frontier was fixed between Staffordshire and Warwickshire. Thus Tamworth was split by the county boundary from its earliest years. The dividing-line between the counties took a zigzag course through the heart of the town. The boundary followed the main north–south axis of the town – Gumpigate was its old name – as far as its meeting with the main east–west route of the High Street. From the cross-road of the High Street with Eller-gate and Lichfield Street the county boundary turned south towards the river along Ladybridge Street and Holloway. On reaching the river, at the bridge close by the castle, the boundary between Staffordshire and Warwickshire then pursued the Tame upstream.

Down the centuries there are many clues to the duality of Tamworth. The place-name element, *gate*, of Danish origin and meaning 'a street', occurs only in the north-western parts of the town that belonged to Staffordshire. We find it in Eller-gate and the ancient street-name of Gumpigate. This fact provides a clue to the long-vanished social geography of Tamworth in the tenth century when the town might have had an Anglo-Saxon core around the castle site in Warwickshire and a Danish-speaking quarter centred on the church of St Editha in Staffordshire.

Until Elizabeth's reign Tamworth possessed two markets. One has been held on the present market place since before the Norman Conquest. The other was held at the junction of Gumpigate, Cross Street and Butcher Street. One probably served the Saxon borough, the other the Danish quarter of the town. Until the building of the Town Hall on Market Place in 1701, Tamworth had two centres of local government. One town hall stood in Lichfield Street and served the Stafford-shire part of the town; the other, for the Warwickshire sector of Tamworth, stood at the junction of Market Street and Ladybridge Street on the site of the Peel Arms Hotel. Each town hall stood in its own county, but the building in Lichfield Street ended its career as a place of government in 1560 when Tamworth received a borough charter from Elizabeth and came under one rule. The Staffordshire town hall was itself demolished in 1701.

Like so many English towns, Tamworth has changed considerably in appearance in the mid-sixties. As part of a general process of urban renewal which is reshaping the cores of many of our cities and towns, the whole area between Market Place and the parish church has been rebuilt. Buildings of little character, built to a common module, are slowly taking the place of the run-down shops and dwellings which crowded the centre of the town. A view of the parish church with its heavy, pinnacled, sandstone tower has been opened up in a town that has concealed its two imposing architectural features in a maze of narrow streets and dull Victorian brick. Down by the river, to the west of the castle, tall tower-block flats have sprouted up in recent years, adding exciting vertical features to the modest red-brick townscape of Tamworth.

The geography of Lichfield today is largely explained by the fact that it has been the most important religious centre of the West Midlands since Mercian times. The first church at Lichfield was founded in A.D. 669 at Stowe on the northern edge of Stowe Pool (1210) (Fig. *3f*). The name *Stowe*, an Old English word, means a 'hermitage' or 'holy place'. The present church of St Chad's stands on the site of Lichfield's first church and beside it you can visit the holy well that was the chief reason for the choice of this place as a religious centre in Mercia. Forty years later, in A.D. 700, another church was built on an outcrop of red sandstone to the north of Minister Pool. This was the cathedral of Mercia. The body of St Chad was taken there and Lichfield became the most important place of pilgrimage in the Midlands. For a brief spell of time about A.D. 800, in the reign of King Offa, Lichfield was raised to the heights of an archbishopric. For a moment of history it was as important as Canterbury.

Two cathedrals have stood on the slopes overlooking Minister Pool before the present building was started at the beginning of the thirteenth century. Its warm, red sandstone was certainly quarried in the neighbourhood of Lichfield. Probably much of the building material came from the hills of Bunter Sandstone that overlook the valley of the Tame at Hopwas (1705), for in 1235 Henry III gave permission to the Dean and Chapter of Lichfield to dig stone in the Forest of Hopwas for repairing the cathedral.

Just as the castle formed the core of Tamworth, so the cathedral and its close are at the heart of Lichfield. In the Middle Ages the cathedral close had more in com-

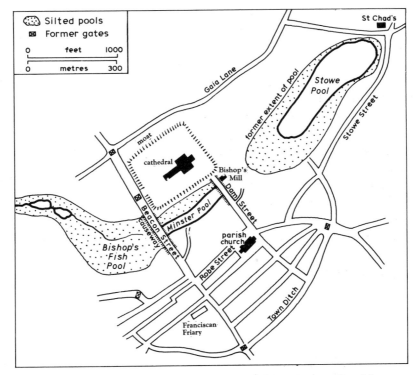

Fig. 3f   The street-plan of the centre of Lichfield with its medieval features

Plate 3g   Lichfield: Minster Pool separates the cathedral close from the twelfth-century town with its rectilinear street-plan. Note the market place (bottom right) and Dam Street with the site of the former bishop's hill at the end of the causeway across the Minster Pool (date of photograph 1964).

mon with Tamworth Castle than it has today because it was fortified with walls and towers under Bishop Walter de Langton between 1296 and 1321. Only fragments of these defences are left in the gardens of the bishop's palace. On the south side of the cathedral close a line of houses stands on the site of the wall, and pieces of this defensive structure and a turret are built into a house at the south-east corner (Pl. 3g).

The twelfth century was a time of great change at Lichfield when a town was laid out on the southern side of Minister Pool. The streets of this planned town were sketched in an orderly way, parallel to each other, and they followed the line of the southern shore of Minister Pool. Today we can see quite clearly the street-plan of twelfth-century Lichfield in the layout at the heart of the modern city. Market Street, Bore Street, Wade Street and Wade Lane were first surveyed about the year A.D. 1130. At the same time the market place was made in the north-east corner of this new town and a town church, St Mary's, was built in the centre of the market square before A.D. 1160. The whole of medieval Lichfield was encircled by a town ditch that ran from the edge of Stowe Pool, along the line of George Lane, and in a semicircle towards the vanished Bishop's Pool. Nothing remains of the town ditch today, but we can trace its influence plainly in the layout of Lichfield and its suburbs. At the heart, within the semicircle of the former ditch, is the regular gridiron plan of streets and the narrow plots of the burgesses' properties. Outside the city boundary only one medieval suburb of any size appeared, and that was around St Michael's Church on the road to the east. For the rest, the two ancient cores of Lichfield – the town and the cathedral close – are surrounded by a modest ring of suburbs that appeared in the nineteenth and twentieth centuries. Immediately to the south of the medieval core is the City railway station and goods yard that brought a suburb into being about 1850. Towards the east, along Trent Valley Road, Lichfield has grown out for a mile towards its main-line station, built in 1847, on the London and North-Western Railway. Now it is the site of the Trent Valley Trading Estate, set up in the past few years with offshoots from firms in the Black Country. They make plastics, furniture and engineering goods. To the north and north-east of the cathedral lies a twentieth-century residential suburb with blocks of council houses, schools and streets of 'semis' put up by speculative builders. The rapid growth of residential suburbs to Lichfield is a symptom of the latest phase in the history of this cathedral city, because it is now favoured as a dormitory suburb for the Black Country and Birmingham.

Further Reading

(*a*) *Tamworth*
Mitchell, H. C. *Tamworth Parish Church* (1935).
— *Tamworth Tower and Town* (1936).
Palmer, C. F. *The History of the Town and Castle of Tamworth* (1845).
Wood, H. *Borough by Prescription* (1958).
— *Guide to Tamworth Castle* (1961).
(*b*) *Lichfield*
Masefield, C. *Staffordshire* (1910).
Thorpe, H. 'The City of Lichfield: a Study of its Growth and Functions', *Staffordshire Historical Collections* (1950–1) pp. 137–211.

Maps

O.S. 1-inch sheet 120 (Burton-on-Trent); O.S. $2\frac{1}{2}$-inch sheet SK 20 (for Tamworth); O.S. $2\frac{1}{2}$-inch sheet SK 10 (for Lichfield), Geological Survey 1-inch sheet 154 (Lichfield).

Suggested Itinerary

Make a comparative study of Tamworth and Lichfield. From the summit of the castle at Tamworth note the chief features of the town's setting and locate the most important buildings. Visit the Castle Museum and its collection of Saxon coins. Pay some attention to Market Place, Town Hall, St Editha's Church, noting the evidence of the Norman church left after the great rebuilding of the fourteenth century. Go on to Lichfield and begin the urban study at St Chad's Well, the first settled site. Study in detail the cathedral quarter. Make a tour of the streets of the planned medieval town to the south of Minister Pool, ending at Market Place with the town church of St Mary's (a nineteenth-century rebuilding on the medieval site) and the birthplace of Dr Johnson with its museum.

Field Work

In your field notebook make field sketches to show the different styles of building in Tamworth Castle. Write a brief note on each sketch giving the age of this part of the castle and say something of the building materials.

Further Work

(*a*) With the help of the air photograph of Tamworth make a sketch-map of the town locating the following features – the main streets, the castle, the market place, St Editha's Church, the site of the town hall that served the Warwickshire part of the town. Sketch in the line of the former county boundary through the heart of Tamworth. Locate the site of the former Castle Green. When and why did it disappear? What is the name of the river in the top right corner of the photograph? How has the town changed since this photograph was taken?

(*b*) Use the air photograph of Lichfield to make a diagram of the main quarters of the city. First mark Minister Pool and Stowe Pool, then indicate, with their chief features, the cathedral quarter, the medieval town and the modern suburban ring.

96

4 The Black Country (i)

WEDNESBURY AND THE TAME VALLEY

The Regional Individuality of the Black Country

The Black Country belongs to the coalfield of south Staffordshire and north Worcestershire. As a region it lacks any physical unity. The coalfield is divided into two by a line of hills pointing north-westward from Rowley Regis (9587) to Sedgley Beacon (9294). To the north Silurian limestones outcrop in Dudley Castle Hill (9490) and the Wren's Nest (9391). At their southern end the central hills of the Black Country reach almost 900 feet above sea level in Turner's Hill (9688), an intrusion of dolerite. The greater part of the Black Country lies to the north and east of the central backbone of hills. Here engineering-works, foundries, housing-estates and the waste land of former coal-mines and blast-furnaces are threaded together by a network of canals, railways and main roads that hum with an endless stream of traffic. It is a flat and dreary district drained by the headwaters of the Tame and it ranks among the regions of England most heavily despoiled by the Industrial Revolution. To the west and south of the central ridge the Black Country presents a somewhat different aspect of itself. Here the River Stour has cut a deep, winding valley across the coalfield. It is a feature that gives unity to the district.

The unity of the Black Country results from the coal-mining and iron-working that gradually covered a once pleasant countryside with chimneys and waste-heaps. The industries that made this region 'black by day and red by night' have almost vanished. Coal-mining is dead on the exposed coalfield. In 1865 there were 172 blast-furnaces in the Black Country; today this industry is represented by two modern iron and steel plants. Nevertheless the Industrial Revolution coined a regional name, the Black Country, that is still very much alive. It has more meaning than some of the older regional labels of the West Midlands such as Feldon or Arden. Today the term Black Country describes not only places and landscapes, but also refers to a distinctive dialect and a peculiar sardonic humour born of the district's industrial past.

The true Black Country that gave birth to this regional name is rapidly vanishing. To grasp its full meaning we have to dip into the pages of the Victorian guide-

97

books. The nameless writer of *Murray's Handbook for Travellers in Staffordshire* gives several vivid pictures of the Black Country in the 1860s. Let us turn to his account of Bilston (9496).

It is one of the busiest towns in the district (pop. 24,192), and is almost surrounded by collieries and ironworks, the 'spoil banks' of the one and the 'cinder mounts' of the other presenting huge barren hills in every direction. Clouds of smoke perpetually hang over it, and the country around at night time is lighted up with lurid flames from the neighbouring blast and puddling furnaces. The fires from the coking-hearths also occasionally burst forth like mimic volcanoes, and the whole scene in a time of active trade is wonderful and impressive. Owing to early and continued mining operations, the neighbourhood of the town, and even some of its precincts, are 'honeycombed', and occasionally subsidences to a considerable extent take place. Many houses and cottages stand awry, and tall chimneys may be seen rivalling in their obliquity the celebrated tower of Pisa.

By the end of this century the name Black Country will no longer be an apt description; it is only half-true today. In the past fifteen years the slag and shale from the waste-heaps of long-vanished coal-mines and blast-furnaces has been rapidly disappearing. Bulldozers flatten the hills and ridges of the derelict land to make sites for council houses. Acres of poor Victorian terraces have been pulled down to be replaced by tall blocks of flats. New factories with long, low sheds of concrete, corrugated asbestos, and an occasional dull, metallic chimney stack are taking the place of the grimy, brick-built foundries. Already in many parts of the region we have to search for evidence of the real Black Country.

Wednesbury and the Tame Valley

Before the spread of coal-mining and iron-making blighted the countryside of the Black Country the life of the region centred on a number of villages and small towns. Wednesbury is already recorded as a settlement in Domesday Book, and the name means *Woden's burh*, which is Woden's fort. Woden was one of the pagan gods of the Anglo-Saxons and his name takes the history of Wednesbury back to a time before the middle of the seventh century. This site on a hill-top between the headstreams of the River Tame was probably one of the outliers of the Midland kingdom of Mercia, a defended place looking westward towards the Severn Valley across a forested countryside that was still not colonised by the Saxons in the eighth century.

Some faint traces remain of this earliest phase of Wednesbury's history. The parish church, on the highest point in the town (988953), seems to stand within the enclosing ditch of an ancient earthwork. Certainly the western boundary of the churchyard looks like an artificial feature. It falls to the street by a steep scarp that has the shape of the rampart of an Iron Age hill-fort. It is likely that the first,

98

Saxon settlers at Wednesbury took a hill-top camp that had been built by a British tribe more than 500 years earlier.

Domesday Book presents the earliest sketch of the geography of Wednesbury. It clearly ranked among the larger settlements of the Birmingham region. Twenty-eight people are recorded among the Domesday population. As these were usually the heads of families it means that Wednesbury had a population of more than a hundred in 1086. Also there seems to have been an extensive tract of arable land around this hill-top village. Domesday Book says 'there is land for 9 ploughs'. It is only when we compare the Domesday facts about Wednesbury with the places round about that we gain a true impression of its importance at the end of the eleventh century. Birmingham had a recorded population of nine. There were sixteen people at Willenhall and eleven at Bilston. Domesday Book shows that the cores of settlement, the hearts of several Black Country towns, were already established by the time of the Norman Conquest.

Although Wednesbury was a flourishing village at the time of the Norman Conquest, scarcely anything of the medieval settlement has survived the Industrial Revolution. The parish church is the only relic of the period before the eighteenth century. The present building of dark, grimy sandstone was the result of a rebuilding towards the end of the fifteenth century of an earlier church. The churches of our industrial towns are not ideal places for the study of medieval architecture. They have had to be adapted to the immense growth of urban populations in the nineteenth century. As a result, medieval buildings have been changed beyond all recognition through drastic enlargements and the addition of galleries. At Wednesbury an enlargement of the building at the end of the nineteenth century resulted in the dismantling of the fifteenth-century apse, stone by stone, and its re-erection a few feet further to the east.

Even though the fifteenth-century parish church has been changed so much, it still contains some fragments of the earlier medieval church that was built on the defensive hill-top site. The restoration work in 1885 uncovered a window of thirteenth-century date – a piece of the church that is first mentioned in a document of King John's reign. This window is in the wall of the north aisle at the west end of the church. The stones at the base of the tower form another fragment of the first church.

The only other surviving feature of Wednesbury's medieval landscape is the pattern of roads in the heart of the town. The main streets, focusing on Market Place (988949) and High Bullen (986951), follow the lines of medieval lanes. This partly explains the many gentle twists and kinks in the road pattern of Wednesbury. By contrast, we notice the straight road that joins Wednesbury to Darlaston, passing through the industrial suburb of King's Hill (9895). This was a turnpike road, built in 1787 across a large open field, King's Hill Field, which still survived in the last years of the eighteenth century.

At the end of the eighteenth century Wednesbury had become a small and busy market centre and the census returns of 1801 show that it had a population of 3077 living in fourteen streets. The rest of Wednesbury's population, about a thousand, lived in hamlets up and down the parish. The Delves, a hamlet with iron-ore workings, had a population of 104 (0295). Another cluster of people gathered at Wood Green (9996), and Wednesbury Forge (002961) recorded a population of 62. The lanes of Wednesbury, as shown on the maps and plans in the last quarter of the eighteenth century, had probably changed little in the previous 500 years. They were to determine the skeleton of the modern town.

The eighteenth-century maps provide some clues to the many vanished features of Wednesbury's medieval landscape. For instance, a parish plan of 1799 shows five patches of open field (Fig. 4a). One of these lay along the flat top of Church Hill eastward of the parish church. Two windmills stood at opposite ends of this open field. Both have disappeared. The site of one is now occupied by a small reservoir (980950) and the name, Windmill Street, preserves their memory. Two large open fields survived in Wednesbury until the end of the eighteenth century. Monway Field (980950) covered the gentle slopes of the Lea Brook in the western part of the parish. By the middle of the nineteenth century most of this common land had been covered by a network of canals and railways and a cluster of small iron-works. Similarly, the King's Hill Field on the northern flanks of Wednesbury (9895) has by now, in the middle of the twentieth century, experienced two cycles of industrial landscapes. The coal-mines and iron-works of the nineteenth century have now vanished. Instead, a modern engineering-plant occupies the tip heaps of

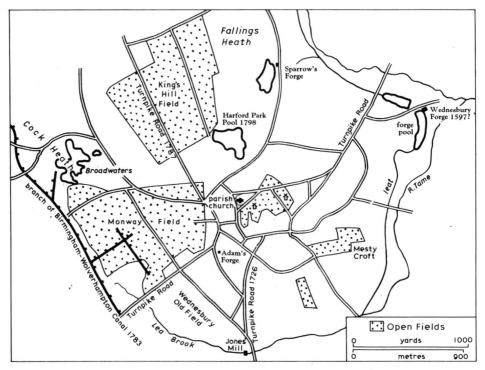

Fig. 4a   The open fields of Wednesbury as shown on a plan of 1799

the Old Park colliery. From the summit of the forlorn hills of shale and slag a huge, harsh, rectangular factory building rises up – a black box in a wasteland. All around are the uniform streets and houses of a twentieth-century council estate. They stand on the bulldozed and flattened derelict land. Beneath the fruitless grey shale lies buried the ridge-and-furrow of King's Hill Field – Wednesbury's lost medieval landscape.

The Industrial Revolution in Wednesbury

Coal-pits are first mentioned at Wednesbury in a document of 1315, and several law cases in the fourteenth century point to the sites of the shallow, bell-shaped pits. By the seventeenth century coal was mined everywhere in Wednesbury on the outcrop of the rich seam of the Thick Coal. Monway Field (980950) and Wednesbury Old Field (985945) were dotted with shallow workings – some active and others abandoned. At this time underground methods of mining came into use. Shafts were sunk to the bottom of the Thick Coal and mining was pursued by the 'pillar and stall' method by which vertical columns of coal were left standing at intervals while the rest of the seam was removed. Wednesbury's parish registers leave a record of an increasing number of mining accidents. During the eighteenth century, industry began to cast an even deeper shadow over the countryside. In 1769 a branch of the Birmingham Canal was opened to the southern outskirts of Wednesbury at Golds Green (984935). In 1783 a new branch of the Birmingham Canal was cut to serve the coal-pits on Monway Field. Several short branches were made to the coal-mines on either hand, one of which allowed barges to reach the collieries at Willingsworth (9694). The branch canals were also intended to collect drainage-water from the mines. In fact, colliery owners were required to pump water from their mines into the canal if they used this new means of transport for getting their coal to Birmingham.

In 1785 an iron-works was built on the banks of a branch canal in Monway Field. It was the first iron-works at Wednesbury to carry out every stage of manufacturing on the same site. Here we can trace the making of one of the earliest industrial landscapes in the Black Country. Coal-mining had been going on for at least 400 years amid the plots and strips of this open field, and it was transformed into an industrial site of first importance by the cutting of the canal. By 1800 the iron-works on Monway Field was bankrupt. An account of the site and plant appeared in a Birmingham paper, *Aris's Gazette*, on 6 January of that year. It shows that a fragment of the industrial landscapes of the Black Country had already come into being.

A capital set of Ironworks, consisting of a Blast Furnace, Foundry, Boring Mill, Forges, Slitting and Rolling Mills, Pattern and Smiths Shops, Warehouses, six Workmen's Houses and every suitable convenience for carrying on a very extensive trade, advantageously situated on the banks of the Birmingham Canal at Wednesbury: the whole comprising about Two and a Half Acres of Freehold Land with valuable mines of Coal, Ironstone and Clay under the same; together with all the Machinery, Implements and Tools now on the Premises.

Nothing is left of Hallens' Iron Works today, but the map of Wednesbury parish, drawn in 1799, shows the site exactly. It stood at the junction of two of the branches of the Birmingham Canal in the former Monway Field (978950). Today, the site is swallowed up in the property of the Patent Shaft Steel Works, one of the biggest engineering companies in the Black Country.

Wednesbury evolved into a true industrial town during the first half of the nineteenth century. The decade between 1851 and 1861 was one of the most impressive in the town's history when population grew more rapidly than at any other time, showing a 50 per cent increase in the space of ten years. Wednesbury had become the chief centre in the British Isles for the manufacture of iron tubes. The industrial boom at the middle of the century was caused by the building of railways both at home and abroad. Two firms towered over the industrial scene in Victorian Wednesbury, specialising in constructional engineering for railways. Lloyds, Fosters & Company at the Old Park Works (981957) made steam-engines, wheels or locomotives and trucks, and turn tables. The Patent Shaft and Axletree Company had been founded in 1838 and after a period of rapid growth in the 1850s, covered twelve acres with its forges, furnaces, engineering-shops and storehouses. They employed 1500 workers, and a description of the time says that 'twelve large steam hammers worked night and day in beating faggots for axles into shape, and in the manufacture of wheels, tyres, rails and boiler plates'.

The landscape of Wednesbury was shaped in these years of industrial boom. Back-to-back houses were built among the scores of pit banks and on land that was already suffering from subsidence. Another piece was added to the Wednesbury scene when the Birmingham, Wolverhampton and Dudley Railway, later swallowed up by the Great Western, passed through the parish. In 1854 a station was opened in the middle of the former Wednesbury Field on a site surrounded by pit banks (983946). Soon after, new streets were laid out close to the station and another element was added to the townscape of Wednesbury with Victoria Street, Albert Street, Stafford Street and Great Western Street.

Since 1870 Wednesbury has had to adjust itself to dramatic changes in metallurgy and engineering that resulted from inventions, the coming of new materials, the rise of industrial rivals at home and abroad, and above all painful periods of industrial depression. Nine firms in the iron trades disappeared in the slump between 1875 and 1886. Only two survived. Other adjustments were made through the founding of new industries or by firms that exploited fresh engineering processes. For instance, drop forging developed in Wednesbury after 1914. Again, in 1939 a hot-dip galvanising-plant for the making of steel windows was built over a rough and useless site of abandoned pit mounds (978958). No coal has been mined at Wednesbury since 1915 and those industries that have weathered a century of almost constant change have been altered out of all recognition. The most conservative feature of this Black Country borough has been the landscape. In the middle of the twentieth century the derelict land, churches, chapels, grey courtyards and shoddy houses are relics of a vanished age.

Wednesbury in the Twentieth Century

One of the greatest problems of the twentieth century in the Black Country has been the legacy of Victorian industrialism in the landscape. Three different features of the landscape have had to be changed or destroyed – the acres of waste-heaps from coal-mines, blast-furnaces and chemical works; cramped and antiquated factories that prevented the use of modern machinery; unhealthy, squalid houses.

In 1930 a fifth of the area of Wednesbury consisted of pit-mounds, slag-heaps and deep, water-filled hollows. This lunar landscape was still liable to subsidence or, worse still, the 'crownings-in' that occasionally brought to the surface subterranean fires smouldering in the shallow coal-seams. The clearance of derelict land began in the economic depression of the early thirties as a means of finding work for the unemployed. In the district of Old Park Road a quarter of a million tons of pit-mounds were levelled with spades, picks and wheelbarrows. Sometimes there was a height difference of seventy feet between the hummocky summits of shale and the floors of the hollows. Since the Second World War derelict land has disappeared at an even greater rate all over the Black Country. This time the work has been done by contracting companies using bulldozers and mechanical shovels. Since 1960 the slag and shale of these Victorian wastelands have gained in value as a material for the foundations of the new motorways. Today, one of the most distinctive features of the Black Country landscape is fast disappearing. It is already hard to find examples of undisturbed derelict land where the steel-grey shale hills fall steeply to the mournful, reed-fringed 'swags'.

The levelled derelict sites provide land for new buildings, for factories and, above all, houses. The first slum-clearance plans began in the Black Country in 1933. Much of the building on derelict land was very costly because the foundations of houses had to be placed on concrete rafts to offset the damage of further subsidence. On Wednesbury's council estates the semi-detached houses and short terraces, each house in its own garden, represent an utter revulsion from the densely built brick deserts of the Victorian back-to-backs. Only recently have revolutionary ideas appeared in the rebuilding of the Black Country towns where some borough councils are building tall blocks of flats on slum-clearance sites.

Over the past twenty years the whole landscape of industry has undergone a violent transformation. New materials and new designs in factory-building stand in stark contrast with foundries, warehouses and offices of the Victorian Age. Low, single-storeyed buildings of concrete, sheet-metal, glass, and even corrugated polythene, replace the picturesque brick buildings of a century ago with their tiny latticed windows. The typical Black Country foundry, a hotch-potch of tiny buildings huddled around a yard and misshapen by subsidence will soon be an irrecoverable piece of history. The new industrial architecture is severely functional and monotonously uniform, as the post-war factory extension of the Old Park Works reveals (984956). There is no greater contrast with the variety of Victorian industrial architecture than this huge, black metal box of the mid-twentieth century.

At Wednesbury the chief industrial locations have persisted since the earliest years of the Industrial Revolution. We have already discussed the part played by Monway Field in the early history of coal-mining, the location of one of the first important iron-works, and in the routes followed by Wednesbury's canals. Even today, this is one of the biggest areas of heavy industry in the borough. Another quarter of heavy industry fills up the spaces between Wednesbury and Darlaston (9797). Here the Old Park Works makes electric locomotives, the sheet-steel frames and undercarriages of railway coaches, and train sets for the London Underground system (Pl. 4b). The first use of this site was for mining coal, ironstone and clay in the early years of the nineteenth century. By the 1850s Lloyds

Plate 4b Old Park Works: on the site of King's Hill Field looking towards the core of Wednesbury around the parish church. There is a patch of derelict land in the foreground with new factory buildings and a house-estate in the distance on restored land. The Wednesbury–Darlaston turnpike road runs across the middle of the picture (date of photo 1949).

Fosters & Company had expanded the Old Park colliery into a plant that was not only mining coal and iron, but smelting the ore and making engines and other railway equipment on a big scale. Old Park Works was one of the earliest examples in industrial history of 'vertical integration' – the participation by one firm in several industrial processes and the making of a varied range of related products. Industry has persisted on this site, formerly the King's Hill Field, although mining ceased here long ago.

The clearest example of the persistence of an industrial site through many changes of ownership is seen at Wednesbury Forge (002961). It was founded towards the end of the sixteenth century at the junction of two of the headstreams of the Tame. The forge is first mentioned in the records of the Quarter Sessions in 1597. Another legal document of 1708 refers to 'the iron mill commonly called Wednesbury Forge'. Towards the end of the eighteenth century this factory site was busy with the making of gun barrels. In 1817 Wednesbury Forge was taken over by Edward Elwell who turned the works into an edge-tool factory. A deed, dated to 1831, provides a picture of this industrial site. There was 'a forge or iron mill, also a grinding mill which had formerly been a windmill, a house, thirteen cottages which had been workshops but which Edward Elwell had reconverted into dwellings, together with adjacent land, a forge pool and a watercourse made to feed it'. Here is a neat sketch of a Black Country factory site in a primitive stage of the Industrial Revolution. Water-power was still important. The master had a house near the forge and his workmen lived close by in cottages. If we visit Wednesbury Forge today, it is still possible to appreciate the continuity and change in this place where the iron trades have been carried on for almost 400 years. The site of the forge is occupied by the buildings of Bescot Drop Forgings. The pool, mentioned in the deed of 1831, has been drained and filled in. A football pitch now occupies the site, but proof of the former existence of the forge pool is seen clearly in the railway that crosses this flat piece of ground on a viaduct of several arches. When the first railway was built through Wednesbury in 1850, it crossed the long pool of the Wednesbury Forge by this viaduct.

Wednesbury Forge is still an active centre of the iron trades. By contrast, on the western fringe of Wednesbury there is a wasteland, the site of Willingsworth colliery, that has passed through the whole cycle of industrial evolution and decline (972945). A substantial grey sandstone farm, Willingsworth Hall, stood here in the seventeenth century. Today its very foundations are lost under the acres of derelict land. This late medieval farm-house is mentioned in a document of 1598. By the end of the eighteenth century the fields around Willingsworth Hall had already become one of the choicest sites for industrial growth in the Black Country. Here were outcrops of the Thick Coal and of iron ore. The industrial value of the site was enriched by the canal cut through the valley of the Lea Brook in 1783 and 1794. By the middle of the nineteenth century the lands of Willingsworth Hall were overgrown with heavy industries. A coal-mine and blast-furnaces stood close by each other. Not far away, attracted by the canal-side site, was Keir's Chemical Works. Willingsworth furnaces were the last to shut down in the district of Wednesbury. They made pig iron until a few months after the end of the First World War. Until the Second World War the blast-furnaces stood idle, falling into ruins. Then they were dismantled.

It is worthwhile to take a walk across the waste lands of Willingsworth today to see a Victorian industrial site in utter decay. If you follow the rough lane from Gospel Oak (968943), the grey pit-heaps of Willingsworth colliery lie on either hand. To the right a still pool, a 'swag' to use a Black Country word for these features, points to the effects of subsidence. Nothing of the colliery remains above ground but a low, circular brick wall that hedges a derelict pit shaft. There is no sound apart from the distant echo of falling water from the depths beneath. Hundreds of thousands of tons of the Thick Coal lie inaccessible and unworkable in the flooded and uncharted mines of the Tame Valley. A few score yards from the colliery the red-brick ruins of Willingsworth furnaces appear on the right and the huge slag hills are now being bulldozed and quarried for ballast. The rough track bends beneath the Great Western Railway, built in the 1850s. Next the road enters a tract of even greater desolation – if that is possible among the derelict land of the Black Country. Here is the waste of Keir's Chemical Works of which every building has disappeared from the ground. The poisonous tips of chemical waste have resisted a friendly garment of vegetation almost completely. The view opens up across a pale grey desert splashed with red and ochre. Through the low hills of chemical waste the track leads down to a bridge across the Walsall Canal that was cut in 1783. Here is the western boundary of Wednesbury and one looks across the canal to an active industrial site with the huge low sheds and metal chimney stacks of the Patent Shaft Company.

If we take to the canal tow-path at this bridge and walk for a few hundred yards towards Moxley (9695), we notice that in places the canal is lined with metal sheeting, a device to offset the effects of subsidence and dangerous burstings of the banks. To the right of the tow-path is the site of Cock Heath, scene of some of the earliest mining at Wednesbury. Now you can see there the making of new a Black Country landscape. A large swag in a deep hollow close to the canal is slowly being filled up with waste material, the rubbish of Wednesbury. On this levelled and reclaimed land the low sheds of new light industries form part of an industrial estate. Here we see the new Black Country of the twentieth century where the schools, council houses and new light industries, powered by electricity, take the place of the hundreds of acres of wasteland created by the heavy industries of the Victorian epoch. Already it is not easy to find an unaltered tract of derelict land dotted with its mournful, reedy swags. Soon some of the dwindling specimens of this kind of country will have to be preserved as examples of a fast-vanishing landscape. The very name 'The Black Country' is now a fossil, and from any hill-top we see a new landscape in the making – a landscape of clusters of giant cooling-towers, cloud-capped under certain weather conditions, of tall blocks of flats in glass and concrete, and long, low, single-storeyed factories that must be the dullest pieces of architecture in the history of civilised man.

Further Reading

Ede, J. F. *History of Wednesbury* (1962).
Birmingham and its Regional Setting, a Scientific Survey, ed. M. J. Wise, 1950.

Maps

O.S. 1-inch sheet 131 (Birmingham); O.S. $2\frac{1}{2}$-inch sheets SO 99 and SP 09 (Birmingham).

Suggested Itinerary (see Fig. 4c)

A field study of Wednesbury should begin on the hill-top crowned by the parish church (988954). Continue northwards to Woden Road. Bear left towards Darlaston Road, the turnpike road that was built in 1787 across the former open field, King's Hill Field. Follow Darlaston Road for almost half a mile through one of the oldest industrial sites in Wednesbury, the Old Park Works. From 981959 take the track to the Holyhead Road (A41), built by Telford in 1826. Conclude the excursion with a walk of about a mile through the derelict sites of Willings-worth to Gospel Oak (967942).

Further Work

1. From either the $2\frac{1}{2}$-inch or the 1-inch maps of Wednesbury draw a large dia-gram of the main roads of the borough. Mark the following features:

(*a*) the probable site of an Iron Age camp
(*b*) Mark and name the sites of two former open fields. What have they in common as landscape features at the present time?

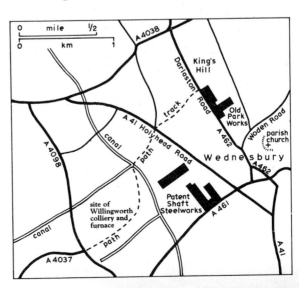

Fig. 4c

Wednesbury,
with the main routes
and features described
in the itinerary

(c) Shade the part of Wednesbury that was favoured in the middle of the nine-teenth century for the homes of the owners and managers of industry.

2. The accompanying air photograph (Pl. 4d) was taken to the west of Wednesbury over Tipton in 1949. The view looks towards the west. Four-fifths of the way up the left-hand margin the band of woodland is on Mons Hill, a continuation of the Wren's Nest Hill. The scene in the foreground contains an example of almost every element in the cultural landscape of the Black Country.

(i)   Use the 1-inch map to identify the location of the air photograph. Give a map reference for the place above which it was taken.

(ii)   Draw a large sketch-diagram from this picture showing:–

  (a) the Birmingham–Wolverhampton Canal
  (b) a patch of derelict land
  (c) derelict land in the process of reclamation
  (d) recent factory buildings
  (e) housing on reclaimed derelict land
  (f) the trunk road between Birmingham and Wolverhampton
  (g) the route of an abandoned canal
  (h) the site of a school. What kind of land was this before the school was built?

Plate 4d

View westward across Tipton with the wooded outcrop of the Wren's Nest ridge in the middle distance (date of photo 1949)

5 The Black Country (ii)

DUDLEY AND THE CENTRAL HILLS

The Black Country is a mosaic of small regions; nowhere is this truth more evident than along the central line of hills. Sharp contrasts in geology underlie the regional variety of this miniature upland. The northern part consists of three steeply folded domes of Silurian limestone – Sedgley Beacon (920934), Wren's Nest Hill (9391) and Dudley Castle Hill (948909). Sandstones and shales of the Middle and Upper Coal Measures outcrop to the south of Dudley Castle. At Rowley Regis (9688) a large intrusion of igneous rock gives rise to another distinctive minor region, one where quarries for road metal make deep scars on the landscape.

The Wren's Nest and Dudley Castle Hill form tiny exposures of the older rocks that lie beneath the coal basins of the Black Country (Fig. 5a). Both are inliers of Silurian rocks, whale-back-shaped domes whose limestones plunge steeply, almost vertically, into the earth. Clays and thin sandstones of the Etruria Marl lap round the flanks of these limestone hills. The exposures of limestone and shale account for the minor features within each tiny upland, features that have been exaggerated as men have quarried the limestones over the centuries. The heart of the Wren's Nest Hill is composed of the oldest of the Silurian rocks, the Wenlock Shales. They are followed by a layer of pale grey limestone, the Lower Wenlock Limestone. At Dudley Castle the Lower Wenlock Limestone forms a ring that completely encloses the summit of the hill. Both of the hills are encircled by an outer belt of limestone, the Upper Wenlock Limestone. The Lower Ludlow Shales form the gentle lower slopes of the hills and dip steeply beneath the rocks of the Coal Measures.

Limestone-quarrying ceased in the early 1920s, and as we walk over the fantastic scenery of these hills we can survey the scars on the landscape of an industry that has run through its whole life-cycle. When it started is far less certain. In the Middle Ages, the quarries were certainly worked for building-stones and the remains of the castle at Dudley contain a large amount of worked blocks of Silurian limestone. By the first half of the nineteenth century the steeply dipping bands of limestone had been followed to considerable depths and the quarrying of the rock under the open light of the sky had given way to mining in echoing sub-terranean caverns. The hard pure Silurian limestone has had several uses. First it was used mainly as a building-stone. By the eighteenth century the rock was quarried as a flux for iron-smelting and limestone was burnt for use as a fertiliser.

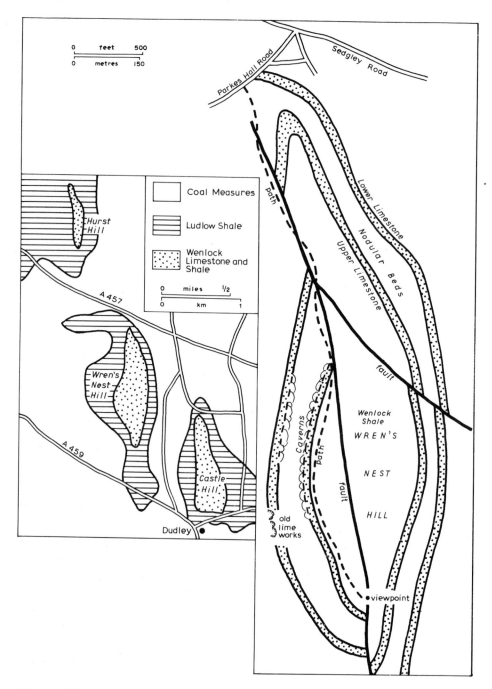

Fig 5a   The geology of the Wren's Nest. Inset: the inliers of Wenlock Limestone
forming part of the dorsal ridge of the Black Country.

Plate 5c The Wren's Nest: abandoned quarries along the outcrop of the Wenlock Limestone marked by white scars and strips of woodland. Council estates on the Ludlow shales.

Plate 5b The entrance to the Dudley Canal tunnel on the eastern flank of the Castle Hill (968917)

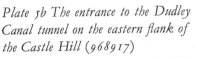

The great age of quarrying around Dudley began with the building of the Dudley Canal in the last decade of the eighteenth century. This waterway cuts through the Dudley Castle ridge in a tunnel (9491) and opened up the depths of the Silurian limestones to water transport. The underground limestone quarries became one of the wonders of the West Midlands in the nineteenth century. A highly romantic account appears in a guide-book to Dudley Castle published by the vicar of Dudley in 1825. He describes 'the Canal Basin, deeply-sunken amid rocks and caves, the sunlight seldom warming its sullen waters, whence diverge four subterranean canals: one for commercial purposes, nearly two miles in length; and three, formed on the same water level, for conveyance of the limestone torn, by explosions with gunpowder, from the bowels of the earth under the neighbouring hills' (Pl. 5b).

The Wren's Nest Hill (see Pl. 5c) bears the scars of centuries of limestone-quarrying. The angle of dip in the Lower and Upper Wenlock Limestones deeply affects the details of the scenery. Along the eastern side of the hill the rocks plunge almost vertically into the ground, and the quarries form deep grooves between upstanding walls of shale (938919). The bands of limestone dip less steeply on the western slopes. Here the rock has been quarried by the pillar-and-stall method, the technique used for the mining of the Thick Coal. Huge shaggy pillars of limestone separate rough-hewn rectangular caverns from which the stone has been taken (936919). The floors and roofs of these abandoned workings follow the steep dip of the rocks and plunge at a giddy angle into the depths of the earth. On the sur-face, above the abandoned quarries, *sinks* and depressions mark the collapse of 'stalls' beneath.

A walk along the path that follows the western flank of the summit of the Wren's Nest Hill shows a landscape that has not changed much since the time when the quarrying industry died. Young trees have sprouted on the spoil-heaps and in the crannies of the limestone. There is a romantic wildness about the place that would have delighted a Victorian guide-book writer. Today Wren's Nest is a place for the day-tripper, a playground for the built-up areas that surround it on every hand.

Quarrying is still the main industry of the central ridge to the south of Dudley. On the southern and eastern slopes of Turner's Hill (969887) a line of huge quar-ries exposes the brown and grey igneous rock, a dolerite that was intruded into the Middle Coal Measures during Carboniferous times in the form of a lens-shaped mass. To east and west, on either side of the Rowley Hills, this igneous intrusion or *laccolith* thins out into fingers of dark rock that penetrate the sandstones, shales and seams of coal. These dykes and veins of dolerite have been explored in great detail as a result of the search for coal beneath the intrusion. One coal-mine, the Grace Mary colliery, stood close to the summit of Darby's Hill at almost 800 feet above sea-level. Its number 2 shaft (969891) cut through the basalt laccolith to reach the Thick Coal at 812 feet from the surface.

The Rowley Regis laccolith, covering a little more than one square mile of country, has given rise to one of the most distinctive minor regions within the Black Country. The dominant feature of the landscape is the collection of huge quarries of such an extent and depth that the cranes, lorries, roadways and all the apparatus for the extraction of the stone are reduced to the scale of toys (Pl. 5*d*). The dolerite occurs as a building-stone in the older cottages around Rowley Regis, and the scraggy, windy fields on the summit of Turner's Hill are fenced with rough walls of shapeless, dark brown lumps of the same rock.

The use of the Rowley dolerite as a building-stone ceased almost two centuries ago when bricks, made from the clays within the Coal Measures, became the uni-versal building material of the Black Country. The rise of the quarry industry on a commercial scale dates only from the 1820s when the hard, smooth rock was used for the paving of new streets in Birmingham and the rapidly growing Black

Plate 5d   Rowley Regis: huge quarries in the dolerite laccolith

Country towns. A native of the Black Country, Walter Allen, has summed up the character of the Rowley dolerite.

The hills themselves resound all day with the thunder of blasting and are scarred and hollowed everywhere by quarries, for they are the source of the hard basalt known as 'Rowley Rag', the horrible stone with which the older streets of Birmingham and the Black Country towns are paved: blue-grey, smooth, shiny, slimy slippery stone that whatever the weather and despite its hardness seems always to exude moisture.

Even though the demands of road-making have changed and paving setts are no longer wanted, the value of the Rowley Regis quarries has not declined. Today the quarries boom as a source of road metal. At the present rate of working the stone will last for another half-century. It is hard to imagine the scene of dereliction on this part of the backbone of the Black Country when the quarrying of dolerite has run through its full cycle.

Dudley

Among all the towns of the Black Country, Dudley carries the strongest impressions of its long history as a settlement (Pl. 5e). Here, we can still see the outlines of a medieval town. The High Street runs southwards from the foot of the Castle Hill along the backbone of the central ridge. It was the focus of the medieval town. At the centre the High Street widens to form an elongated market place; for at least eight centuries this has been a place of trade and commerce. Churches stand at either end of the High Street, landmarks at the approaches to the medieval town. St Thomas looks along the axial street from the south. The church that we see today was rebuilt in 1819 on the site of its medieval forerunner. It is typical of so many churches of the Industrial Revolution. The dark and heavy stained-glass windows create an overpowering sense of isolation from the world outside, as if the architect wished to make a haven from the smoke and fire of the furnaces and coal-mines that once surrounded the Dudley ridge on every hand.

Dudley High Street ends abruptly in the col at the foot of the Castle Hill. Above a ring of woods, on a limestone hill-top, stands the finest medieval building in the Black Country. Domesday Book says that Dudley had a castle in 1086: 'the said William held Dudley, and there is his castle'. We can still see some of the features of the first castle that might have been built by the William, William Fitz-Ausculph, named in the pages of Domesday Book. These features are the huge, grass-grown mound beneath the keep and the ditch that surrounds it.

For two centuries Dudley Castle has been a total ruin. Its roofless buildings and broken walls of pale Wenlock Limestone form the most picturesque piece of architecture in the whole region. The present state of decay is largely the result of a fire that swept through the castle buildings in 1750. Booker describes the burning of the castle for three days and nights in his *Descriptive and Historical Account of Dudley Castle*, published in 1825. He was able to use the eye-witness accounts of old people

Plate 5e   Dudley Castle Hill: an inlier of the Wenlock Limestone crowned by a medieval castle whose Norman mound is clearly visible. In the foreground the north end of the High Street and St Edmund's Church.

in Dudley, and his pompous, clerical language provides an account that must have delighted his readers. 'Conflagration rapidly completed that work of ruin which the mighty hand of time and the violence of War had failed to accomplish. . . . Its roof, chiefly of lead, poured down fiery torrents resembling burning lava, previously to the timbers giving way which supported it. These, falling at intervals, were followed by smothered explosions, like distant thunder; while columns of flame rose up to an astonishing height, visible, especially throughout the hours of darkness, for many miles.'

Despite the fire, the main stages of Dudley Castle's building-history may be traced clearly in the ruins. The gatehouse, the wall and the two-storeyed stone keep that crowns the Norman mound all date from about the year 1320. The last stage of building took place in Henry VIII's reign when the castle had become the property of Sir John Dudley, later the Duke of Northumberland. He employed Sir William Sharington, an eminent Tudor architect. The centre-piece of this work is a Great Hall, built over the foundations and cellars of a fourteenth-century structure. With its tall mullioned windows the Great Hall foreshadows the style of the grand country mansions of the reigns of Elizabeth and James I. Close to the castle stood the priory, founded in the middle of the twelfth century as a daughter of the great monastery at Wenlock. Little remains today, apart from fragments of the walls of the church of St James.

The great castle on Dudley Hill played a very important part in the development of the town. Powerful lords were able to call into existence markets and fairs, and the broad High Street, stretched beneath the Castle Hill, reminds one of the part played by the castle in the creation of an urban community. Dudley failed to gain the full status of a borough until the nineteenth century, but with its weekly market and three fairs a year it had all the life and activities of a town.

For centuries the town has lived under the wing of the earls of Dudley; they have left their mark upon its topography in so many ways. In 1819 the Earl of Dudley helped to pay for the rebuilding of St Thomas's Church. At the close of the eighteenth century the reigning earl engineered the conversion of the limestone quarries on Dudley Castle Hill into a park with pleasant footpaths and drives for carriages. Booker, in his *Guide to Dudley Castle*, recalls this transformation of a piece of the Black Country's landscape. He explains that it happened when the working of limestone in open quarries 'was superseded by the more rapid and profitable system of tunnelling'. In his picturesque language Booker describes the change: 'the abrupt superficies of the glade before us, as well as several other parts of these grounds, whose whole substratum is Lime Rock, were judiciously softened off and planted. Thus, in little more than twenty years, these parts are indubitably rendered more beautiful, as now transformed, than they were in their tamer state of nature.' The ornamental fountain that stands on Market Place was a gift of the Earl of Dudley, put up on the site of the Old Town Hall.

Among the Black Country towns Dudley has been set apart both by its site, astride the dividing ridge of the region, and by the character impressed upon the place through centuries of association with powerful aristocratic families. Today, it is a regional shopping-centre midway between the dreary industrial settlements of the Tame and Stour basins. Above all, it is a pleasure resort for the Black Country, a character that Dudley acquired towards the end of the eighteenth century as a result of the 'improving works' of the earls of Dudley upon the Castle Hill. The ruined castle, the stupendous viewpoint at the summit of the keep (a building miserably neglected by its present owners) and the shady walks through plantations in the abandoned limestone quarries epitomised the Victorian idea of an inland pleasure resort. Dudley Castle Hill has not lost its reputation as a pleasure ground; today it houses the Black Country's zoo.

Further Reading

Allen, W. *Black Country* (1946).
Whitehead T. H. and Pocock, R. W. 'Dudley and Bridgnorth', *Memoirs of the Geological Survey of Great Britain* (1947).

Maps

O.S. 1-inch sheet 131 (Birmingham); O.S. 2½-inch sheet SO 99; Geological Survey 1-inch sheet 167 (Dudley); Geological Survey 1-inch sheet 168 (Birmingham).

Suggested Itinerary

A day excursion by car or coach might begin at the Wren's Nest Hill. Take the lane (936922) into the saddle between Mons Hill and the Wren's Nest. Follow on foot the path that leads southwards to the summit of the Wren's Nest Hill. Return to 936922 and drive to the Birmingham–Wolverhampton trunk road at 943922; follow this road towards Tipton and at 951917 stop to explore the site where the Dudley Canal and its underground feeders emerge from the tunnel (947917). This place clearly illustrates the theme of the Black Country's changing industries. We can see the derelict canal basins, abandoned limestone quarries in the slopes of Dudley Castle Hill and a stainless-steel tube works, the most modern of industries, on the site of the former lime-kilns. Follow the main road to the centre of Dudley; view the chief features of the town.

Follow the main road A461 to Dudley Port, a canal settlement. Dudley Port stands on the original 473-foot level of the Birmingham and Wolverhampton Canal. It is worthwhile taking a walk for a third of a mile from the canal bridge on the A461 (963913) towards Tividale Aqueduct (968909). This canal tow-path presents several features of a Black Country industrial landscape. We note that short branch-canals lead into factory yards. Industry now has little use for its canal-side sites, transport is mainly by road. From the Tividale Aqueduct walk to the mouth of the Netherton tunnel (967908). This was the last great feature of the Canal Age and was built in 1855.

Return to 963913 and follow road A461 to the junction at 964914; turn right to Brades Village (9890) and Oldbury. The industrial landscapes here are typical of the north-east of the Black Country; much derelict land is now levelled and partly built over with modern factories.

From Oldbury follow Newbury Lane (9788), to Portway (973884). Newbury Lane climbs steeply across the outcrop of the Middle Coal Measures. Some classic features of the Black Country scene may be observed here. To the left of the road the sites of old coal-pits have been cut away to expose the Etruria Marl for the extraction of clays used in brick-making (980887). The latest stage in the development of the Black Country may be seen in new factories sited on derelict land, and council houses on similar sites. At Portway (973884) turn right and climb steeply to Turner's Hill (968887) and Darby's Hill (9689), the summits of the dolerite laccolith. Note the long line of active and derelict quarries on the eastern flanks of these hills where the igneous rock takes the place of the marls and sandstones of the Middle Coal Measures. The Rowley Hills give fine panoramas over the eastern and western sectors of the Black Country.

Field Work

Prepare a large sketch-map of the country covering the squares on the 1-inch or $2\frac{1}{2}$-inch maps bounded by the grid lines 96/98 and 87/90. Using your sketch-map in the field plot the quarries in the Rowley Regis area today, indicating with different colours the active and abandoned workings.

Make enquiries from the quarry companies about the places to which the road metal is sent. Make a sketch-map to show the extent of the market for this rock.

Further Work

From either the 1-inch map or the $2\frac{1}{2}$-inch maps make a tracing of the country between Sedgley (9193) and Rowley Regis (9587) to show the features of the Black Country's dorsal ridge. Trace off the main roads as a means of locating other features.

(1) Mark and name two hills where the Silurian limestones outcrop.
(2) Roughly shade the area of outcrop of an igneous rock. What is its chief use?
(3) Mark two canal tunnels through the Dudley ridge and write down the dates of their construction.
(4) Indicate the site of:
   (*a*) a former important lime-works
   (*b*) the site of a priory
   (*c*) the site of a colliery that is today a brick-works.

6 The Black Country (iii)

A TRANSECT OF THE STOUR BASIN

The south-western part of the Black Country has a clearly drawn character. Hills fall steeply to the valley of the Stour and they have made a deep impression on the topography of industrial settlements. Brierley Hill (9186) and Netherton (9488) crown the summits of hills. Their rows of terraced houses and Victorian streets seem to flow down the steep surrounding slopes. Other places, such as Lye (9284), Cradley (9485) and Quarry Bank (9386), cling to the sharp bluffs that rise from the river. Their streets and lanes often follow the contours, and the settlements have a stepped and terraced appearance. In many places wide views open up across the Stour Basin and the elements of the industrial landscape – derelict land, factory buildings and red-brick cottages – are arranged in a new order against a background of hills. There is a certain beauty about the landscapes of the south-western part of the Staffordshire Coalfield that is lacking from the urban sprawl of the Tame Valley. Part of the attraction of these landscapes lies in the fact that Victorian industrialism has not subdued the natural scene completely.

The Stour winds through a rapidly deepening valley cut across the clays, shales and sandstones of the Middle and Upper Coal Measures. Between Halesowen and Stourbridge the river falls almost 200 feet, and a few miles below Stourbridge it empties into the Severn. Since the latter part of the Ice Age, when the spilling over of a glacial lake in central Shropshire caused the cutting of the Ironbridge gorge, the Severn Valley has been rapidly deepened. The Stour responded to the deepening of the Severn and its own valley has undergone rejuvenation. Hence the strong topography of the present landscape.

Rock structures add another set of distinctive features to the scenery of the south-western part of the Black Country. The Netherton anticline, an upfold in the older Silurian rocks, occupies the central part of the coalfield. In one small area, on the crest of the anticline, the Silurian rocks are exposed at the surface. Between Black Brook and the Lodge Farm Reservoir (9387), the Upper Ludlow Shales outcrop. The Middle Coal Measures, with their productive seams, outcrop on the eastern and western sides of the Netherton anticline and curve in a tight arc around the blunt northern nose of this Silurian dome. Two basins filled with Carboniferous rocks lie on either side of the anticline. To the east occurs a thick deposit of the Etruria Marl. This series of red and purple clays is the source of the famous Staffordshire blue bricks and around Cradley the formation has a depth of 800 feet. Collieries have reached the rich Middle Coal Measures through the cover of the Etruria Marl, and this is a region of clay-pits, brick-works and much derelict land. Westward of the Netherton anticline the Coal Measures are preserved in the Pensnett Basin. Here the Middle Coal Measures crop out at the surface. They include nine coal-seams, but even so only two per cent of the rock series consists of coal; the rest is shale, sandstone and fire-clay. The Black Country's most important seams of fire-clay are found between Stourbridge and Gornalwood (9191), and the fire-clay mines that are still active give the district a special character as an industrial landscape.

The separation of the south-western sector of the Black Country into two small coal-basins by the Netherton anticline has had a deep effect upon the progress and character of mining in the region. Coal was much less accessible than in the Tame Valley. Around Wednesbury, Tipton and Bilston the thirty-foot seam of the Thick Coal could be mined at only a few feet from the surface over many acres of land. In contrast, on the flanks of the Netherton anticline the Coal Measures plunge steeply to great depths; mining in its early primitive stages was much more difficult here.

Halesowen and the Upper Stour Valley

Halesowen, like Dudley, belongs in part to the Black Country and its heavy industries, but also presents features that do not typify the region. Dudley stands above the coal-basins on the dorsal ridge; Halesowen lies on the edge of the productive Coal Measures. To the south the land rises by billowy folds to the summit of the Clent Hills at a thousand feet above sea-level. In an amphitheatre of woods, fields and isolated farms tiny streams gather together to form the Stour. It is country left unspoilt by the Industrial Revolution because the underlying rocks are almost barren of coal. They belong to the Upper Coal Measures and consist of a thick series of grey-green and reddish sandstones. Even though the countryside to the south of Halesowen escaped the effects of the Industrial Revolution, it now stands in the shadow of a greater threat from the expansion of the huge Birmingham conurbation. The dull suburbia of Quinton (9884) shows only too plainly what could happen to the lanes and footpaths of Illey (9881) if the laws that created Birmingham's 'green belt' were to disappear.

The outlook towards the north-west of Halesowen presents a very different scene, one where we can recognise most of the industrial elements that have given the Black Country its regional name. The Stour flows northward across the outcrop of the Etruria Marl. The Dudley Canal, cut in the closing years of the eighteenth century, follows the contours of the eastern slopes of the Stour Valley. In the distance, at Coombeswood (971853), a steel-tube works straddles the banks of the canal and displays the part played by the Black Country canals in fixing the sites

119

of industries in the first half of the nineteenth century. Clay-pits and brick-works, the waste land of collieries, and hillsides splashed with Victorian terraced housing make up the rest of this landscape. Even the place-names of the landscapes taken in by the panorama from Mucklow Hill (978847) reflect the contrasted historical development of the two tracts of country. To the south the scattered farms and tiny hamlets point to a region of late medieval colonisation. For instance, the suffix 'ley', meaning a woodland clearing, occurs in the name Illey (9881). Names such as Oatenfields Farm (9682) and Dovehousefields Farm (9681) recall the features of a countryside untouched by Victorian industry. In the view towards the north-west the Industrial Revolution has added its own place-names to the land-scape. Just to the north of Halesowen, we note The Furnace (966845) and Furnace Hill (967842) – names that take the mind back to the beginnings of industry in the West Midlands.

Halesowen, like Dudley and Wednesbury, has had a long history as a settlement. Domesday Book shows that it was flourishing in the eleventh century. In fact, the details of plough-teams and population at Halesowen in Domesday Book suggest that it was the largest and most important settlement in the region. The core of Halesowen, on the steep western bank of the Stour, has a medieval street-plan. The parish church is one of the best medieval buildings in the Black Country, its earlier parts dating from the twelfth century. Outside Halesowen, the ruins of an abbey stand amid the fields on the further side of the Stour Valley (976828). It was founded in 1214 when King John gave the manor of Hales to the Bishop of Winchester with the instruction that a monastery should be built there. A farm now occupies the site. The open space that was enclosed by the cloister is now a stock-yard and a wall of the abbey church can still be seen as part of a barn. In the fields around St Mary's Abbey are the traces of a moat and the grass-grown embankments of the monastery's fish-ponds (Pl. 6a).

At least 200 years of industrial development are represented in the topography of Halesowen. The Furnace (966845) was one of the most important iron-making centres of the Black Country before 1700 when Halesowen was making scythes, spades and other agricultural tools, nails and gun barrels. By the early nineteenth century the borough's industrial reputation rested mainly on the manufacture of nails. Nail-making persisted as a domestic industry long after the factory system on a large scale had invaded iron manufactures and the many branches of engineering. The nailers lived in cottages, each with its own nail shop. In the first years of the nineteenth century a nailers' suburb was added to Halesowen. Small terraced houses and nail shops grew up in the district of the Stourbridge Road (964837). Today this part of Halesowen is changing rapidly as a redevelopment project of 1959 has led to the demolition of the primitive nailers' cottages.

The latest phase in the evolution of Halesowen belongs to the middle of the twentieth century. The town spreads across the summit of the broad spur that

120

Plate 6a Halesowen Abbey: a view towards the Clent Hills. In the foreground is the grass-grown dam of a former fish-pond; in the distance the abbey ruins stand up incongruously amid a nineteenth-century farm.

divides the Stour from the Lutley Brook (948835). At Queensway a new town centre has been built over a former piece of parkland. Housing-estates built in the boom of the late fifties cover all the fields that sloped gently to the valley of the Lutley Brook. Within fifteen years Halesowen has more than doubled its built-up area and rebuilt much of the town centre, proof of the pressure for building-space on the fringes of the Birmingham and Black Country conurbation. No part of the ring of country around the vast midland conurbation is more attractive than its south-western fringe with views of the Clent Hills and easy access to the unspoilt scenery of the Severn Valley. In the age of the motor car Halesowen sums up the struggle between town and country on the fringes of the expanding conurbations.

Cradley and Cradley Heath

The industrial settlements of Cradley (9485) and Cradley Heath (9486) have grown on the coal basin that lies to the east of the Netherton dome. Here the Stour flows in a deep valley and before the age of steam provided valuable water-power sites for the forges and slitting-mills of eighteenth-century industrialists. At Cradley one is overwhelmed by the feeling that this place went through the most vital phase of its development in the first half of the nineteenth century. Chain-making has remained its chief industry since the beginning of the Industrial Revolution. Like the nail-makers at Halesowen, the men who made chains at Cradley had small forges behind their cramped cottages. Their red-brick cottages still form the dominant impression of Cradley where they stand scattered about the steep valley side above the Stour.

Below Lyde Green (936854) a minor stream, the Mousesweet Brook, joins the River Stour. Here we find only a patch of derelict land and the dull concrete and asbestos sheds of a small factory estate, but the name, Cradley Forge, commemorates one of the earliest events in the Industrial Revolution. At this place, where the Stour provided water-power, Dud Dudley managed a forge early in the seventeenth century and made the first experiments in the smelting of iron with coal. Almost a century later, Abraham Darby experimented on the same lines and successfully smelted iron with the aid of coke at the Coalbrookdale works in Shropshire. Perhaps the site of Cradley Forge should be added to the small list of recognised monuments of the Industrial Revolution – names that should rank alongside Runnymede and Bosworth Field in England's historic places.

Place-names often keep alive the memory of a vanished landscape. Cradley Heath (9486), on the north bank of the Stour, was one of the many commons that once occupied a considerable area of the Black Country. Another vanished common is remembered by the name of Blackheath, a mile to the south-east of the Rowley Hills (9786). During the eighteenth century chain-makers and nailers settled on Cradley Heath and Blackheath; squatters' cottages were scattered irregularly over the commons. Later, in the second half of the nineteenth century, Cradley Heath vanished beneath the streets of a drab industrial settlement (see Pl. 6b). Part of the stimulus to its growth came from the opening of the railway between Stourbridge

Plate 6b Cradley Heath: twentieth-century housing-estates cover the derelict land of former collieries, patches of which still remain in the centre and top of the picture. The older, Victorian part of Cradley Heath is in the background beyond the railway.

Plate 6c

*Mushroom Green:
a cottage in a
squatters' hamlet of
the early years of the
Industrial Revolution*

Junction and Birmingham in 1861. By 1900 Cradley Heath had rapidly outstripped Cradley. Parallel streets of late Victorian terraced houses took the place of the former heath and the railway encouraged the growth of factory sites on the gently sloping land of the north bank of the Stour. Cradley Heath makes chains, cranes and lifting-gear; its grimy industrial buildings threaded with mineral lines are typical of the late nineteenth century.

A fragment of the Black Country's earliest industrial landscapes has survived at Mushroom Green (938865). It consists of tiny brick cottages scattered at all angles in the floor of a narrow tributary valley of the Stour. A century and a half ago its inhabitants worked in the nearby colliery of the Earl of Dudley at Saltwells (939863). Mushroom Green is typical of the unplanned squatter hamlets that grew up in the early years of the Industrial Revolution (see Pl. 6c). Many of them have disappeared amid the factory buildings and streets of terraced houses that came with the full spate of the Industrial Revolution after 1840. Mushroom Green preserves the atmosphere of the years about 1800 when the countryside still predominated in the most industrialised parts of England. Until the 1840s the works of industry formed only a minor and subdued element in the landscape of the Black Country. Since the Second World War, Mushroom Green has been reduced in size by the removal of some of its inhabitants to the new council estate that covers the derelict land on the higher slopes of the valley. What remains of the hamlet should be preserved as a national monument, a museum piece that forms a fossil landscape of the first years of the Industrial Revolution. Mushroom Green's neatly kept kitchen vegetable-gardens and higgledy-piggledy pattern of narrow cottages could belong to the period and landscapes of Charlotte Brontë's *Shirley*, to a time when the full effect of the new inventions and manufactures on England's economy, population and scenery were undreamt of.

The country between Quarry Bank (9386) and Brierley Hill (9186) belongs to the most westerly coal basin of the Black Country, the Pensnett Basin. Here the seams of the Middle Coal Measures are accessible at the surface and, as in the Tame Valley around Tipton and Wednesbury, mining started at an early date. The rich seam of the Thick Coal outcrops on the flank of the Netherton anticline at Quarry Bank. Less than a mile to the west, near Stourbridge, it appears again at the surface. There is documentary proof that coal was being worked near Amblecote early in the fourteenth century. By the end of the eighteenth century the valley slopes to the south of Brierley Hill were dotted with small coal-pits, and the place-name Delph (919862) recalls that coal-mining from shallow workings was once the chief occupation of the district.

Apart from coal, the chief resource of the country between Stourbridge and Gornal is the thick succession of bands of fire-clay beneath the coal-seams. These grey clays are resistant to high temperatures, and for more than two centuries they have been used in the manufacture of pots and containers for the glass industry. Fire-bricks, crucibles and sanitary ware are also made from the same fire-clays.

The presence of fire-clays encouraged the growth of the glass industry in this region during the eighteenth century. At Stourbridge and Amblecote (9085) a few of the curious conical shaped glass-houses still survive. William Pitt, author of a *Topographical History of Staffordshire* (1817), mentions the part played by fire-clay pots in the glass industry of the time. 'The clay possesses this peculiar excellency, that a pot made of it, with a proper heat, will melt almost anything into glass, provided it be fluxed with proper salts. The largest pots made of this clay are for crown glass, plate glass, broad glass and bottles, and hold from 15 to near 30 cwt each. . . . The largest will last from one or two months, the smallest from nine to twelve months.' The glass industry also needed large amounts of coal, but an equally strong inducement to its location on the south-western fringe of the Black Country must have been the short life of the glass-house pots and the presence of fire-clay from which they were made.

In the Coalbournbrook Valley (9186), one can see so many features of the earliest and latest phases of the Industrial Revolution. Delph (9186) was the scene of some of the earliest coal-mining and fire-clay pits. Today this landscape, despoiled in the first years of the Industrial Revolution, is being worked again by the methods of open-cast mining. Along the lane that drops down the valley side from Amblecote Bank (917857) to Delph Locks (917863) we can see the recent work of bulldozers over former derelict ground. Huge pits, fifty feet and more in depth, make harsh gashes in the hill-side. On their freshly cut, vertical walls the grey fire-clays are exposed to the light of day as well as the contrasting black bands of coal-seams. Already some of the open-cast quarries are worked out, and the land has been levelled for building. Victorian industrialists practised a wasteful robber economy that consumed the riches of the earth without forethought. The un-planned mining of the Thick Coal in the country around Tipton and Wednesbury in the first half of the nineteenth century provides an outstanding example of such indiscriminate exploitation of natural wealth. Today many millions of tons of coal are inaccessible in the flooded and uncharted mines. How will the future judge our own period in the continuing industrial revolution? The pace of change is far greater than anything experienced in the Victorian industrial revolution, and the scars on the skin of the earth seem infinitely deeper. Meantime, as we follow the lane down to Delph Locks, we can see the earliest and the latest stages in the technology of the Industrial Revolution. The Coalbournbrook Valley, is thickly dotted with the sites of works that use the local fire-clays. Some are located in a maze of clay-pits; others have been built on the banks of the Stourbridge Canal that encircles Brierley Hill on the south, west and east like some medieval moat. This canal was cut in the 1770s. Its most impressive feature is a huge flight of locks that climbs through eighty feet from the head of the Coalbournbrook Valley. The Delph Locks were built by the Dudley Canal Company to make a link between their system and the Stourbridge Canal. Little traffic passes that way now, and the canal is another item in the archaeology of the Industrial Revolution.

The topography of Brierley Hill summarises so many features of the history and geography of the Black Country. A wide view across the coalfield opens up from its hill-top churchyard. On the north-eastern fringe of Brierley Hill, at Round Oak (921877), we find one of the last surviving iron and steel works of the region (Pl. 6d). It was founded in 1857 and has been converted into one of the most

Plate 6d   Brierley Hill: the main axis of the settlement lies along a former turnpike road. The Round Oak steelworks is in the left foreground, and streets of Victorian terraces occupy the ground between the railway and the eighteenth-century parish church (date of photo 1960).

modern steel plants in the West Midlands. Today Round Oak produces a quarter of a million tons of several grades of steel from its five open-hearth furnaces. To the south-west Brierley Hill shares the industrial pattern of Stourbridge and Amblecote with glass-works and the manufacture of refractory bricks. For the rest, with its clay-pits, derelict land, and abandoned canal basins Brierley Hill is a characteristic sample of the Black Country's industrial landscapes.

Brierley Hill grew in the large medieval parish of Kingswinford (8989), first among the royal manors of Staffordshire in Domesday Book. The Manor Court Rolls of Kingswinford first mention Brierley Hill as an inhabited place in 1619. Already squatters were beginning to exploit the resources of this wild and open common that was crossed by the lane from Stourbridge to Dudley. By the middle of the eighteenth century an industrial community had emerged on the heath at Brierley Hill, a community that lived by its pits, forges and furnaces, brick-kilns, glass-houses, nail and chain shops. In 1765 a chapel was built to serve this new settlement and a decade later the cutting of the Stourbridge Canal gave an added impetus to the growth of industry. William Pitt mentions this fact in his *Topographical History of Staffordshire*, published in 1817, where he notes under 'Brierley hill Chapel' that 'a vast trade in glass is carried on in the neighbourhood, which has been greatly promoted by the Stourbridge canal'.

The oldest part of Brierley Hill, the eighteenth-century squatter settlement, occupied the steep flank of the Coalbournbrook to the south of the parish church. On the summit of the ridge, northward of the church, a zone of industrial buildings is succeeded by the quarter completed by the end of the nineteenth century. This part of the settlement with its streets of Victorian terraced houses ends abruptly against the railway tracks. Beyond lies the development of the twentieth century where grey-green fields form patches between the semi-detached council houses that have sprung up on former derelict land.

Brierley Hill not only shows clearly its main stages of growth between the eighteenth and twentieth centuries, but today it provides one of the best examples of redevelopment or urban renewal, a process that is rapidly transforming the landscapes of the Black Country. Close to the centre most of the early squatter-settlement has been demolished and now tall skyscraper flats have arisen on the site. From the valley of the Coalbournbrook they dominate the skyline and dwarf the squat tower of the eighteenth-century church that once gave character to the view of this hill-top industrial settlement.

A mile to the west of Brierley Hill a fault draws an abrupt line along the edge of the coalfield. Beyond the fault, rocks of Triassic age, mainly Bunter sandstones and conglomerates, underlie the landscape. To the west the landscapes of the Industrial Revolution come to a sudden end. Not that this region has been completely free from the influence of its grimy neighbour. Kinver (8483) has long been a favourite resort for day-trippers from the Black Country towns and only the laws that attempt to preserve a green belt to the west and south of the Birmingham conurbation prevent the city from spilling over into these pleasant pastoral landscapes.

Further Reading

Buchanan, K. M. *Worcestershire*, pt 68 of the Land of Britain series, ed. L. D. Stamp (1944).

Myers, J. *Staffordshire*, pt 61 of the Land of Britain series, ed. L. D. Stamp (1945). See appendix by S. H. Beaver, 'The Black Country'.

Excursions Guide to the Birmingham Region, ed. H. Thorpe (1965).

Maps

O.S. 1-inch sheet 130 (Kidderminster); O.S. $2\frac{1}{2}$-inch sheet SO 98; Geological Survey 1-inch sheet 167 (Dudley); Geological Survey 1-inch sheet 168 (Birmingham).

Suggested Itinerary

Begin the transect to the east of Halesowen on Mucklow Hill (978847), where there is an excellent view of the upper part of the Stour Basin. Descend Mucklow Hill, noting industrial sites on the banks of the derelict Dudley Canal, and turn right on entering Halesowen (971838) to follow the secondary road to The Furnace (967846). From the site of Halesowen Forge return to the centre of the town and the parish church by the lane that climbs Furnace Hill (967843) past the grammar school. Examine the parish church and the street-plan of the core of Halesowen. Take the road B4183 westward from the redeveloped town centre of Halesowen. Turn northwards at 956828 through the new housing-estates on the hill-top above Halesowen, reaching the Cradley road (A458) at 959839.

Follow A458 towards Cradley. The site of a former forge is passed in the deep valley of the Lutley Brook (951841). The lane that follows the south bank of the Stour closely from Overend to St Peter's Church, Cradley (942852), gives a good impression of this early industrial settlement with cottages scattered irregularly on the steep valley side. At Cradley take the footpath from St Peter's Church across the open hillside to Netherend (935852) and walk northwards along the road to rejoin the bus in the Stour Valley at the site of Cradley Forge (935857).

From the historic site of Dud Dudley's early seventeenth-century forge drive into Cradley Heath. Take a left turn at the cross-road (944859) and follow the minor road to the site of Saltwells colliery and Mushroom Green. It is better to study this squatter settlement of the late eighteenth century on foot. Take the footpath through Mushroom Green that follows the floor of the valley to join the road again at 936867. Note a similar squatter settlement across the valley on the outskirts of Quarry Bank.

Rejoin the bus and drive through Quarry Bank to the scattered ridge-top settlement of Mount Pleasant (921859). This can be made the beginning of a walk that unfolds the details of the historical and economic geography of the Coalbournbrook Valley. Leave the bus at the cross-road (917856) and follow the lane northward towards Delph Locks (917864). Here are some fine views of an early mining area that is now being re-exploited by open-cast methods. Already, much land has been worked out and levelled as a preparation for building. The site of an abandoned fire-clay mine still survives as one approaches Delph Locks. Finally, follow the tow-path by the eight Delph Locks until the canal is crossed by road A4100. At this point rejoin the bus and drive into Brierley Hill. Conclude the transect of the south-western part of the Black Country with a study of Brierley Hill, comparing the features of the town with those of Halesowen. Note that the earliest topographical feature of Brierley Hill, the parish church, belongs to the second half of the eighteenth century and compare this with the evidence for a flourishing medieval town at Halesowen. Pick out the nineteenth-century features of architecture and street-layout in Brierley Hill and conclude the transect at the Round Oak Iron and Steel Works (9287).

Field Work

(*a*) On a visit to Halesowen Abbey try to recognise the pieces of medieval building that still remain. Draw a sketch-plan of the present farm buildings and mark the parts that seem to belong to the former abbey.

(*b*) On the transect from Halesowen to Brierley Hill make a series of panoramic sketches at good viewpoints to illustrate the chief features of the geography of the south-western sector of the Black Country. Name the towns, important industrial sites and physical features taken in by your views.

Further Work

Construct a simple sketch-diagram from the air photograph of Brierley Hill. Insert the following features to help locate the detail – the main road A461 that forms the busy axis of the settlement, the Worcester and Wolverhampton railway in the foreground, and the Stourbridge Canal that crosses the picture in the distance.

Insert the following features:
(*a*) the parish church. When was this founded?
(*b*) Indicate part of the site of the Round Oak Iron and Steel Works. When was this plant founded? What is its average annual output of steel today?
(*c*) Locate the site of the Delph Locks.
(*d*) Mark an area of nineteenth-century houses and an area of twentieth-century building.

128

7 The Landscape of Extractive Industry Around Nuneaton

Although the West Midlands is often thought of as a vast industrial region, many of its individual industrial units are very compact and self-contained and form ugly blots within a predominantly rural landscape of green pastures and high hedgerows. This applies to the narrow belt of country in east Warwickshire running northwards from the outskirts of Coventry through Bedworth to Nuneaton and beyond (Fig. 7*a*). In this strip of country there is a concentration of workings connected with quarrying and mining, all loosely connected in that they are primary extractive industries. The reason for this concentration in a narrow north–south belt lies in the geology of the area. Starting to the north-west of Nuneaton there is a ridge of ancient hard rock (Pre-Cambrian), mainly quartzite. This forms a sharp upfold and gives rise to Caldecote Hill (3493) and Hartshill (3394). On its north-eastern side it ends in a fault scarp overlooking the wide Anker Valley and the red Keuper Marl plain of west Leicestershire beyond. On the other flank of this ridge of old resistant rock the land slopes gently westward to form a dissected plateau 400–500 feet high. This is the area of the East Warwickshire Coalfield. In the east of the coalfield the coal seams come to the surface as a series of steeply dipping beds where they have been folded against the Pre-Cambrian ridge. Farther west the seams dip more gently under a thick cover of barren beds. There are about fourteen workable seams in all and rather fortuitously in places like Newdigate (3387), Arley (2889) and Keresley (3284) collieries, six or seven seams have come together to form the Thick Coal, 23 feet thick in places. Associated with the coal are thick beds of clay which are worked in open pits for brick and tile-making. The distinctive Staffordshire blue bricks are also made in the area from the clays of the Etruria Marl, which lies above the Coal Measures. Beds of ironstone, pyrites, fire-clay and limestone were also worked at one time in this tract of very diversified geology. As most of these were worked in open pits, the whole landscape is scarred with hollows, now often filled with water. South of Nuneaton the outcrops of the various geological formations run approximately from north to south and, as a result, the different extractive industries form narrow belts trending in this direction. This is most clearly seen from the high ground of Caldecote Hill where the distinctive lines of the coal-tips, the chimneys and ovens of the brickworks and the open chasms of the stone quarries lie in parallel belts.

129

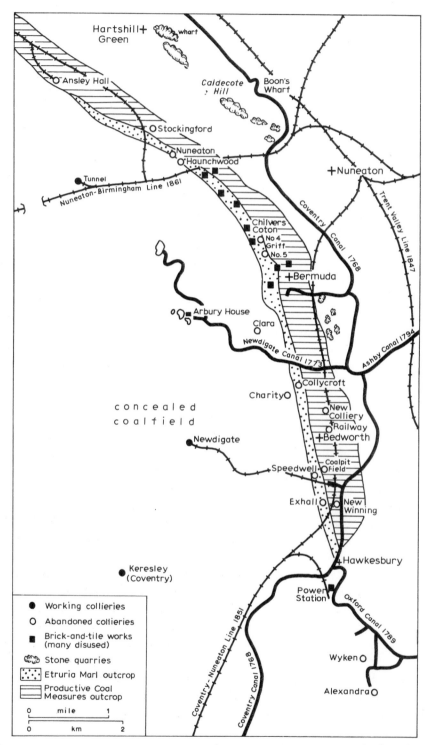

Fig. 7a Extractive industries of the belt of country between Nuneaton and Bedworth

Coal-mining

The earliest record of coal-working in this area goes back to the thirteenth century. The coal was obtained from the surface outcrops, particularly the Thick Coal, around Nuneaton. Open pits and short, sloping adits following the individual seams were used to win the coal. Both, however, suffered from bad drainage, the open pits because they filled with water and the adit workings because the water drained towards the working coal-face. The problem which the early miners must have faced was illustrated until recently at Bermuda (3590) where the bottom of the big open pit was flooded prior to its use as a refuse dump. This same pit also shows the steep dip of the coal-seams which is a feature of the edge of the coalfield.

Some of the earliest workings in the area were owned by Nuneaton Priory and provided a source of income for this religious house. After about 1550 the mines were taken from the priory and given to the Constable family who allowed various owners to work the coal. Under this arrangement, the coal-workings gradually extended southwards along the outcrop and by the early seventeenth century some of the biggest mines were in the Bedworth area (3587). In 1622 no fewer than 500 miners were employed at the great coal-mine there. Bedworth still has the appearance of a mining town with its rows of terraced houses, working men's institutes and co-operative shops. New council estates are built around the old overgrown pit-heaps, particularly in the area of Coalpit Field (3686). As much of the spoil is clay and shale, vegetation can take a hold on the pit-heaps and so they are not as bare or unsightly as in many coal-mining areas. The great coal-mine of seventeenth-century Bedworth has long since closed and the present-day miners have to travel to more distant collieries like Newdigate (3387). As a town, Bedworth, sited on a patch of glacial gravels, has always suffered in competition with Coventry and to a lesser extent, Nuneaton. It benefited, however, in that the silk industry of Coventry was established here in the nineteenth century, at first as a cottage industry and then in small factories. Until recently one of these early factories remained near the centre of the town, with its living-quarters on the ground floor and the silk shops above with their long windows. The building, a good example of nineteenth-century industrial architecture, has regrettably been pulled down during redevelopment.

While Bedworth was developing other industries like silk-ribbon manufacture, tapes and hats, the coal-workings had now moved farther south towards Coventry and westward on to the concealed coalfield. The working of the deeper seams was made possible by improved methods of draining the mines. Deep mining, as opposed to the open pits working the outcrop coal-seams, can be said to date from about 1778 when James Watt installed a powerful steam-engine for pumping at Hawkesbury colliery (3684). The greatest development of the East Warwickshire Coalfield did not come until after 1880 when the better seams of the South Staffordshire Coalfield were worked out and the Black Country became an importer rather

Plate 7b   Griff No. 5 colliery being dismantled as part of a policy of concentrating coal-working in a few large pits (347905)

than an exporter of coal. A number of new collieries were opened up on the concealed coalfield between 1880 and 1910, including Haunchwood (3191), Griff Clara (3489), Newdigate (3387), Arley (2889) and Keresley (3284) (Pl. 7b).

Some of these later collieries like Arley and Haunchwood were sunk close to existing railway lines to take advantage of good communications for exporting the coal. The most recent colliery of Daw Mill (2690) is sited on the Nuneaton to Birmingham line. At an earlier date it was the canals that provided the means of transport. The Coventry Canal, which was begun in 1768, was designed to bring coal from the collieries on the exposed coalfield to meet the ever-increasing demand of the Coventry industries. James Brindley, the great canal engineer, was in charge and the first section between Coventry and Atherstone was completed very quickly. This length ran from the canal basin close to the centre of Coventry (332796), through the industrial quarter to the north of the city and then close to Hawkesbury Colliery *en route* to Bedworth. Here the canal crossed the watershed into the Anker Valley system in a cutting through Bedworth Hill (3686). From Bedworth its route lay mainly to the east of the coalfield passing west of Nuneaton, around the southern end of the quartzite ridge and then along the foot of the fault scarp bordering the Anker Valley as far as Atherstone. In order to serve the many small collieries which lay close to the canal, small feeder branches were built. One ran west through Griff Hollow to the hamlet of Bermuda (355899), an early nine-teenth-century mining settlement with two rows of houses bordering a single, tree-lined street. At the southern end lay the canal wharf, now derelict with a half-sunken barge as the only link with the past. Tramways ran down to the canal basin from the many collieries of the area. Another feeder to the main canal ran for three miles from Arbury Park (3389). This was the home of the Newdigate family who had considerable interests in the coal-mining and even had small pits within the parkland setting of their estate at Arbury. The feeder canal was designed by Sir Richard Newdigate to take the coal from these small pits to Coventry and Nuneaton. Built in 1773 it must be one of the first private canals in the country and, as it ran close to his stately house, Sir Richard Newdigate went to great pains to harmonise the canal with the parkland landscape. The bridges which took the main drives across the canal were built of red sandstone and the lakes in front of Arbury House served the dual purpose of being both ornamental and acting as feeder basins for the canal.

Even when the railways reached the area after 1840, a considerable amount of the coal was still carried by the canal system. Tramways were laid to connect the collieries of Bedworth Heath (3486) with the Coventry Canal and one was in use until quite recently from Newdigate colliery (3387) running down to the basin off the main canal near Bedworth Hill. Another similar canal basin, now overgrown with reeds and used as a dump for the surrounding neighbourhood, lay near Potters Green (371824) on the north-east outskirts of Coventry. This served the Wyken Alexandra colliery of which now little remains save the overgrown spoil-heaps and some crumbling brickwork. The whole area around is one of fairly recent abandonment with the embankment of the old mineral line, the incongruous level-crossing gate, the flat-topped and grassed-over spoil-banks with their scatter of young thorn bushes, the subsidence flashes, all very much in evidence. Across this area the council house estates of Coventry have spread in recent years but because no real attempt has been made to restore the landscape before rebuilding, development has been haphazard due to the need to avoid the dereliction caused by past mining.

When Brindley built the first part of the Coventry Canal, he had in mind a much bigger scheme to connect the Trent–Mersey system with the Thames. Although he died in 1772, his dreams of a waterway across England gradually came about. This was made possible by the building of the Oxford Canal which joined the Coventry Canal at Hawkesbury (3684). Here a small canal settlement grew up with an inn, a shop and a few cottages lining the canal wharf. A fine single-span cast iron bridge built by John Sinclair in 1837 still spans the junction of the two canals. An early nineteenth century pumping-house to maintain the water level in the canal stands near by, and this was also built by Sinclair. Until quite recently it housed a very early Newcomen pumping-engine which was brought here from

Griff colliery. Hawkesbury, although a typical canal hamlet of a bygone era, still has its barges carrying coal to the near-by Coventry Power Station but this seems unlikely to continue much longer (Pl. 7c).

Brick-and-Tile Industry

Associated with the coal-seams are the beds of clay which form the basis of the brick industry. In addition there are beds of Etruria Marl which are used for making blue bricks. The clay-pits and brick-fields are therefore located close to the coal-mining areas, reaching their greatest development in the Stockingford–Chilvers Coton (3491) area. The industry has always been on a small scale, with numerous small open pits and brick-works located along the length of the clay outcrop (Pl. 7d). Flooding of the pits and a collapse of their sides has tended to limit the size of the workings but even so they occupy large areas. Although difficult to reclaim, the large pit near Bermuda (355903) is at present being filled in with refuse from Coventry. Large-scale reclamation has been carried out in the area near Stockingford Station (338918) where there was formerly a working for Etruria Marl. The ground is first levelled and then the topsoil is put back before reseeding. Land reclaimed in this way can be used either for playing-fields or for housing, as, unlike in coal-mining, long, continued subsidence is not a problem. At Chilvers Coton (3591), a suburb of Nuneaton, a school and housing-estate have been built on reclaimed land of an earlier clay-working (Pl. 7e). Although there is much still to be done by way of reclamation, the problem is not likely to be aggravated by the opening up of new clay-pits. In recent years, most of the smaller brick-and-tile works have been forced to close down in face of competition from the bigger and more highly mechanised units of places like Peterborough and the Bedford area.

Plate 7d   Brick-and-tile works alongside the railway at Stockingford. The flooded clay-pit cut in Etruria Marl lies next to the works, and other abandoned workings occur beyond the railway (3392).

Plate 7e   Chilvers Coton on the western outskirts of Nuneaton with its abandoned clay-pits lying alongside the reclaimed land of the school playing-fields. The Coventry Canal with its large factory runs across the top of the photograph (3591) (date of photo 1961).

Plate 7f
The working-face of
the diorite-pit at
Griff Hollow with
the massive rock
removed by blasting
and then broken up
for road metal

Stone-quarrying

The great upstanding ridge of hard quartzite rock, with bands of diorite running through it, extending north-west from Nuneaton, has been extensively quarried since about 1840. Huge pits have been opened up around Hartshill (3394) and these extend with only a short break to Tuttle Hill (3492) close to the outskirts of Nuneaton. The road which runs along the crest of the ridge from Abbey Street Station in Nuneaton (3592) to Hartshill Green (3294) gives excellent views of the quarries. The great vertical rock faces which are exposed clearly show the steep dip of the quartzite beds. Unlike in so many of the clay-pits, little difficulty is experienced with water and there seems no limit to the depth of the hole. The quartzite is a very jointed rock and this makes for easy quarrying. Before the days of mechanical diggers the quarry-men used to descend the working face on the end of a rope and simply dislodge the rock by means of a crow-bar. Only occasionally was blasting necessary to bring down the rock. In places there are dirt beds and, as some of the quartzite is brittle, there is quite a high percentage of waste which has to be dumped in great conical spoil-heaps which recall the coal-mining areas.

The diorite is a tougher rock than the quartzite and requires more blasting to dislodge it. In the nineteenth century it was extensively used for making paving-setts and kerbstones in the rapidly growing industrial towns of the Midlands. Today both the quartzite and the diorite are used mainly as road metal. Much of the stone is now carried away by road but in the mid-nineteenth century the Coventry Canal acted as the main artery of transport. Both the Hartshill and Tuttle Hill groups of quarries had wharves on the canal near by, at Anchor Inn (335947) and Boon's Wharf (347933). Later the railways took over some of this traffic as the quarries lay close to the main Nuneaton to Atherstone line running along the Anker Valley (Pl. 7*f*). The diorite quarries which occur around Griff Hollow (3689) are also connected with the railway, although here again much of the stone is now transported by lorry.

Further Reading

Milburn, D. *Nuneaton – the Growth of a Town* (1963).

Mitcheson, J. 'The East Warwickshire Coalfield', *Birmingham and its Regional Setting, a Scientific Survey*, ed. M. J. Wise (British Association for the Advancement of Science, 1950).

Redmill, J. 'The Rise of Population in the Warwickshire Coalfield', *Geography*, vol. XVI (1931) pp. 125–40.

Maps

O.S. 1-inch sheet 132 (Coventry and Rugby). This is adequate to follow the text, but for greater detail, especially in relation to the field work, the O.S. $2\frac{1}{2}$-inch maps, sheets SP 42 and SP 41, are of value.

Suggested Itinerary

The area forming an arc around the western fringes of Nuneaton, from Hartshill Green (3294) in the north to Bedworth (3686) in the south, displays most of the features described in the study. Starting from Hartshill Green, the route should run along the top of the quartzite ridge past the large stone-quarries, to the outskirts of Nuneaton. At Chilvers Coton (3490), the brick-and-tile works, now abandoned, can be seen. Close by, near the mining hamlet of Bermuda (353900), the steep dip of the outcropping coal-seams can be seen on the rim of Coventry's refuse tip. At the southern end of Bermuda, the old wharf of one of the many feeder branches to the Coventry Canal and the mineral lines which were connected to it, are seen. The third element in the landscape of extractive industry in this region, namely the coal-mining, can be seen around Griff and Collycroft (3587) as well as along the lane leading southwards from Bedworth to the Coventry Canal at Bedworth Hill (3686).

Further Work

Using either the 1-inch or $2\frac{1}{2}$-inch Ordnance Survey maps of the Nuneaton district, choose an area of about 50 square kilometres (50 grid-squares) and trace off on to squared paper (*a*) the areas covered by housing, (*b*) the areas devoted to coal-mining, clay-workings and brick-and-tile works, and stone-quarrying. From this, calculate the percentages of the total area given over to housing and industry.

137

8 Coventry – A Medieval City and a Modern Industrial Centre

Sir Basil Spence, architect of Coventry's new cathedral, calls his book *Phoenix at Coventry*. The phoenix was the mythological bird that burnt itself on a funeral pyre and then rose, full of youth, from its own ashes to begin another life-cycle. The burnt-out shell of Coventry's fifteenth-century parish church stands at the threshold of the twentieth-century cathedral, a symbol of the war-scarred city's new life-cycle. New buildings face us everywhere in Coventry; in the central shopping-sector, the new Technical College and Belgrade Theatre, in the scores of flats and suburban housing-estates. But the present time is only the latest of several periods of renewal in the long life of the city. The second half of the fourteenth century, for instance, was a period of expansion in the history of Coventry. Buildings of this medieval golden age still survive, despite the fire-bombs of the Second World War. Coventry's medieval wool and cloth industries have vanished completely, and since the sixteenth century several industrial cycles have given periods of prosperity to the city. The making of silk ribbons occupied Coventry in the first half of the nineteenth century. After 1860 bicycles and sewing-machines dominated the city's business life. Coventry's chief industries changed again in the twentieth century. Cars, lorries and farm machinery became the main industrial products. Each life-cycle in the city's history has left its mark on the urban landscape – in architecture, the layout of streets, the names of buildings and places. The past can never be completely obliterated, not even by war.

Medieval Coventry

Towards the end of the twelfth century urban ways of life were planted at Coventry. About the year 1181 Earl Ranulf of Chester gave the inhabitants of his manor at Coventry their first charter of liberties. The details of this charter show that Coventry was already changing from a village into a town. Earl Ranulf promised that its inhabitants should 'have the free and good laws of the burgesses of Lincoln'. Also, the charter of 1181 stated that 'incoming merchants' were 'not to be injured or unjustly treated'. Coventry, it seems, was already a place where traders met.

If we turn back a century from Earl Ranulf's charter to the Domesday Survey, it is certain that in 1086 Coventry was nothing more than a village. Warwickshire had only two towns at that time – Tamworth and Warwick. Domesday Book says

Plate 8a Coventry: in the foreground the new shopping-centre and precinct. The spires of Holy Trinity and St Michael's mark the core of the medieval town, and in the distance is the industrial quarter that developed in the Sherbourne Valley at the end of the nineteenth century (date of photo 1964).

that there was 'land for twenty ploughs' at Coventry and that '50 villeins, 12 bordars and 7 serfs' were living there. There is no mention of anything like a town. Coventry was a village in the eleventh century with a population of between 300 and 400. Its farmsteads probably stood on either side of the Earl's street – a name that has persisted to the present day. Earl Street is now part of the busy spinal road of Coventry cutting through the heart of the city from east to west.

The earls of Chester were not the only landowners in medieval Coventry. Before the Norman Conquest, in 1043, Leofric Earl of Chester, had given land for the foundation of a monastery. The monastic estate lay in the northern part of the town and until the middle of the fourteenth century Coventry was divided into two distinct parts, the *Earl's Half* and the *Prior's Half*. The boundary between the two estates still runs through the heart of the city as the line separating the parishes of St Michael and Holy Trinity. The effects of the medieval division between the *Earl's Half* and the *Prior's Half* are not completely lacking in the modern landscape. It accounts for the positions of two churches, side by side, in the centre of the city (335791). Holy Trinity served the Prior's part of the city; St Michael's was the parish church of the growing settlement of merchants and traders that gathered along the street beneath the castle of the earls of Chester. The castle still stood at the head of Broadgate in the sixteenth century, but it has since vanished from the scene as completely as the huge abbey church that served as Coventry's first cathedral.

A time of great prosperity and of rapid growth followed the granting of Coventry's first royal charter of incorporation in 1345. The poll-tax returns of 1377 show that Coventry had a population of 7000 and as the fourth city of England stood not far behind London, Bristol and Norwich. By the fourteenth century Coventry was the greatest road-centre of the English Midlands. A glance at the modern one-inch map shows the spider's web of roads at Coventry that is a legacy of these medieval communications.

Coventry's period of prosperity in the fourteenth century has left its marks on the topography of the city. It explains the dominance of the Perpendicular style with its large windows and magnificent clerestorys in the city churches. Much of Holy Trinity Church was built at this time. St John's Church (331791) was built by the Guild of Saint John the Baptist founded in 1342. Light pours through its tall clerestory windows into the chancel. Another feature of Coventry's medieval churches is the number of side chapels belonging to the various crafts and trades. St Michael's, whose burnt-out shell stands by Sir Basil Spence's cathedral, had six chapels belonging to the dyers, cappers, mercers, smiths, girdlers and drapers.

Plate 8b   Coventry in the early seventeenth century: the town is still contained within its medieval walls apart from the suburbs which extend beyond each of the main gates. The garden and orchards behind the burgesses' houses were to be closely built up in the early years of the nineteenth century.

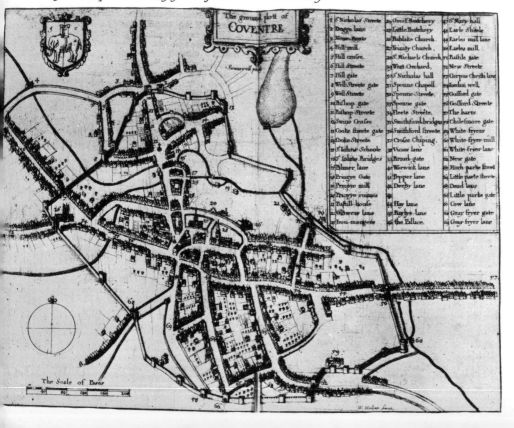

Despite the destruction in the great air-raid of 1940, you can still appreciate their influence on the layout of the church in its unusual width.

The golden age of the fourteenth century witnessed the building of the 300-foot tower and spire of St Michael's Church. The work started in 1373 and was finished in 1398. Two of Coventry's important citizens, the brothers William and Adam Botoner, directed the building. St Michael's spire is still the grandest feature of Coventry's skyline and it formed the starting-point in the design of the twentieth-century cathedral. The construction of the city wall began in 1355. When the task was finished, after half-a-century, the wall was three miles long with 12 gates and 32 towers (see Pl. 8*b*). Little remains, apart from two gates and fragments here and there. Until the wall was dismantled in Charles II's reign it must have formed one of the most striking features of the topography of the city, because a sharp line was drawn between the built-up interior, the medieval core, and the expanse of open fields and commons that lay without. Even today the line of the former city-wall may be discerned in the street-plan of the central part of Coventry. The medieval lanes and gently curving streets of the medieval core may be distinguished from the suburbs of the nineteenth century that were laid out upon the sites of the open fields. The city gates acted as places where roads converged, and their role in the topography of the city is still clear where five roads converge on the site of the former Bishop Gate (333794).

A few examples of domestic architecture survive in Coventry from the Middle Ages. Among the most remarkable are the terraces of timbered houses in some parts of the city. The finest examples today remain in Spon Street (328790) where, within a few yards, there are three separate groups of these houses whose upper storey is made of close-set vertical timbers separated by narrow panels of plaster. Another distinctive feature is the projection of the upper storey above the ground floor. This style of late medieval domestic architecture is widespread in Kent and Sussex, and such buildings with oversailing first floors are known as *Wealden houses*. The north side of Spon Street has the finest example of Wealden houses in any Midland town. These wooden houses with their massive frames of timber probably date from the end of the fourteenth century. They are examples of speculative building in the golden age that saw the creation of so many features of the medieval town. It is likely that Coventry's period of prosperity in the second half of the fourteenth century saw the establishment of a new suburb on the road leading westward from the city beyond the Spon Gate. This idea is confirmed by a similar pattern of growth in Far Gosford Street (342789) on the road to Leicester. Here another tiny cluster of Wealden houses has remained until the present time. Both of these medieval extensions of Coventry beyond the city wall were along the main road that for centuries has formed the spine of the city.

The heart of Coventry, the part that lay within the medieval wall, contains both the oldest and the newest. The vast shopping-precinct of the mid-twentieth century lies only a stone's throw from Holy Trinity and St Michael's tower. Despite the fire and desolation of the Second World War and the drastic surgery of town-planners, Coventry still exposes its medieval past. Much Park Street and Little Park Street lie in a part of the city seared by the air raids of 1940, but their names tell us that they once led to the two deer parks created on the south side of Coventry by the earls of Chester soon after the Norman Conquest.

Coventry in the Nineteenth Century and the Second Industrial Revolution

The population of Coventry rose rapidly between 1800 and 1860. The census of 1801 records 16,049 people in the town. By 1841 the number had risen to 30,781 and in the following twenty years the population climbed to 40,936. Coventry was one of the most vigorous towns in Victorian England.

The expansion of Coventry's population was set against a great scarcity of land for new houses and workshops. The peculiar politics of the city prevented the use of the wide girdle of open fields and commons for new building. Each of Coventry's freemen possessed grazing rights on the open fields and meadows, and the rights of a freeman were granted to all who completed their apprenticeship in one of the city's medieval crafts or trades. Consequently, by the nineteenth century Coventry had a body of citizens who jealously kept their grazing rights in the common fields, even though most of them never had any animals to turn out to the winter stubble. The power of the freemen lay in the fact that until the 1860s they were almost the only people in Coventry with the right to vote at the election of Members of Parliament. As a result, they were able to use this strength to preserve their rights in the common fields. No Member of Parliament for Coventry could guide through the House of Commons an 'act' for the enclosure of the city's common fields. It was only after 1860, when the voting-power of the freemen was overthrown, that the enclosure and development of the common lands began.

The common fields, known as the Lammas and Michaelmas lands, surrounded Coventry on almost all sides (Fig. 8c). Only towards the north-east, in the quarter known as Hillfields (345795), was land available for the expansion of the town. Here a number of landowners and small farmers were glad to sell fields at high prices for building or to take part themselves in the boom of developing a new town on the north-eastern outskirts of Coventry in the 1840s. For the rest, the population of Coventry doubled between 1800 and 1840, but there was no room for the physical growth of the city. Thirty thousand people had to cram themselves into the space encircled by the former city wall on a tract of land that had housed a medieval population of no more than six thousand. The effect of this process in the first half of the nineteenth century was to make Coventry one of the most tightly packed cities in the country. The gardens and allotments behind the main streets and medieval lanes gave way to a maze of alleys, courts and weavers' cottages. In the quarter of Much Park Street speculators bought up half-timbered medieval houses and handsome Georgian town-houses for the sake of their gardens. If the garden was wide enough, it was made to take two rows of cottages divided by a narrow alley. The plan of buildings and courtyards looked like a honeycomb on large-scale maps and plans. These congested quarters of the city became the slums of the twentieth century and the massive rebuilding of the city's heart since 1950 has erased most of them.

Before 1860 Coventry could break through the iron band of its encircling common fields in only two directions. Towards the north-east, the suburb of Hillfields was already developing in the 1830s. Between 1840 and 1860 two thousand new houses were built there in long, red-brick terraces, forming a separate new town of the silk-weavers. A second distinct suburb, Chapelfields, grew to the west of Coventry during the 1850s (318789). It was possible to develop Chapelfields before the general enclosure of the common fields because the land belonged to Coventry Corporation. Sir Thomas White had given the land to the Corporation of Coventry in 1551 and in 1845 an Act of Parliament was obtained to permit its enclosure and development. What had been given over to market gardening in the 1840s became the watch-makers' suburb of the following decade.

A walk through the streets of Hillfields and Chapelfields today reveals many features of this phase of mid-nineteenth-century development. Both display a gridiron street-pattern, a layout so frequently adopted by the speculative builder of the Victorian period. The houses are built in long brick terraces, but a detailed examination of these two suburbs on the ground uncovers many minor differences.

Fig. 8c   Coventry as it appeared in 1835

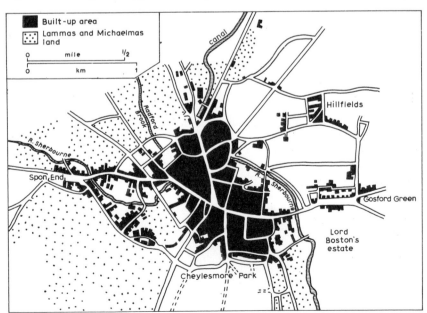

Plate 8d

A terrace of cottages in the silk-weavers' suburb of Hillfields. Note the large windows of the 'topshops'.

Plate 8e

The front of Eli Green's factory at Hillfields: one of the latest examples of domestic industry's attempts to compromise with the factory system

Plate 8f

The topshops of Eli Green's factory face on to an inner courtyard where the power-house stood

In many details of their architecture they reflect the differences between the two industries of silk-weaving and ribbon-making.

A middle class of freemen weavers settled at Hillfields in the 1840s and the suburb grew rapidly. The domestic character of the silk industry is written into the style of its buildings. Many terraces survive with huge upper windows, designed to let as much light as possible into the workshop. In some tall, three-storey cottages the rest of the house with its sash windows and narrow Georgian doorway is utterly dwarfed by the vast upper window of the loomshop – a glass oblong made up of sixty or eighty separate panes. The rows of weavers' cottages scattered around the streets of Hillfields commemorate one of the most fascinating phases of the Industrial Revolution in England (Pl. 8*d*). Here we can see, expressed in bricks and mortar, the transition from a cottage industry to the beginnings of a factory system and its use of steam-power. For a brief period of twelve years, between 1847 and 1859, groups of tall, three-storeyed houses were built in Hillfields with a steam-engine attached. The engine occupied an outhouse at the end of the row of cottages and power was supplied to each weaver by shafting that ran through the upper storey, the 'topshop', from house to house through the dividing walls. Thus the conservative middle-class weavers of Hillfields made their compromise with progress. For a brief time they were able to enjoy the advantages of the new power along with the independence of the old domestic system – a freedom that allowed them to work long irregular hours interspersed with days squandered in idleness and drink.

The most ambitious cottage factory of all in Hillfields still stands. A wealthy ribbon-manufacture, Eli Green, built sixty-seven houses in a triangle. The houses of the long terraces are three-storeys high, and the big rectangular windows of the topshops look over the tiny gardens inside the enclosure (Pl. 8*e* and Pl. 8*f*). The central enclosure contained the engine house, the source of power for all the loomshops. As you walk down Berry Street, you can still see the place where the shafting passed across to the tall row of cottage factories on Brook Street. Another cottage factory, built by the Cash brothers in 1857, can still be seen on the bank of the Coventry Canal (336806) (Pl. 8*g*). Tall windows flood the topshops with light and the pointed gables have black and white timbers in a mock Tudor style. John and Joseph Cash were kindly Quaker capitalists who had grown rich in the ribbon trade. They felt a concern for the social problems of the rapidly growing industrial towns of Victorian England. Their factory cottages, overlooking the stagnant waters of the canal, remain as a memorial to Robert Owen and all those Victorian idealists who wanted to find a system in which the master and his men, capital and labour, could live and work in harmony.

Chapelfields (317787), the watch-makers' suburb, was built at about the same time as the laying out of several streets in Hillfields. But the buildings of Chapelfields show us many of the small differences between the two crafts. The watch-

*Plate 8g The factory built by the Cash brothers on the banks of the Coventry
Canal in 1857 – the end of an epoch*

maker needed very little space to carry on his trade; a small upstairs room with a
bench under the window was enough for the putting together of the tiny parts of
a watch. In common with the ribbon-manufacturer he wanted as much light as
possible, so the watch-maker's shop contained a large rectangular window that
filled almost the whole of one wall. It was possible to hide the whole of Coventry's
watch industry in the back rooms of the long terraces of Chapelfields. From the
streets there was hardly any suggestion of a thriving industrial suburb, as busy as
the noisy weaving district of Hillfields where steam-engines and the whirr and
clank of shafting in the topshops threw out the harsh sounds of an industrial
quarter. The watch-maker lived in a neat suburban house, and not, like the ribbon-
weaver, beneath a small factory. Watch-making, too, was a highly skilled trade
that showed its specialised and superior character because women and children
were not employed. And here lies the main clue to the appearance of Chapelfields
today, although the watch trade vanished long ago. The watch-maker, a hundred
years ago in Coventry, stood higher on the social scale than the weaver. He lived
a comfortable life and was a member of that subtly graduated stratum of Victorian
society, the middle class; and as such all signs of trade and industry had to be kept
away from the front of the house. Today, as we explore the streets of Chapelfields,
we have to search in the back gardens for the architecture and archaeology of

Coventry's watch industry. The development of Chapelfields began in the late 1840s; it was completely built up by 1870. For a long time it remained isolated from the rest of Coventry – a suburb devoted entirely to the craft of watch-making. And as we walk through its quiet streets today, Chapelfields still has an air of Victorian respectability. To the south-west this suburb ends abruptly against the open space of Hearsall Common – a far older element in the landscape of Coventry.

Coventry's Third Industrial Revolution and the Shaping of the Modern City

The shaping of Coventry's topography as we know it today entered its final phase in 1860. From the collapse of the ribbon trade and the cottage industries, Coventry emerged to embark on a third industrial revolution. In 1860 an Act of Parliament permitted the enclosure of the Michaelmas and Lammas lands. The iron band of the common fields encircling Coventry on almost every side was broken.

Coventry's industrial revival in the second half of the nineteenth century came with the planting of new kinds of industry. The bicycle industry appeared in the 1860s. The manufacture of sewing-machines belongs to the same period. From these two branches of the Victorian engineering industry Coventry developed the mass manufacture of cars, lorries and tractors – the occupations that overshadow every other activity of the city today. Close to the city centre and especially towards the north and east the large factories of the engineering and vehicle industries were built at the end of the last century. They belonged to the pioneer firms of the new industries – Rudge, Singer, Hillman and Whitworth. This suburb (339793) with its severe brick-built factories, four and five storeys high, came to fill the valley floor of the Sherbourne Brook that separated medieval Coventry from the weavers' quarter of Hillfields. Until the 1840s building had been impossible along the flood plain of the Sherbourne because three water-mills blocked the flow of the stream. At times of heavy rain stagnant flood waters made a moat around the northern and eastern flanks of the city. The threat of regular flooding disappeared only when an Act of Parliament, obtained in 1844, allowed the mills to be pulled down. Ford Street and Lower Ford Street were made in the 1850s and the slow development of this industrial quarter started.

The most recent phase of Coventry's industrial history started in the years after the First World War. The car industry developed at an astonishing pace and new methods of manufacture have left a deep impression on the geography of the city. The techniques of mass production demanded a new kind of factory with single-storey buildings, covering acres of ground, where cars could be carried in long lines through all the stages of assembly. The cramped factories of the older industrial quarter around Ford Street could not be adapted to these new processes. Consequently, a new ring of twentieth-century industries arose on the fringes of the city. Some of these modern mass production plants lie close to the ring road in

147

the west (3078) and near to the railway (3279). Another large cluster of car and machine-tool factories lies in the south-east, and still more have covered waste land on the banks of the Coventry Canal to the north of the city (3480).

The vigorous growth of Coventry's new engineering industries in the first half of the twentieth century drew a strong flow of migrants towards the city. Between 1901 and 1960 the population rose from 70,000 to 310,000. Outlying hamlets and villages that stood utterly aloof from the city until the last years of the nineteenth century have been swamped by the rapid expansion of housing-estates and factories. Expansion around the rim of Coventry has proceeded at unequal rates. Growth to the south of the city has been moderate; nevertheless, Earlsdon (3177), Stivichall (3276) and Pinley (3577) have disappeared as separate settlements. To the north, Coventry exploded untidily in the past hundred years, taking in the poor lands of heaths and commons on the southern fringe of the East Warwickshire Coalfield. Here Radford (3280), Keresley (3182), Foleshill (3582), Wyken (3680) and Stoke (3579) are caught up in the tentacles of the expanding city. The number of place-names that contain the term 'heath' in the northern suburbs reminds us of a land-scape that disappeared so recently. We notice Little Heath (3482), Great Heath (3481) and Parting of the Heaths (3482) among other names of the same kind.

The years since the end of the Second World War witnessed rapid changes in Coventry and have been a period of unequalled prosperity. The most dramatic transformations have taken place in the heart of the city where two closely built quarters to the west and south of the cathedral were seared by fire-bombs and high explosive. The western sector of rebuilding (332789) now forms the chief shopping centre of the city. Between the shops and stores are arcades and a spacious central street reserved for pedestrians. The busy traffic that flows through Coventry's centre has been diverted around the flanks of the shopping-precinct; formerly, the busy road that led out to the west, Smithford Street, ran through the core of this quarter now free of traffic.

The southern and eastern parts of the heart of Coventry have changed almost as much as the new shopping-quarter of the city. Here, between Little Park Street and Much Park Street, a densely packed industrial and residential quarter of airless courts and alleys has been swept away. An occasional lonely Georgian house stands amid the dull glass and concrete buildings, a reminder of the past.

The heart of Coventry presents a fascinating piece of the English landscape. It is a mosaic composed of fragments of many different ages. Within a few yards you can step from Greyfriars Lane, a medieval street where the octagonal steeple of the monastery church still stands, to the new shopping-quarter that was shaped by the ideas of town-planners in the middle of the twentieth century and built in the materials of this age. Amid this mixture of buildings and architectural styles stands the new cathedral, huge, squat, and rock-like, a link between the medieval and the modern in its style and purpose.

Further Reading

Jones, S. R. and Smith, J. T. 'The Wealden Houses of Warwickshire and their Significance', *Transactions and Proceedings of the Birmingham Archaeological Society* vol. LXXIX (1960–1) pp. 24–35.

Poole, B. *Coventry, its History and Antiquities* (1869).

Prest, J. *The Industrial Revolution in Coventry* (1960).

Spence, B. *Phoenix at Coventry* (1962).

White, F. *History and Antiquities of Coventry* (1874).

Maps

O.S. 1-inch sheet 132 (Coventry and Rugby); O.S. 2½-inch sheets SP 38, SP 37.

Suggested Itineraries (see Fig. 8*h*)

Coventry possesses all the variety and richness of a natural region. As an urban region it contains the material for several field excursions.

(*a*) An excursion may be devised to illustrate the various aspects of the medieval core. Begin with the cluster of churches in the heart of the city – Holy Trinity, the shell of St Michael's and the post-war cathedral (336791). Explore next the district of Much Park Street, Little Park Street and Greyfriars Lane, noting the contrasts in building-styles in this partly rebuilt district that preserves several medieval features. Visit Ford's Hospital and return to the city centre at Broadgate; note the site of the former castle long since vanished from the landscape. Turn westward into the new shopping-centre and conclude the excursion in Spon Street with its examples of timbered Wealden houses, noting *en route* the guild church of St John, the former site of the Spon Gate and the wall that stood immediately west of the church (330791).

(*b*) An excursion may be arranged to study the industrial suburbs of the middle of the nineteenth century. From a starting-point in the centre of the city cross the Sherbourne Valley to Ford Street, noting the immense changes in the landscape in little more than a century. Even the river is now lost to sight in a culvert. From the east end of Ford Street (340793) follow Raglan Street to the junction with Hood Street and East Street (343793). In this part of the excursion one skirts the industrial quarter that developed about 1900 when the engineering industries passed through the first phase of their evolution. Bear northwards along Brook Street to the intersection with Yardley Street. (344795). Here one reaches Eli Green's triangular-shaped cottage factory, the most interesting attempt to compromise with the problems of the Industrial Revolution in the ribbon-weavers' suburb of Hillfields.

A comparison of Hillfields should be made with the watch-makers' suburb at

Chapelfields (3178). From the centre of the city follow Spon Street towards Spon End (324790) where the character of the Sherbourne Valley may be appreciated better than on the excursion to Hillfields. Note the medieval houses in Spon Street as proof of this fourteenth–fifteenth-century suburb outside the wall of the city. Explore Chapelfields with its many examples of houses where the watch-making industry was carried on. Take in Broomfield Place (321790), Mount Street (318788) and some of the houses of the wealthier watch-makers on the Allesley Old Road. The excursion may be continued to Hearsall Common (314785), a descendant of the common lands that once encircled Coventry and which is now a public park. To the west, between Hearsall Common and the Outer Ring Road, is the site of one of the twentieth-century car plants – an example of the latest phase of industry in Coventry.

(c) Longer excursions may be planned to include the growth of Coventry in the nineteenth and twentieth centuries.

  (i) A walk along the tow-path of the Coventry Canal provides a good view of industrial sites in the northern suburbs. It includes the cottage factory of the Cash brothers (336807). The excursion may be ended at Navigation Bridge (350815) or extended beyond Little Heath (348829).

 (ii) With the help of a bus a great variety of routes may be worked out to expound the geography of Coventry and its suburbs. They should be designed to illustrate some of the main phases in the growth of the city. A start should be made on foot with a glimpse of the medieval heart. This should be followed by a mid-nineteenth century industrial suburb in either Hillfields or Chapelfields. Finally take in some of the features of the explosion of Coventry into the surrounding countryside in the twentieth century – car factories, housing-estates and swallowed-up villages. On the north-eastern fringe of the city the most recent incursions of Coventry may be seen. There, at Potter's Green (3682), tall blocks of flats, suburban housing and single-storeyed factories are beginning to invade the landscape of abandoned collieries on the southern tip of the East Warwickshire Coalfield.

Field Work

(a) Prepare a sketch-plan of the streets in the centre of Coventry. As you do your field work in the central part of the city locate on your map the sites of (i) medieval buildings and (ii) buildings of the twentieth century.

(b) From a large-scale street-plan of Coventry draw a sketch-diagram of the Hillfields district. As part of your field work mark the sites of all houses with topshops. OR In a survey of the streets of Hillfields count the number of topshops of the ribbon-weaving industry in this quarter.

(c) Make a transect diagram based on a field excursion along the tow-path of the Coventry Canal through the northern suburbs of the city. Plot the industries on either bank and name the firms and products produced in these factories. Did they depend upon the canal for their location? OR Make a similar transect diagram to study the industries of the Outer Ring Road.

Further Work

(*a*) Using either the 1-inch or the $2\frac{1}{2}$-inch maps make a tracing of the main roads that centre on Coventry and mark the course of the River Sherbourne and the city boundary.
  (i) Mark the line of the Coventry Canal. Find out the date of its construction and put this on your diagram.
  (ii) Mark the site of the cathedral and a medieval guild church.
  (iii) Mark the site of a former medieval deer park.
  (iv) Name and locate two villages that have been swallowed up in the growth of Coventry.
  (v) Locate the sites of two gates in the vanished city wall. When was the wall built?
  (vi) Shade a district where the city is expanding in the 1960s.

(*b*) Use the air photograph of Coventry on page 139 to make a sketch-diagram of the main features of the city centre. Mark the following with distinct symbols and colours:
  (i) the shopping-quarter built since 1945. Mark the former route of Smithford Street.
  (ii) Indicate a church that stood in the *Prior's Half* and another that was in the *Earl's Half.*
  (iii) Mark the site of the castle that disappeared four centuries ago.
  (iv) Mark roughly the course of the River Sherbourne.
  (v) Show an industrial quarter that developed in the last part of the nineteenth century.

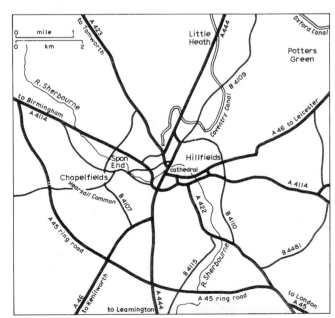

Fig. 8*h*

Approach roads around Coventry

9 Deserted Villages in South Warwickshire

Many villages of the English Midlands disappeared before the end of the sixteenth century. You can recognise their sites in the landscape today by the low grass-grown mounds, footings of farmsteads and cottages, and the hollow ways that represent the lines of former lanes and streets. Sometimes a church still stands alone in the fields to betray the site of a former village.

Over the past twenty-five years historians have uncovered the sites of scores of deserted villages in several English counties. Almost seventy have been found in Leicestershire and an even greater number in east Yorkshire. Warwickshire alone has 113 deserted villages. They are thickly clustered in the southern half of the county, in the district that bears the old regional name of the 'Feldon'. Here, on the heavy soils of the Lower Lias Clays, was a landscape of large clustered villages and of open-field farming before the centuries of enclosure. Today you can still recognise traces of this vanished medieval farming-system written on the landscape in the form of gently curving, grass-grown ridges and furrows.

The main road that runs from Southam (4161) towards Banbury passes through a countryside rich in deserted-village sites. Parishes lie side by side without churches or villages. Hodnell (4257) stands on an isolated hill surveying the Lower Lias clay plain of south Warwickshire. From the bare fields on its summit around the Manor Farm the view extends northwards to beyond Southam; to the south the prospect is closed by the small and shapely hills of the Marlstone. Within the compass of this single viewpoint are the sites of six deserted villages.

Hodnell belongs to the kind of deserted village that today is represented by only a single farm. Apart from the abundance of stone in the fields close to the Manor Farm, there is little trace of the former village on the ground. But the air photograph of Hodnell clearly picks out the earthworks of a former settlement. Within the perimeter of ridge-and-furrow, one-time strips in Hodnell's open fields, we see the sharp shadow of a former street and the unmistakable outlines of a simple church (Pl. 9a).

Domesday Book records a population of 31 at Hodnell in 1086. Because William the Conqueror's taxation survey only mentions the heads of families and the more important people in a settlement, it is likely that the true population of Hodnell in the eleventh century reached between 120 and 150; about the same as Wormleighton at the present time.

152

Plate 9a   Hodnell: the Manor Farm occupies the site of a deserted village of which traces are clearly visible in this photograph. Note the rectangular shape of a church to the right of the farm buildings, a sunken lane and the foundations of houses towards the left, and the ridge-and-furrow of the former open field abutting against the village (4257).

If Hodnell was a village full of life at the end of the eleventh century, when was it laid waste? The exact date and cause of its desertion is not fully known, but it is named as an empty and depopulated place in a history book written in 1486 by John Rous who was a priest in Warwick. The book, a history of England, contains a list of deserted villages in the Midlands and John Rous mentions 48 in Warwickshire. In an account of the Norman Conquest he deals with the destruction of villages by the armies of William the Conqueror and diverts history into a passionate description of desertions in the Midland countryside during his own lifetime. He wrote, 'what shall be said of the modern destruction of villages bringing want to the state. The root of this evil is greed. The plague of avarice infects these times and avarice blinds men. They are not sons of God, but of Mammon.' Again John Rous writes, 'as Christ wept over Jerusalem so we over the destruction of our own times. How many outrageous things do men perform? They enclose the area of the village with mounds and surround them with ditches. In such places the king's highway is blocked and poor people can neither enter nor leave.' John Rous's vivid sentences show that he himself had seen some of the destroyed village sites in Warwickshire. Clearly, he witnessed the making of mounds and ditches that were to leave their marks on the landscape right down to the present day.

153

Hodnell had gone by 1486. The cause of its destruction was a change in farming that was sweeping the country, and especially the Midland counties, during the fifteenth century. Because of the growth of the cloth industry, wool prices were rising. Sheep-farming became a profitable business. Some landlords began to specialise in sheep-rearing, and it could be done only if large tracts of open field were turned into permanent pastures. The monasteries, particularly the Cistercian order, were pioneers of large-scale sheep-farming in England after the Norman Conquest. The spread of monastic sheep-farming in the counties of Midland England caused a deep disruption of the life of the countryside. Deserted villages in which the monasteries have played a part can be counted in hundreds between the the Severn and the Lincolnshire coast.

Although the story of the disappearance of Hodnell is not known in any detail, the chief agents in the desertion seem to have been Nuneaton Priory and Combe Abbey that owned tracts of land there. Towards the end of the twelfth century Combe Abbey was given land at Chapel Ascote, Watergall, Radbourn and Hodnell. There is some evidence that the monks of this great Cistercian abbey, just outside Coventry, turned their lands in the Hodnell district over to grazing. For instance, the great seventeenth-century topographer, William Dugdale, mentions that the monks of Combe Abbey had received a grant of land at Radbourn and that there was pasture for 600 sheep. It seems likely that decades before the final destruction of this group of Warwickshire villages pastures had been made amid the open fields to graze the flocks of sheep owned by distant monasteries.

John Rous tells us that Hodnell was a deserted site by 1486, but there is a shred of evidence that the village community decayed long before this date. Another medieval document, the *Feudal Aids*, tells us that Hodnell had only four house-holders in 1428. The total population of the settlement was probably less than 30. The hill-top site was approaching desertion by the beginning of the fifteenth century. Extensive enclosures for sheep-farming, made by the monasteries, must have helped to break up the life of Hodnell and Chapel Ascote, but one also wonders whether the Black Death that swept through England in the middle of the fourteenth century did not speed the destruction of the settlement by killing off a third or even a half of its population.

Lower Radbourn lies in the shallow valley to the east of Hodnell (441570) (Fig. 9*b*). The 2½-inch map marks the site of a church a few yards from the northern bank of the stream that flows towards the Itchen. This church is mentioned in a will of 1616 as 'the ruined church of Radbourn'. A century earlier, a survey of church property in 1535 mentions the 'parish church' of Radbourn and the rector is recorded as receiving 'a yearly payment of £5–6–8*d*. from Richard Catesby'. This date helps us to discover the time when the church was abandoned. The last year in which the Catesby family appointed a rector to the living at Radbourn was 1573. The church was probably a ruin by that time. Nothing is to be seen of the chapel at Lower Radbourn, but a careful search of the farm buildings close to the site and an examination of their stones will show carved and worked blocks of limestone that have come from this vanished medieval chapel.

The destruction of Lower Radbourn was probably the work of the Catesby family. They first entered the history of this Warwickshire parish in 1369 when John de Catesby acquired the manor of Radbourn. The exact date of the desertion is not known. The desertion of the village certainly took place before 1486 because the name occurs in John Rous's list of deserted villages. The church seems to have continued for almost a century after the decay of the village and the conversion of its open fields to pastures – hence the appointment of rectors in the Tudor period, probably to serve the small population of shepherds.

Lower Radbourn covers an extensive site with grass-grown mounds and hollow ways that mark the former built-up part of the village. Its farmsteads and cottages seem to have been arranged around the sides of an open village green. It has a square-shaped plan, unlike the narrow rectangle that defines the shape of former street-villages. On the edge of the village lies a cluster of grass-grown basins, the site of the former fish-ponds. One of these, a large pool that possibly served as a mill-pond, still contains water and today it is used as a decoy for wild duck.

In contrast to the other deserted sites of south Warwickshire a village has survived at Wormleighton until the present day (4453). A walk round the centre of this parish reveals many features that suggest a long and complicated history.

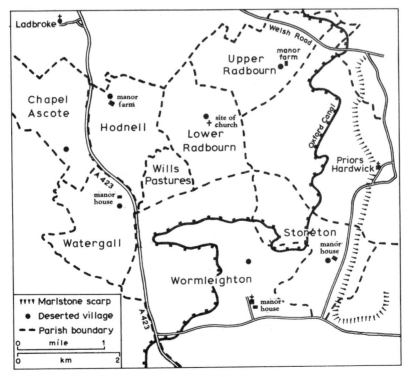

Fig. 9b   The group of deserted villages on the Lias Clay near Southam

The village stands on a low hill of glacial sands and gravels rising sharply from the Lower Lias Clay plain. The deeply-weathered, brown marlstone church dates back to the early years of the twelfth century. As in most churches, the different parts and pieces of the building were put up in years that are widely separated from each other. Only the stones of the four corners of the nave give proof of the plain church that was built here soon after the Norman Conquest. The squat tower and the two narrow aisles were added almost a century later, about 1200. Early in the thirteenth century the chancel was rebuilt. Two hundred years later the roof of the nave was raised, and the clerestory with its slit-like windows was added. Here, in the parish church of St Peter, is proof of an active community at Wormleighton through all the centuries from the Norman Conquest until just before the Tudors came to the throne.

Another and very different feature of Wormleighton is the fragment of the manor house, built at the beginning of the sixteenth century by the Spencer family after they had bought the estate. This red brick building of Tudor date is now a farm-house in the middle of the village. A century later, in 1613, the first Lord Spencer added an elaborate gatehouse of the rich, brown Marlstone that was quarried in the steep face of the escarpment at near-by Stoneton (4654). These two buildings in Wormleighton tell of the period from 1506 until the middle of the seventeenth century when the Spencer family flourished from the rewards of sheep-farming here and on the lands of neighbouring deserted villages. Another period of the history of the Spencers at Wormleighton is illustrated by the later buildings of the nineteenth century. By that time the lands of the parish had been divided up into holdings worked by tenant farmers. The descendants of the great sheep-farmers of the Tudor period were content to draw rents and to keep a fatherly watch over their manor. The neat row of estate cottages, built in 1849, tells of this phase in Wormleighton's history. There is still no public house in the village – another sign of the will of the ruling landlord.

The various dates of the buildings of Wormleighton remind us of the continuous life of the settlement down the centuries, at least from the time of the Norman Conquest. But if we take the footpath that branches to the left near the church we find that it bends through a wood to emerge on to a steep grassy slope. In the distance is the sinuous line of the Oxford Canal. Not many yards away, at the foot of the slope, are the grass-grown mounds and hollows that betray the site of a large deserted village. A careful inspection of the former village will reveal other features. For instance, there is an impressive string of fish-ponds. A rectangular hedged enclosure in the upper part of the huge field was the site of a large fish-pond, and in the far corner of the field, close to the canal, there is the deep moat of a manor-house now filled with a lush greensward. This was the medieval fore-runner of the red brick mansion that John Spencer built on the hill between 1516 and 1519. More faintly one can trace the site of a village green. Plainest of all is the old boundary between the former village, with its farm-houses, barns and gardens and the enveloping open fields. A sharp line separates the hummocks, squares, rectangles, and hollow ways of the former village from the long, gently curving ridges and furrows of the strips that lay in the medieval open fields (Pl. 9c).

The history of the destruction of Wormleighton is known in some detail. The Lay Subsidy of 1327 shows that Wormleighton was flourishing early in the fourteenth century when the village was expected to pay 62 shillings. Both Hodnell and Radbourn are listed in this document as liable for 22 shillings and 9 shillings and 6 pence. The Lay Subsidy also mentions the number of tax payers; Wormleighton has twenty-two, whereas Radbourn can only muster six. Wormleighton survived until the last year of the fifteenth century. The revolution in Wormleighton's economy began when William Cope, a civil servant at the Court of Henry VII, was granted the manor in 1498. During the following months Cope bought up the land of minor owners in the parish. In 1499 he was master of the whole parish and set about the destruction of the village and its conversion into a sheep and cattle farm. Twenty acres of arable land were enclosed and converted to pasture; sixty peasants were turned off the land and driven from their homes. They took to the roads as beggars and tried to find homes and work in other parishes or else in the thriving industrial town of Coventry.

Plate 9c   Wormleighton: the present estate village is in the lower foreground. The rest of the picture shows the site of the deserted village and its open fields. Note the line of former fish-ponds beyond the large enclosure and the site of a moated manor-house by the Oxford Canal.

William Cope did the deed of destruction at Wormleighton, but he only kept the manor for another seven years. In 1506 he sold Wormleighton to John Spencer for £1900 – a vast sum of money at the beginning of the Tudor period and an indication of the profits that could be drawn from specialised sheep-farming. The Spencer family already owned or rented pastures in many parishes of the Lower Lias Clay country in south Warwickshire. We find them at Burton Dassett (3951), Hodnell, Radbourn, Stoneton and Ladbroke (4158), to mention only some of the places. The Spencers now began a centuries-long connection with Wormleighton. It was the first Spencer there who resited the village on the hill-top around the medieval church. As we have already noticed, we can still see some of the remains of his early Tudor manor-house that was built to replace the ruined moated mansion in the fields below the hill.

The estates of the Spencers stretched eastwards into Northamptonshire and south Leicestershire, and their chief residence was at Althorp in Northamptonshire. The absence of elaborate family tombs and monuments in the parish church at Wormleighton shows that they did not reside there. Only one member of the family, another John Spencer who died in 1610, lies buried in a huge white stone tomb in the chancel. For the Spencers Wormleighton was the centre of a number of large sheep and cattle ranches in this part of south Warwickshire. When the wool trade stood at the height of its prosperity in the second half of the sixteenth century a huge wool barn and shearing-yard stood close to the manor-house at Wormleighton. Not a trace of it remains today and the estate cottages, built in the Victorian age, occupy the site.

With the passing of large-scale sheep and cattle-farming, after the middle of the seventeenth century, the pastures at Wormleighton were divided into smaller fields. It was a long, slow process, a revolution that only the historian can unravel as he works on the estate plans and maps of the succeeding three centuries. By the end of the eighteenth century two farms had come into being among the fields outside the village; both stand on the long spur that is now half encircled by the canal (4355). Soon after 1800 the revolution in land-holding speeded up. The manor was broken up into smaller farms and the tenant farmers could build their homes outside the village in the midst of their own fields. Wormleighton Hill Farm (434546) was built in 1834, and about the same time Glebe Farm (446557) came into existence on the northern edge of the parish. It was a small holding of only forty acres. Many of the field boundaries that we see today were made in the first half of the nineteenth century.

Despite the deep changes in the features of Wormleighton's landscape in the nineteenth century, you can still recapture some of the atmosphere of the Spencer family's great sheep farm. If you stand on the slope to the north of the present 'estate village', looking across the green banks and hollows of the settlement that was deserted in 1499, you can still see a fragment of the landscape of Tudor Worm-

158

leighton. The 'old town', as it is called, stands in a vast field with winding and rather irregular boundaries. Large fields with uneven hedges are characteristic of the late medieval and Tudor enclosures for sheep-farming in many parts of the Midlands, and the field that contains the 'old town' is a fossil landscape feature dating from the first enclosure of William Cope. But at Wormleighton the ancient boundaries that enclosed the open fields have a most peculiar feature; they consist of double banks and ditches, many of them set with tall trees. The south-western boundary of the field containing the deserted village possesses a double hedgerow and there are several other examples in the parish which may be picked out on the $2\frac{1}{2}$-inch map or air photographs. This trivial feature of Wormleighton's landscape, the double hedgerow, takes us back to the most critical years in the history of the village. John Spencer mentions these same boundaries in a letter to Wolsey's *Commissions of Inquiry*. In order to justify the enclosures, John Spencer described the severe shortage of timber in south Warwickshire. 'There was no wood nor timber growing within twelve or fourteen mile and the poor folk had to burn the straw that their cattle should live by,' he wrote. Then John Spencer describes how trees were planted along the hedgerows. 'Acorns were set both in the hedgerows and also betwixt the hedges adjoining to the old hedges that William Cope made before.' This sentence tells us exactly how these field boundaries were made in two stages between 1499 and 1519. William Cope had the first banks raised and then John Spencer added another hedge after he had purchased Wormleighton in 1506. Down to the minutest detail we can trace the hand of man in the making of the landscape of the English parish.

Further Reading

Beresford, M. W. 'The Deserted Villages of Warwickshire', *Transactions and Proceedings of the Birmingham Archaeological Society*, vol. LXVI (1946) pp. 49–106.
— *The Lost Villages of England* (1954).
Mawer, A. and Stenton, F. M. *The Place-Names of Warwickshire* (English Place-Name Society, vol. XIII, 1936).
Thorpe, H. 'The Lord and the Landscape', *Transactions and Proceedings of the Birmingham Archaeological Society*, vol. LXXX (1962) pp. 38–77. An excellent study of landscape-history at Wormleighton.
Victoria County History, Warwickshire, vol. V (1949).

Maps

O.S. 1-inch sheets 132 (Coventry and Rugby); 145 (Banbury); O.S. $2\frac{1}{2}$-inch sheet SP 45.

Suggested Itinerary

Hodnell, Chapel Ascote, Watergall and Wormleighton may be visited in short asides from the main road, A423, between Southam and Banbury. The hill-top site of Hodnell with its lonely Manor Farm is an excellent place from which to survey the setting of the deserted villages in clear weather, but it is essential to get permission from the owner beforehand. Most time should be given to Wormleighton where the elements of the deserted village are so clearly distinguished. The lonely site of Lower Radbourn is best approached from the lane, the Welsh Road, that runs from Southam to Priors Marsh. Leave this road at 451588 following the made track past Upper Radbourn Farm (this can be very confusing because it is not marked on the 2½-inch map and only on the 1-inch sheet).

Field Work

(*a*) From the air photograph make a large sketch-plan of the deserted village at Wormleighton. Include the bounds of the field that contains the site of the medieval village and the Oxford Canal; indicate the pattern of ridge-and-furrow and the mounds and hollows of the vanished village. Use this sketch-plan as you examine the site in the field and name the fish-ponds, the site of the moated manor-house, the line of a former lane.

(*b*) From the hill-top site at Hodnell make a panorama field-sketch in your note-books of the country to the south bounded by the Middle Lias Marlstone escarpment. Mark boldly with arrows the approximate sites of Lower Radbourn, Stoneton, Wormleighton and Watergall.

Further Work

(*a*) Use the 2½-inch map (sheet SP 45) to trace the present boundary of Wormleighton parish. Add to your tracing the line of the Oxford Canal, the site of the village, and the metalled roads through the parish. Finally trace on to your map the field boundaries that are printed with a faint double grey line.

What is the approximate age of these double hedgerows?

Try to find a similar field boundary elsewhere on the map.

(*b*) Take the 1-inch map, sheet 132 (Coventry and Rugby), and try to find the sites of four deserted villages in addition to those we have studied around Hodnell and Wormleighton. As a clue look for parish names printed in fine, sloping capital letters (compare with the printing of Hodnell in square 4256). Note this kind of type is used to name parishes that contain two villages, but an examination of the map will soon show the presence of settlements today. The absence of a village, a single farm with the name of the parish, an isolated church or a great house in its park are all further clues to prove the presence of a deserted village.

10 Glacial Lake Harrison

Stretching south-westward from Rugby to Moreton in Marsh is a strip of country which to many is typical of the Midland landscape. Although pleasant and surprisingly rural throughout, it lacks the impressive scenery of the adjacent Cotswolds which form a natural boundary on its south-eastern side. Its valleys are wide and open, drained by rivers like the Avon and its tributaries the Leam and Itchen which meander slowly across their gently falling valley-floors. In between, the low plateaus are flat and featureless with open views on every side. Only occasionally, where a more resistant bed of limestone within the softer clays gives rise to a minor scarp or broad-topped ridge, like Christmas Hill near Bishop's Itchington (3756), is there a break in the rather monotonous scenery.

Yet to the physical geographer this stretch of country is not without interest in that it preserves in its landscape a record of a major episode in the glaciation of the Midlands. At one stage during the Ice Age (corresponding to the Gipping glaciation in East Anglia), this whole area was the site of an extensive lake to which the name Lake Harrison has been given (Fig. 10a). At its maximum extent this lake was hemmed in by ice on its northern and western side and by the Cotswold scarp on its eastern margin. Into this lake meltwater streams from the ice front brought great quantities of sands and clays which were laid down on its bed. At a later date, the ice advanced from the north over the whole lake floor laying down coarse gravels before it and then hummocky masses of boulder clay, a true glacial deposit. Ultimately the ice front reached within a mile of Moreton in Marsh and here it has left behind a surprisingly impressive end-moraine with its outwash fan beyond it. Thereafter the ice retreated northwards and as it did so Lake Harrison began to form once again. There were thus really two Lake Harrisons, one formed before the ice advance and the later one developing as the ice retreated. The lake was big enough for quite large wind waves to be formed and these cut a bench in the soft rocks along the shoreline at a constant height of about 410 feet. This wave-cut bench is particularly well seen along the foot of the Cotswold scarp where it can be traced for many miles. Thus we have a record of the former existence of Lake Harrison in its sequence of lake and glacial deposits, in its wave-cut bench and associated overflow channels and finally in the end-moraine country around Moreton in Marsh. All can be studied in the field and used to give reality to an episode in the Ice Age which occurred perhaps 150,000 years ago.

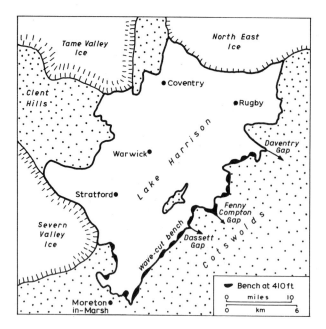

Fig. 10a

Lake Harrison at its maximum extent with the various overflow outlets through the Cotswold scarp

The Lake and Glacial Deposits

As the River Avon and its tributaries developed on the floor of the former lake, they have cut down through its soft deposits, and in the valleys the lake sediments have been completely removed. On the flat-topped ridges and valley-side slopes, however, the various beds of sand, gravel and clay are preserved and can be seen in the many quarries which have been opened up to work the deposits. At Wolston (4175), on the flanks of the Avon Valley, the old gravel-pits by the side of the road leading up to Dunsmore Heath (411749) show a good sequence of the lake beds (Pl. 10*b*). In the bottom of the pit are the Baginton Gravels (a name taken from a nearby village), now largely removed and covered by the flooding of the pit. They are mainly rounded pebbles up to six inches across and form a bed up to fifteen feet thick. They were probably laid down by a river on the floor of an old valley which ran to the north at a time before the main ice reached the area. Above the gravels in the Wolston pit there is a bed of sand, rusty brown in colour and up to fourteen feet thick. On the southern edge of the pit, this sand layer (Baginton Sand) forms a low platform which has been extensively gullied by stream action since the pit was abandoned. This Baginton Sand is also looked upon as a river deposit laid down on the floor of the same valley as the Baginton Gravels. The climate was becoming colder as the ice front lay not very far away. As a result the rivers were less active and were able to carry sand and not the heavier gravel. With the ice front coming ever closer from the north the valley in which the gravels and sands had been laid down was now blocked, and a lake formed. As more and more water entered the lake, its level rose steadily so that in time it covered the

162

whole area below the 400-foot contour between Rugby and Moreton in Marsh. Deposits of fine silt were laid down on its bed, and today these form the red clays which occur near the top of the face in the Wolston pit. The topmost beds in the sequence are the gravels of Dunsmore Heath. When these were deposited as the outwash fans of the advancing ice sheet, the ice was in the immediate vicinity of the Wolston area and was about to override the deposits of Lake Harrison. The ice sheet finally covered the whole of the lake bed and came to a halt in the end-moraine country around Moreton in Marsh.

The character of the glacial and lake deposits has influenced the vegetation of the region. Near the main road (A445) at Ryton Police College where the Baginton Sand is exposed (375729), the now cultivated fields at one time carried open heath vegetation. Only a field away, where the sand is replaced by the lake clay, the vegetation changes to woodland. Indeed the rather extensive area of woodland here, like Ryton Wood (3772), Bubbenhall Wood (3671) and Wappenbury Wood (3770), follows the outcrop of the Wolston Clay with its heavier soils so suited to the oak and elm. On the ridge top at Dunsmore (4372), the natural vegetation was again heath, as is evident from the place-name of Dunsmore Heath. At the beginning of the nineteenth century this area was transformed by marling the sterile gravelly soils. This involved the digging of scores of shallow pits through the thin gravel cover in order to reach the more fertile clay beneath. Over the years the pits have become overgrown and flooded so that the surface of Dunsmore Heath today has its myriad of tiny ponds.

Plate 10b   Glacial beds exposed on the edge of the Wolston sand- and gravel-pit (410750)

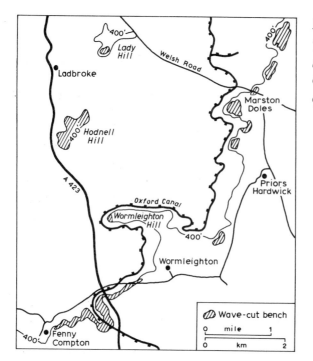

Fig. 10c

The lake bench features cut along the edge of the Cotswolds in the vicinity of Fenny Compton

The Lake Bench and Overflow Channels

At one stage in its history Lake Harrison must have stood at a height of about 410 feet for a considerable length of time. This is shown by the existence of a wave-cut bench formed in the softer rocks along the foot of the Cotswold scarp (Fig. 10c). The bench is best seen between Fenny Compton (4152) and Napton on the Hill (4661). Near the farm at Marston Doles (465580) it forms a broad flat just above the 400-foot contour backed by a steep bluff on its inner side which probably marks the line of a small lakeside cliff at the shoreline. The feature continues northwards from Marston Doles with much the same form and at the same height to beyond Potash Farm (478593). Farther south at Fenny Compton, the lake-side bench lies on either side of the gap. On its north side the bench is very distinct, being cut in clay and studded with isolated oak trees alongside the Oxford Canal (434533). From here it continues across the main road (A423) and enters the gap as far as the point where the road crosses the railway and canal. On the other side of the gap the bench is equally distinct, following the 400-foot contour as far as Fenny Compton village.

For the waters of Lake Harrison to have remained at a constant height of 410 feet for a sufficiently long period to enable the bench to be cut, there must have been an outlet at this same height. As the western gaps were probably continuously blocked by ice, the most likely outlet would be through one of the low cols in the

Cotswold scarp. Three gaps exist which might have functioned as overflows, those at Daventry, Fenny Compton and near Avon Dassett. Of these possible escape-routes for the lake waters we have the most direct evidence from the Fenny Compton gap where, as we have seen, the lake bench continues into and runs through the col. From here the lake waters would enter the upper Cherwell Valley. This valley is very wide and open and unlikely to have been formed by the present stream, which is a misfit in relation to the size of the valley floor.

Towards the end of its life Lake Harrison must have drained away rapidly, to leave its bench as a prominent feature of the present-day landscape. The final draining was probably brought about by the withdrawal of the ice from the western margins of the lake in the area of the Severn Valley. Once the lake was drained, the River Avon quickly cut down through the soft lake and glacial beds and in time established its drainage basin over the whole of the former lake floor.

The Moreton in Marsh end-moraine country

The ice advance from the north which brought about the destruction of the first glacial Lake Harrison moved steadily southwards before finally coming to a halt near Moreton in Marsh. Here it laid down a thick deposit of boulder clay in the form of an end-moraine. The line of the end-moraine can be clearly seen in the rather broken country which runs from near Dorn Farm (205345) past Lemington Grange (218337) to Wolford Wood (2333) (Fig. 10*d*). In many parts the heavier soils of the boulder clay are still under deciduous woodland, mainly oak. On its

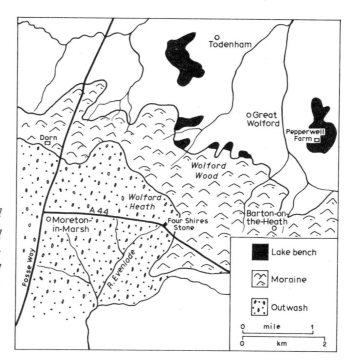

Fig. *10d*

The end-moraine and associated features at the southern end of Lake Harrison near Moreton in Marsh

northern side the relatively steep slope of the moraine has been deeply cut into by the headwater streams of the River Stour, a tributary of the Avon. We have seen that the River Avon has been able to cut down rapidly into the soft lake clays and sands of Lake Harrison and this in turn affected its tributaries right to their source. Compared with the headwaters of the River Stour, those streams of the River Evenlode to the south of the moraine make very little impression on the open landscape around Moreton. This flat and featureless country represents the outwash from the ice sheet. The sand and gravel spreads were laid down by meltwater streams from the ice which had finally come to a halt along the line of the moraine. The remarkably flat terrain is particularly well seen on either side of the A44 road to the east of Moreton. In its natural state much of this sandy and gravelly soil was under heath, as is apparent from surviving names like Wolford Heath (2332), Batsford Heath Farm (220327) and Heath Farm (234319). Today the heath has been largely reclaimed and is now farmed.

After the retreat of the ice front Lake Harrison came into being for the second time. At first it was quite small, but as the distance between the ice margin and the moraine became greater so the lake grew in size. Much of the country between Todenham (2335), Great Wolford (2434) and Stretton on Fosse (2238) still preserves remnants of the old lake floor. To the west of Todenham village there is an extensive flat at about 410 feet. At Stretton on Fosse there is a similar feature at about the same height extending westward from the village along the ridge top. On its southern margin pits working the sand and gravel deposits have been opened up in recent years and, like those at Wolston described earlier, give a clear picture of the lake deposits. Here the main bed is a pinkish sand with strings of pebbles running through it and often showing current bedding. Above is a thin bed of gravel and near the top of the pit a thin deposit of chocolate-coloured clay, a true lake silt deposit. In addition to these flats, which can be looked upon as surviving remnants of the lake floor, there is the wave-cut bench along the former shoreline of the lake. This is well seen on the spurs between the deeply cut valleys on the northern flanks of the end-moraine around Great Wolford (2434) and Barton on the Heath (2532). A wide expanse of the old lake bed has been preserved near Pepperwell Farm (265341). In appearance these lake-side benches are very similar to those previously described farther north around Fenny Compton, and indeed form part of the same sequence which occur at intervals along the lower face of the Cotswold scarp.

Further Reading

Bishop, W. W. 'The Pleistocene Geology and Geomorphology of Three Gaps in the Midland Jurassic Escarpment', *Philosophical Transactions of the Royal Society*, series B, vol. CCXLI (1958) pp. 255–306.

Dury, G. 'A 400 foot Bench in South-East Warwickshire', *Proceedings of the Geologists' Association*, vol. LXII (1951) pp. 167–73.

— *The Face of the Earth* (Pelican Books, 1958) pp. 171–2.

Shotton, F. W. 'The Pleistocene Deposits of the Area Between Coventry, Rugby and Leamington', *Philosophical Transactions of the Royal Society*, series B, vol. CCXXXVII (1954) pp. 209–60.

Maps

O.S. 1-inch sheets 132 (Coventry and Rugby), 145 (Banbury) and 144 (Cheltenham and Evesham).

Suggested Itineraries

The following excursion can be undertaken as a whole or in three separate visits:

(*a*) the area of glacial and lake deposits around Wolston

(*b*) the lake bench around Marston Doles and the overflow channel at Fenny Compton

(*c*) the end-moraine country around Moreton in Marsh.

(*a*) From Wolston village (4175) take the lane which leads up Knightlow Hill to Dunsmore Heath. The old gravel-pits with their exposures of glacial and lake deposits are seen on the west side of the road (411746). The 'reclaimed' landscape of Dunsmore Heath with its late enclosure and old marl-pits can then be visited. Around Stretton on Dunsmore the varied landscape developed on the different sand, gravel and clay formations can be appreciated.

(*b*) From Stretton on Dunsmore take the Fosse Way as far as Princethorpe (4070) and then continue along the A423 to Southam (4161). From here follow the Welsh Road to Marston Doles (4658) where the old lake bench is clearly seen within a loop of the Oxford Canal (465580). Continue along the by-roads through Priors Hardwick (4756) to Fenny Compton. The lake-side bench running into the overflow channel can be seen on both sides of the A423 road from the canal wharf (432537) to The Tunnel (435524).

(*c*) The Moreton excursion should begin with a visit to the sand- and gravel-pits at Stretton on Fosse (220382) which show some of the deposits which underlie the area. From here the route should pass through Todenham (2335) where the lake bench is well developed, Great Wolford (2434), amidst the dissected hummocky end-moraine country and finally across the outwash fan of Wolford Heath towards Moreton in Marsh.

11 The Avon Valley from Stratford to Evesham

The River Terraces

After the disappearance of glacial Lake Harrison (Study 10), the River Avon began to establish its drainage basin on the former lake floor. From its junction with the River Severn at Tewkesbury it cut back steadily into the soft deposits of sands, clays and gravels. Its earliest valley floor was broad and open and at a much higher level than at present. Today we must look for the isolated hillocks capped with gravels lying about 150 feet above the present valley, as these represent the only remnants of this first-formed valley floor. In this section of the valley between Stratford and Evesham, the flat top of Welford Hill (1550) rising to 270 feet, with its thick capping of gravel, is one such remnant (Fig. 11a).

After the formation of this earliest valley floor, a change in sea level occurred and this had the effect of rejuvenating the river, which involved cutting down into its original bed. In time, a new valley within the old was formed. As a result of this change of level, the old valley floor was left as a marginal terrace about sixty feet above the newly formed flood plain of the river. Later river erosion has destroyed the greater part of this second valley floor and again we must look to the isolated hillocks along the valley side for any remains. The flat, low top of Clifford Hill (1852) about two miles south-south-west of Stratford, rising to a height of 208 feet is a remnant of this phase. This process of rejuvenation, in response to changes of sea level, went on frequently during the later stages of the Ice Age so that, in all, five sets of terraces were formed in the Avon Valley. At present they are arranged as a series of steps above the flood plain. At no point in the valley is the staircase complete, for the river, in creating a lower step, often destroys all trace of the old terrace. This is happening at Luddington (1652) where, near the church, the river is gradually cutting back into the edge of the low (number 2) terrace. Each terrace is flat or gently sloping towards the river. On its lower side it often ends in a low bluff about ten feet high while its inner edge is marked by a steeper slope up to the next terrace. The upper terraces (numbers 3, 4 and 5) are usually formed of gravel under the thin soil cover. In contrast the lower terraces are much sandier and this gives rise to a light, easily worked soil, ideal for market gardening. Many of the place-names in the valley, like Sandfield Farm (161531) and Weston Sands (165515), give a clue to the soil conditions of these lower terraces.

168

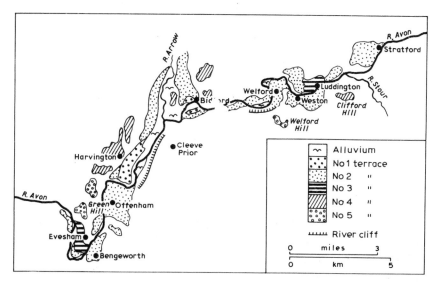

Fig. 11a   The terraces of the Avon Valley between Stratford and Evesham

Of all the five terraces developed at various places along this section of the Avon Valley, it is the second lowest (number 2) which has been best preserved. It is well developed at Welford (1452) within a large meander loop of the river. At this point the terrace lies about thirty feet above the flood plain and obviously makes an ideal dry and extensive site for the open plan of the village. At Evesham, also within the meander loop, a sequence of three terraces has been preserved. The highest and oldest (number 5) forms an area on the outskirts of the town on the main road to Birmingham at Green Hill (0445). The main part of the old town, including the site of the abbey (037437) occupies the extensive number 3 terrace. Between it and the lower number 2 terrace there is a drop of about ten feet, a feature clearly seen as a low bluff in the abbey gardens.

In those parts of the Avon Valley where the terrace features have been destroyed by river erosion, their place has been taken by a prominent river cliff. These often provide good vantage-points from which to study the terrace features. One such viewpoint lies about half a mile south-west of Welford (140514) where the minor road to Welford Pastures climbs to just over 180 feet. From the roadside the abrupt slope of the river cliff drops quickly to the flood plain. The extent of this is brought out by the strip of permanent pasture along the valley bottom across which the meandering river swings lazily from side to side. Across the valley, the wide flat of the number 2 terrace forms an extensive area of arable land with large fields and few boundary hedges. On its lower edge it falls quickly over a small rounded bluff to the flood plain.

The river cliff of Cleeve Hill (0749), close to the village of Cleeve Prior, is also a good viewpoint from which to appreciate the terraces of the Avon. Due to the development of a north–south upfold of the rocks, the red Triassic marls are brought to the surface and as a result Cleeve Hill is one of the most striking land-forms of the valley. On its western edge, the upfold has been undercut and cliffed by the meanders of the Avon. Due to the presence of beds of limestone within the marls, the river cliff is almost precipitous in places and runs without a break from Marlcliff (0950) to Bennetts Hill Farm (0645). At its foot it is being steadily eroded at the present time by the river. On the opposite bank towards Harvington (0548) a large fragment of the lowest number 1 terrace has been preserved. The village of Harvington itself lies on the higher number 4 terrace, well above the flood level of the river.

The successive rejuvenations of the River Avon which have led to the formation of the terrace sequence, have also created breaks in the long profile of the river termed knickpoints. In their natural state these knickpoints simply represent a slight increase in the fall of the river bed, where flow is more rapid in contrast to the more placid waters of the intervening stretches. The increased gradient at the knickpoints, however, has been used by man to provide a head of water for a mill wheel. At various points along the valley artificial weirs have been thrown across the river and water led away in a side channel to the mill. At the end of the lane from the church at Welford (1452), the old corn mill with its broken wheel still stands as a reminder of the time when the river provided an important source of power. The Avon was also an important artery of trade and at one time boats used the river as far as Stratford. At the weirs the boats had to be hauled up sloping ramps to the next section of the river. In places like Pershore (9445) and Nafford (9441) locks were also built in the attempt to make the Avon an important navigable waterway.

Market Gardening

The terraces of the Avon Valley and the adjoining claylands, particularly around Evesham, have long been noted for their market gardening and fruit-farming. Although 'garden' cultivation on a small scale was practised in the eighteenth century, it was not until the coming of the railways into the area about the middle of the nineteenth century that the greatest development occurred. The railways allowed the fresh vegetables to reach markets like Birmingham while still in prime condition. A further extension of market gardening took place after the breaking up of the large estates following the agricultural depression of the 1870s. Agricultural labourers were able to rent small strips of land and work them on a part-time basis. With careful management they were able to buy other strips until in time they had built up a smallholding which could fully support the tenant and his family. As a result of this rather piecemeal acquisition of the land, the smallholding today often consists of a number of scattered strips sometimes even in different parishes. Although this might seem uneconomic to work, the system has the advantage in giving the smallholder different types of land where he can grow different crops. If one should fail, due to frost damage for example, he is not wholly dependant on it for his livelihood.

The system of land-holding known as the 'Evesham Custom' has also played an important part in the development of market gardening. Each tenant farmer has the right to develop the land as he pleases, adding value to it by his careful cultivation and manuring. When he wishes to part with his rented land, he has the right to nominate his successor and ask him to pay for the improvements he has made. It is this unique system which has led to the steady improvement of the land under market cultivation and the continued growth and prosperity of the industry. Many believe that it is this human factor more than site, situation, soil type and climate that has been responsible for the development and progress of the localised horticultural industry of the Avon Valley around Evesham.

The landscape of smallholders' strips is well seen around Offenham (0546) on one of the Avon terraces (Pl. 11b). Farther east on the higher claylands of Cleeve Hill there is an equally impressive development of strip cultivation. In both situations, the individual strips are long and narrow, often separated only by a furrow or a narrow path. The fields are large and open, and hedge boundaries are rare. Seen from the main road across Cleeve Hill, the pattern of colours of the different crops and the varying alignment of the strips recall the medieval open-field landscape. Although the use of mechanical aids to cultivation like the hand-rotovator has increased in recent years, much of the land is still dug with a spade.

Plate 11b   The lower terraces of the Avon around Evesham, used for market gardening and fruit-growing. The railway, after crossing the river, cuts through a remnant of the number 4 terrace (1544).

During the winter months, it is not uncommon to find the smallholders laboriously digging over their plot, adding manure and making ready for the two or three crops which they hope to grow in the coming season. Some form of rotation is practised by many of the smallholders although this is by no means universal or closely followed from year to year.

Although the whole of the Avon Valley between Stratford and Evesham is dominated by market gardening, there are noticeable variations from place to place. Around Stratford, the land is farmed by capitalist and businessmen farmers on an extensive scale. A farm like Sandfield in Luddington parish (161531) extends over a considerable area and includes two of the river terrace levels. On the upper (number 4) terrace, fruit orchards have been planted in recent years to take advantage of the better frost drainage of the upper slopes. On the lower terrace, typical market garden crops like cabbage, brussels sprouts, peas and beans are all grown, each crop occupying a strip in the large open fields. Farming here is on an extensive scale and much use is made of mechanical aids like tractors. In places the old hedge field-boundaries have been rooted up to facilitate extensive mechanised cultivation.

In contrast to this area near Stratford, the market gardening around Cleeve Hill near Evesham is organised on a completely different basis. Here on the low plateau top well above the Avon Valley the flat land has been parcelled out into strips, each individually rented by smallholders as part of the 'Evesham Custom'. As there is less likelihood of frosts on the plateau top compared with the valley bottoms, there are extensive plum orchards. The clay soil also favours fruit-growing in this area compared with the lighter soils found on the river terraces. To make the maximum use of the available land, the smallholder usually practises under-cropping of vegetables amidst the fruit trees. In certain areas, like the parish of Badsey (0743), specialised crops such as asparagus form an important part of the market gardening economy. Everywhere the landscape is open with few field boundaries or houses to break up the all-round views. The smallholder lives in villages like Littleton and Badsey and not amidst the strips which he works.

Settlement Geography

The south bank of the Avon Valley, below Stratford, contains parishes of very different sizes and shapes and with contrasted features of settlement-history. For instance, Welford is a comparatively large parish with a long frontage on the river, while its neighbour, Weston on Avon, is only half the size and possesses a mere thousand yards of river bank.

Welford on Avon straggles across the neck of a big meander loop of the river (1952). Most of the village stands on the level surface of the second river terrace. This is a complex settlement of three distinct parts. A cluster of farmsteads and cottages gathers around the church in the north-west corner of the village (1452).

Another core of settlement forms around the triangular village-green and stretches along a lane to the river (149518). A third part of Welford consists of a 'street village' of widely spaced farmsteads along the road that climbs gently southwards over the flight of river terraces from the crossing of the Avon at Binton Bridges (145531).

The name *Welford* provides the first clue to the history of the settlement. It means 'the Welshmen's ford' and tells us that the settlement is named after the ancient crossing-place over the Avon close to the church (143521). The name also shows that this place was associated with Welshmen, descendants of the Romano-British people of the Midlands. From this dark hint in a place-name we can only guess that there was a settlement of Celtic-speaking people in this meander loop of the river at the time when the Saxons first appeared in the Avon Valley. But this surmise may throw light on the unusual plan of Welford at the present day. The part of the village clustered around the church may well be on the site of a pre-Saxon settlement, a hamlet that stood close to the Welshmen's ford. The second part of Welford, on the eastern side of the river terrace around the green, has probably grown from a later Anglo-Saxon settlement (see Pl. 11c).

Welford on Avon seems to have evolved from two settlements that originated at different periods of time. Other facts from the history of the place support this idea. For instance, the ownership of land down the centuries is split between two manors. One manor belonged to the priory of Deerhurst in Gloucestershire before the Norman Conquest, and in 1467 it was given to Tewkesbury Abbey by Edward IV. It rested in the hands of the abbey until the dissolution of the monasteries in Henry VIII's reign. The second manor at Welford first appears in the records

Plate 11c   Welford on Avon: the three units of the village are clearly visible – the cluster of cottages around the church at the former ford of the Avon, the centre around the triangular green, and the street settlement on the left of the picture.

towards the end of the fourteenth century when it is mentioned in the will of Sir Thomas West who died in 1316. A later will of Elizabeth I's reign makes is clear that there were two settlements and two manors at Welford. Ludovic Greville died in 1589 and his will says that he owned 'the manor commonly called Welnsford Grevill, and another manor there commonly called Abbot's Welnesford, late belonging to the monastery of Tewkesbury'. The second manor at Welford is probably represented by the village centred upon the triangular-shaped green, and we note that the name Manor Farm still survives there (153521).

Besides the split between two manors, Welford on Avon also possessed two water-mills for grinding corn. They were sited at the crossing-places of the Avon where the course of the river is broken by small islands. One mill stood at the ancient ford near the church whose use probably dates back into prehistoric times; the other was on the northern boundary of the parish at Binton Bridges (145531). One mill worked for the monastic lord and the other for the lay lord of Welford. The crossing-place over the Avon below Welford church has now vanished; not even a footpath strikes over the fields on the other side of the river. The ford over the Avon belonged to a medieval route between Bidford and Stratford; parts of it may still be followed along footpaths and lanes. For instance, the track that connects Bidford with Hillborough Manor (1351) and its deserted village is a visible survival of this route. Eastward of Hillborough all trace is lost until Welford where the road continues again by tracks and footpaths through Weston and Milcote Manor (1752) – the site of still another deserted hamlet. Welford's other crossing of the Avon at Binton Bridges presents another historic feature of this landscape. There was a narrow packhorse bridge here in the thirteenth century. It did not span the whole river, but reached only from the north bank to the southernmost island, from which a shallow ford led to the Welford bank.

Welford on Avon contains some thirty timber-framed cottages and farm-houses. Most of these date from the late seventeenth and early eighteenth centuries and display a rural style of architecture using wood, plaster and a pleasant warm red brick. Facing the church, a later and more elegant style of building is seen in the Georgian architecture of Church Farm. Two villages have grown together to make Welford on Avon. Perhaps the most striking feature of its evolution was the division of the parish between two counties. Until the tidying up of the county boundaries, first in 1894 and finally in 1931, Welford on Avon was split between Gloucestershire and Warwickshire. The manor that belonged before the Norman Conquest to Deerhurst Priory was part of Gloucestershire; the other lands of Welford belong to Warwickshire.

Bidford on Avon arose at a crossing-point in the valley that was fairly free from extensive flooding. The Romans chose this crossing of the Avon when they built Ryknield Street, a route through the heart of the Midlands that linked Cirencester and Derby. The Roman road was the first important influence in the shaping of

Bidford. It entered the village just below the site of the parish church by a ford, and today we can follow Ryknield Street through the village as the lane that runs along the eastern wall of the churchyard. In the first long phase of its history, from the time of an Anglo-Saxon settlement until the turn of the twelfth century, Bidford was probably a small street-village laid out along the north–south axis of the Roman road. The church marked the south end of the settlement, and to the north a number of farmsteads straggled along the road.

If we examine the topography of Bidford at the present time, we notice that the part of the village around the parish church stands isolated from the main part of the settlement along the High Street. The ancient ford has been disused for centuries and the main road that once ran by the churchyard now comes to a dead end on the steep bank above the northward-swinging meander of the Avon. Today, the main road from the south enters Bidford across a bridge that was built about the middle of the fifteenth century. It stands a quarter of a mile below the ford established by the Romans, and the diversion of the medieval road from the line of Ryknield Street, made at the time of the building of the Avon bridge, is still clearly visible (102514).

The fifteenth-century bridge that spans the Avon at Bidford leads the road into the west end of the High Street. It is not the first bridge across the river at this place. Whenever the first bridge was built, and history has preserved no record of it, it must have deeply changed the geography of Bidford. Its construction, at some time before 1450, led all the trade into the west end of the High Street and left the part around the church as a quiet backwater.

One can only guess at the time when these changes took place, but some events in Bidford's history suggest that it was about the middle of the thirteenth century. Bidford is one among many of the failed towns of England. It never had the full rights and status of a borough, but at least it was much more than a village. It held markets and fairs. Bidford first struggled to become a town in the thirteenth century. At that time it was owned for a few years by Llewelyn, Prince of North Wales, who had acquired lands in the Avon Valley as part of a dowry when he married King John's daughter, Joan, in 1206. In 1220 Llewelyn obtained the right to hold a weekly market at Bidford. In the years after 1220 Bidford probably became a busy trading-centre; and merchants, shopkeepers and artisans set themselves up in the High Street. Markets were held in the triangular open space that stood to the north of the church, which today is largely filled in by buildings dating from times after the middle of the sixteenth century.

Another clue to the making of a small town at Bidford in the thirteenth century may be found in its appearance at the present time. The cottages and houses that flank the High Street have a continuous built-up frontage on to the pavement. There are no gardens in front of the houses and no spaces between. A large-scale map shows that this continuous line of buildings occupies a series of long, narrow plots leading back at right-angles from the street. These are identical with the 'burgage tenements' that are a basic feature of the geography of medieval towns.

Two other features of Bidford suggest that it was a growing place in the thirteenth century. The present church of St Lawrence dates mainly from about 1250. The nave was probably built on the foundations of an earlier church – the simple chapel that was part of the parish of Salford Priors. The rebuilding and enlarging of Bidford's church suggests a growth in population and rising prosperity. A few years later, in 1264, Bidford got the right to hold two annual fairs – a fact that also points to the rise of a busy little trading-centre at this crossing of the Avon. Although we do not know when the first bridge was built across the Avon into Bidford, it is most likely that it happened sometime between 1220 and 1260 when the growing traffic compelled the construction of a good stone bridge to replace the hazards and delays of a ford that must have been impassable when the river ran high with flood waters.

Below Bidford the face of Cleeve Hill rises steeply from the Avon's flood plain. Until the middle of the nineteenth century, Cleeve Hill was an important source of building-stone. The thin bands of Liassic limestone were quarried for building materials, for the headstones of graves, and the rock was burnt for lime to improve the heavy clay soils of this belt of country. The grass-grown pits and the disturbed ground of the forgotten quarries can be easily traced and below the escarpment, on the bank of the Avon at the Fish and Anchor ford (065471), there is a ruined lime-kiln. Formerly lime was sent by water in the days when the Avon was a busy navigable river. The limestone quarries of this district have been worked for many centuries. The earliest and most vivid reference to the industry occurs in Domesday Book where we read, under the entry for Offenham (0546), that a team of oxen was used to draw stone from the quarries 'to the church'. Rarely does this tax survey of the Norman Conquest produce so vivid an aside on the life of medieval England. But here we are told that stone was dragged from the quarries, scarcely a mile away on the face of Cleeve Hill, to the church that was being built about the year 1086 on the dry terrace above the marshy flood plain of the Avon.

North and Middle Littleton is a twin settlement eastward of the crest of Cleeve Hill. The first settlement here was Middle Littleton with its church and manor-house. North Littleton, a few hundred yards away, began as an offshoot of the main village. This event must have happened in the first decades of the Saxon colonisation because both places were in existence when the Littletons were granted to Evesham Abbey in A.D. 703 by the King of Mercia. The shape and layout of North Littleton also points to its origin as a daughter settlement; its farmsteads and cottages are arranged in an open plan along a lane forming a loop across the stream that drains the Littletons.

The open fields of these villages lay on the gentle slopes to the east of the crest of Cleeve Hill. At North and Middle Littleton the open fields were not enclosed

176

until the second decade of the nineteenth century. On the other hand, the enclosure of most of the open arable fields at South Littleton took place two centuries earlier. A land survey of 1635 says that there was 'an exchange division and inclosure agreed betweene the lord and tennents of the whole fieldes in the first or second year of King James' reign'. If we look at the field boundaries of these parishes on the 2½-inch map, we can distinguish the two periods of enclosure. At North and Middle Littleton the results of the Parliamentary Enclosure Award of 1811 may be noticed in fields that are mainly square in shape. By contrast the fields of South Littleton form long and narrow rectangles that point to the enclosure of bundles of strips at the beginning of the seventeenth century.

The parishes to the north of the Avon Valley display several different features of settlement geography from the places that straddle the Cleeve Hill escarpment. Both Salford Priors (0751) and Norton (0448) are much bigger than the average parish of the left bank. Salford Priors covers almost 5000 acres. Each parish contains an ancient mother village that dates back, at least, to the first period of the Anglo-Saxon settlement in the Avon Valley. In the outlying parts of the parish are a number of daughter settlements. Some are of pre-Domesday date; others came into existence in the great phase of colonisation and woodland clearance during the twelfth and thirteenth centuries. In contrast, the parishes to the east of the Avon have no outlying hamlets and the lonely, separate farm is a rare feature of the landscape.

Norton, the mother settlement of Norton and Lenchwick, is a 'street village'. Its farmsteads and cottages stand in a line along the main road from Evesham to Alcester. The parish church (042478), dedicated to St Egwin, stands at the south end of Norton village. St Egwin was the founder of Evesham Abbey, and this dedication points to one of the chief themes in the medieval history of this part of the Avon Valley. For 800 years Evesham Abbey was the greatest landowner in this district; it has left its mark on the landscape not only in saintly dedications but also in the history of forest clearance and settlement.

The place-name, Lenchwick, helps us to unravel something of its early history. The suffix *wick* means an 'outlying pasture' or 'dairy farm'. When Lenchwick (034472) was named in the eighth-century document of the gift to Evesham Abbey there was only one house at this place – the single dairy farm remembered in the place-name. Lenchwick reappears in the history of Evesham Abbey at the beginning of the fourteenth century when there is a record of 'land that was cleared and brought into cultivation by Abbot Randolph'. The same document mentions that between 1214 and 1229 he built a grange there and made a fish-pond. Here we observe the role of the abbey as an agent of colonisation and a destroyer of the primitive woodland. Even today we can locate the site of the medieval fish-pond in the valley of the tiny brook that flows through the parish to the Avon (033469).

The pattern of settlement in the larger parish of Salford Priors resembles that of

Norton. Around the core-village, close to the north bank of the Avon, lie a number of outlying hamlets. Abbot's Salford (0650), Wood Bevington (0553), Cock Bevington (0552) and Dunnington (0653) are all outlying settlements in this large parish. Several phases of settlement history may be discerned here. Wood Bevington is typical of the woodland colonisation that appeared after Domesday times. A few timber-framed cottages are scattered along a lane that ends at the site of a manor-house. Cock Bevinton reveals still another aspect of the development of this complex parish. Here, at Bevington Hall (056526), is the site of a hamlet that was deserted in 1506 when William Grey converted 64 acres of arable land to pasture. Forty people of this large hamlet became homeless. The change-over to sheep-farming was continued by his son and, in 1547, more houses had been pulled down and another 180 acres enclosed as pasture.

Along the main road that crosses the parish to Alcester, still another type of settlement emerged in the eighteenth century. Here, around Iron Cross (061523), a number of roadside cottages were built in the 1780s. This resulted from the enclosure of Dunnington Heath (0652) in 1783. Twenty-five cottages were scattered over Dunnington Heath before the enclosure converted the common waste to hedged fields; the inhabitants of these squatters' cottages were rehoused along the post-enclosure road.

The evolution of the landscape of Salford Priors had not come to an end with the enclosure of the heath in the eighteenth century. On the western boundary of the parish place-names point to a former tract of woods and waste land. Bevington Waste (042534) was an extensive tract of tangled woodland that was cleared and ploughed up for the first time in 1872.

Stratford on Avon and Evesham

Stratford on Avon and Evesham both stand at important crossing-places of the river. Stratford means 'the street ford', and there a Roman road crossed the Avon. It was a minor road, joining the Ryknield Street at Alcester with the Fosse Way. Evesham cannot claim a road of Roman origin, but it was certainly an important medieval crossing of the river. At the time of the suppression of the monasteries, in Henry VIII's reign, the royal commissioners described Evesham as 'a great thoroughfare from the Marches of Wales to London'. But no town owes its origin to the facts of geography alone. Towns are made by men, and in their beginnings they are the expression of the will of human beings.

Evesham ranks among the earliest towns of the West Midlands, owing its origin to the monastery that was founded there at the beginning of the eighth century. The exact date when a town came into existence at the abbey gates is not known. Certainly it was before the Norman Conquest, because Edward the Confessor granted Evesham the privileges of a *port* and gave the Abbot the right to hold markets there in 1055. In Anglo-Saxon England the granting of the rights of *port* meant that a place was able to develop trade and commerce. Evesham must have been a lively and growing town by the first half of the eleventh century.

Stratford on Avon belonged to the bishops of Worcester, part of an estate which had been in their hands since the end of the seventh century. The core of the property lay at Old Stratford on the north bank of the Avon, and now in the part of the town around Holy Trinity Church. Stratford remained a rural estate of the bishops of Worcester until the close of the twelfth century. Then, in 1196, Bishop John de Coutances secured from Richard I the right to hold markets there. Half a century later, in 1252, a survey of Stratford on Avon mentions that it had 240 burgages. In half a century an urban community had come into being on the bank of the Avon. The date of its creation must have been about the year 1200. Stratford seems to have grown little in the following three centuries because another survey of the town, in 1590, notes that it had 217 houses 'belonging to the lord of the manor'.

The outline of the town created by the bishops of Worcester can still be recognised in the street-plan of Stratford on Avon (see Fig. 11d). Between the Memorial Theatre and Clopton Bridge (206548) a regular gridiron of streets extends westward from the bank of the Avon and marks the core of the medieval town. Three streets run parallel to the river and another three streets lie at right-angles. The first buildings in the bishops' new town were probably put up along Bridge Street, just to the west of its crossing of the Avon. Here the road from London opened up into a wide market place. By the end of the fourteenth century the open space of the market had been largely filled in with buildings between Wood Street, Henley Street and Guild Street (Pl. 11e).

Evesham did not receive its first borough charter until 1604, threequarters of a century after the oppressive control of the abbey had been removed. Stratford on

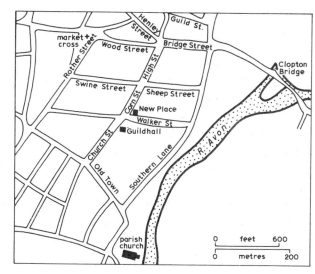

Fig. 11d

Town plan of Stratford with its medieval features and gridiron pattern of streets

Avon waited until 1553 for a borough charter, more than 300 years after its foundation. Both towns never had any defensive walls. This was a usual feature of monastic towns and places that grew up under the wing of the church. Evesham, even more than Stratford, reveals its history through its layout and architecture. The abbey site still dominates the town, even though for decades after the dissolution of the monasteries it provided one of the richest quarries for building-stone and lead. The town's two chief churches, St Lawrence and All Saints, stand side by side within the abbey wall, where they were founded by the monastery as chapels for the inhabitants of Evesham (see Pl. 11*f*). The town of Evesham clung to the walls of the monastery. The market place flanked the abbey to the north-west, and under the northern wall of the monastery, in Bridge Street, the first merchants and traders of Evesham built their houses. To the north of Bridge Street, the narrow streets and lanes show traces of a rectangular layout and suggest the site of a small medieval planned town. Perhaps this is the quarter of Evesham that is called 'the new borough' in a document from the end of the twelfth century. This document contains a list of the inhabitants of Evesham who paid rents. There are nearly 200 of them, and they are divided between four parts of the town – Evesham, Greenhill, the Barton, and the new borough (*de novo burgo*). The last phrase suggests that a new part had been added to Evesham in the second half of the twelfth century with some of the rights and status of a borough. The oldest part of Evesham, which had been in existence from before the Norman Conquest, probably belonged to the High Street and the vicinity of the main gate of the abbey.

Plate 11e   Stratford on Avon: the regular street-plan of the town created at the end of the twelfth century by the Bishop of Worcester. Note the large filled-in market site at the northern edge of the medieval town (date of photo 1963).

At Evesham much of the site of the medieval town has been built over with red-brick terraces, small factory buildings and warehouses. The line of a former street now ends abruptly in a factory yard. It is likely that this piece of Evesham became derelict after the closing of its great abbey in 1539; trade declined and the town no longer had a large community of monks calling on its services. The land was redeveloped in the eighteenth century as the life of Evesham slowly expanded. A handful of industries developed there making woollen goods, linseed oil and bone-manure; but the most important was the manufacture of silk ribbons, and it was in the lanes behind Bridge Street that the industries of this period intruded.

At both Evesham and Stratford the initiative of the church and the influence of a great monastery led to the creation of active medieval towns. There is nothing in the physical geography of the Avon Valley that determined the development of towns at these particular places. In fact, the possibilities for town growth were equally great and favourable at both Bidford and Welford on Avon.

Further Reading

Buchanan, K. M. *Worcestershire*, pt 68 of the Land of Britain series, ed. L. D. Stamp (1944).
Fox, L. *The Borough Town of Stratford-upon-Avon* (1953).
Tomlinson, M. 'The River Terraces of the Lower Valley of the Warwickshire Avon', *Quarterly Journal of the Geological Society*, vol. LXXXI (1925) pp. 137–69.

Plate 11f Evesham: a pre-Domesday town that grew at the gate of an abbey. Bridge Street occupies the centre of the picture and to its right lies the quarter of the new borough laid out in the twelfth century (date of photo 1956).

Maps

O.S. 1-inch sheet 144 (Cheltenham and Evesham); O.S. $2\frac{1}{2}$-inch sheets SP 15, SP 25, SP 05 and SP 04.

Suggested Itinerary

A survey of the different forms of rural settlement may be made by car or bus. Leave Stratford by road A439 and after one mile take the lane (left) to Luddington (1652), a small linear settlement where the church was rebuilt on a new site close to the river in 1872. Return to the main road and at 145533 follow the lane into Welford. Make a study on foot of Welford and Weston on Avon. Take the road along the south bank of the Avon to Bidford. Note the excellent viewpoint above the river cliff about half a mile from Welford (141514). At 130513 stop to survey the site of the deserted village of Hillborough that can be seen clearly across the Avon. At Bidford examine the line of the Roman road across the Avon; note also the architectural features that give this place the appearance of a town. From Bidford take the road to Evesham through Cleeve Prior and Offenham. *En route*, note the wide use of the Lias limestone as a building material in Cleeve Prior; examine the escarpment of Cleeve Hill and trace out the evidence of former quarrying. At Offenham note the former ford across the Avon (065471), the market gardening at the foot of the Cleeve Hill escarpment and on the site of a former open field, the street form of this village that once belonged to Evesham Abbey.

Field Work

(*a*) For each settlement on the traverse between Stratford on Avon and Evesham note the various kinds of building-material.

(*b*) Select a part of the Avon Valley which shows two or more terraces in its cross-section, as for example around Luddington (1652) or Harvington (0548) (see map), and attempt to trace the edge of the terrace features on the ground and note their degree of preservation. Why are the lower terraces flatter and less dissected?

(*c*) For a small area which you can select between Cleeve Prior (0849) and North Littleton (0847), find out the ownership of the individual strips and make a map of the holdings of a single farmer.

Further Work

Using the $2\frac{1}{2}$-inch Ordnance Survey maps as a base, trace the course of the Avon between Stratford and Evesham. Plot the distribution of orchards in this tract of country. What kinds of land do they avoid and which sites are favoured by this type of farming? Can you suggest any reasons for the abundance of market gardening and orchards close to Evesham?

12 Withington – the Historical Geography of a Cotswold Village

Withington stands on the River Coln, a headstream of the distant Thames, not far from the crest of the Cotswold escarpment above Cheltenham. Here, only four miles from its source, the Coln is scarcely two yards wide and meanders through the rank pastures of the valley floor as a misfit stream. The main valley at Withington swings from side to side in sweeping curves. We note the great loop in the valley's course half a mile to the north-east of Withington church (0316). Again, the stretch of the Coln Valley between Withington mill and Cassey Compton (0515) swings through a long curve in the opposite direction. The stream today has little to do with the larger landforms of the valley that were probably shaped by a more powerful forerunner of the Coln, swollen by snow and glacial melt waters in the last phases of the Ice Age.

The dip-slope plateau of the Cotswolds, into which the Coln Valley is cut to a depth of 300 feet, is composed of the creamy limestone of the Inferior Oolite. The rock can be seen in the abandoned quarries close by the road from Withington to Compton Abdale where it crosses the summit of the plateau (044162). These shallow overgrown pits in the limestone were worked for local building-stone, and particularly for the thin grey slabs used in the making of walls at the time of the enclosure of Withington's open fields in 1819. We can see the limestone in cottages, farm-buildings and boundary walls, and everywhere on the plateau top, especially after a fresh ploughing shows the red-brown soil with a dense speckled rash of chunks of creamy rock.

The Upper Lias Clay lies beneath the Inferior Oolite and it is exposed in parts of the floor of the Coln Valley (Fig. 12a). For instance, the outcrop of the clay explains the broadening of the valley above Withington. The biggest of Withington's former open fields, the North Field, once stretched across the heavy soils of the Upper Lias Clay in this part of the valley. Geology accounts for the subtle differences in the landscape to the south of the village. Here, below the site of the mill, the Coln runs into a shallow gorge before the valley begins to open out once more towards Cassey Compton (0515). This miniature gorge-section is explained by the crossing of a tongue of the Inferior Oolite and the disappearance of the outcrop of the Upper Lias Clay.

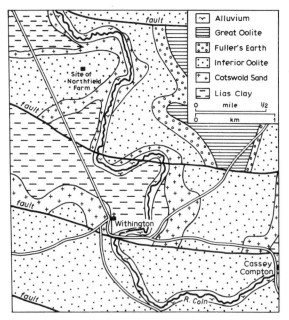

Fig. 12a Geology of the Withington area

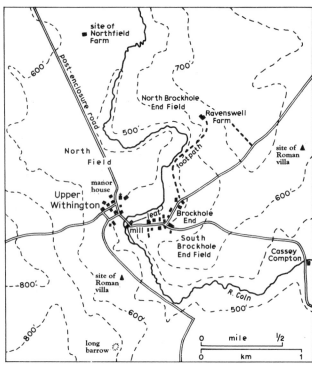

Fig 12b Withington and the sites of the former open fields

The Settlement Pattern of Withington Parish

If we take the $2\frac{1}{2}$-inch map and look at the arrangement of the buildings in Withington parish, we are soon able to recognise different kinds of grouping. In the main village the farms and cottages have two distinct patterns. Part of Withington is clustered around the parish church (031156). It has a compact shape and the manor-house, rectory and church stand opposed to the row of cottages and farmsteads along the lane that climbs westward from the village centre. The rest of Withington lies to the south of the church on the other side of the River Coln. Here the farms and cottages are stretched out for almost half a mile along the lane that leads over the limestone hill to Compton Abdale. Here the buildings are much more widely spaced than in the main part of the village around the church and manor-house. The grey stone houses and barns are interspersed with gardens and orchards. Several have been built on narrow plots of land and their gable-ends abut on to the road. This part of Withington has the typical arrangement of a street-village, and until about a century ago it had a separate name. On the Ordnance Survey map of 1828 it is labelled 'Broadwell End', and in earlier manorial records the name 'Brockhole End' refers to the same part of Withington. In fact, Withington seems to be made up of two villages; but the old name of the 'street settlement' has gradually fallen out of use over the past century (Fig. 12b).

184

Beyond the nucleated settlement that forms the core of Withington parish are a number of hamlets and isolated farms. Some of these date back before the Norman Conquest; some sites seem to have been inhabited in prehistoric times. For instance, at Foxcote (013183) relics of the Iron Age have been discovered, including the bones of animals and pottery that date back to the first century B.C. A hoard of Roman coins, dating from the third and fourth centuries A.D., suggests that Foxcote was inhabited in late Roman times. Pegglesworth, a hamlet on the north-western margin of the parish (9918), was a Saxon foundation. The name means 'Paeccel's clearing' and a farm was probably made there at some time between the eighth and the tenth centuries. Upcote (022160), half a mile to the west of the main village, is another old settlement, because it is named in a tax survey at the end of the twelfth century. Some of the outlying farms are much younger. For example, Northfield Farm (028172) dates from the time of the enclosure of Withington's open fields in 1819.

The Prehistoric and Roman Features of Withington's Landscape

The oldest man-made object in the countryside around Withington dates back for at least 4000 years. It is the long barrow that stands on a spur above the twisting stream of the Coln (031142). Today you climb up to the barrow by a zigzag grassy track through a close coppice wood. The barrow, an untidy hummock overgrown with bramble and almost a hundred feet long, lies in a tiny clearing. Like the other long barrows that occur in nearly every parish on the Cotswolds, this was a communal burial place of Neolithic times. A fine example of this Cotswold type of grave may be seen a few miles to the north of Withington at Belas Knap (021255).

The Withington barrow is the most striking proof that men lived and died here in Neolithic times. Another piece of evidence from this period of prehistory between 3000 and 2000 B.C. comes from Foxcote (0118), in the form of a Neolithic stone axe. An analysis of the rock from which it is made shows that the axe originated 200 and more miles from Withington, in the Lake District. It is a product of the prehistoric axe factory that exploited the hard igneous rock outcropping on the steep slopes at the head of Great Langdale. Some kind of trade among the first farming peoples of the British Isles must have brought this axe from the chipping-floors of Langdale to this secluded Cotswold valley.

Another prehistoric feature of Withington's landscape is a trackway that ran northwards from Cirencester along the broad ridge of open country between the valleys of the Churn and Coln. Today this ancient road is part of the tangle of lanes and footpaths along the summit of the limestone ridge to the west of Withington.

The site of a Roman villa represents the next stage in man's use of the landscape of Withington. The villa stood on a flattened spur a few feet above the Coln, and only a quarter of a mile from the village centre on the lane to Chedworth (031148). Nothing can be seen of the villa today in the cornfield that stretches up the slope to the green curtain of Withington Woods. But if you visit the site after ploughing, proof of this villa whose buildings were 160 feet long can soon be found. Among the lumps of cream-coloured limestone that are a common feature of almost every Cotswold field you come across pieces of rich red tile from the remains of the Roman buildings that lie a yard deep beneath the soil.

Withington's Roman villa was excavated in the year 1811 by Samuel Lysons, a well-known archaeologist. At that time the open fields of Withington had not been enclosed and the site of the villa lay in Wood Field – a southward extension of the huge North Field. The discovery of bits of mosaic during the ploughing of 1810 had given rise to the suspicion of a buried Roman building. Samuel Lyson's excavation uncovered the remains of walls that were still four feet high and plastered on the inside. They were built of the local limestone and doubtless many of the pieces of stone that can be picked up in the field today belong to the villa. Eight of the rooms had tessellated pavements, and one of the mosaics – a picture of Orpheus – is now in the British Museum. It dates from the first part of the fourth century A.D. and provides proof that this piece of Withington was occupied and farmed in the late Roman period. After Samuel Lysons had finished his excavation of the Withington villa in the spring of 1812, the topsoil was put back and nothing remains on the ground today to point to the buildings beneath. If we want to form a clearer impression of the Roman villas in the Cotswolds, we have to visit the next parish, Chedworth, where a magnificent villa site has been excavated and is preserved by the Ministry of Works for all to see. Its discovery was just as much a piece of luck as the find at Withington. The site was located by bits of mosaic found in the soil of a rabbit warren in Chedworth Woods on a ferreting expedition in 1866.

Some other features of Withington parish probably date from Roman times. The lane that crosses the Coln on the south-eastern border of the parish at Cassey Compton (0515) is probably of Roman origin (see Pl. 12c). Today it climbs the hill slopes to Compton Abdale and probably began as a minor road joining the Roman villa estates in Compton Abdale, Withington and Chedworth with the regional capital at Cirencester. The parish boundaries in this part of the Cotswolds possibly date from the same time. Each parish hereabouts – Chedworth, Withington and Compton Abdale – contains a Roman villa, and it is likely that the modern parish coincides with the country covered by the Roman estate. The present parish boundary between Withington and Chedworth was probably first sketched as a line of demarcation between the two villa estates. H. P. R. Finberg belives that the site of the main village, around the church, was first occupied at this time by slaves who worked on the villa estate, and the North Field may well have formed the chief tract of arable land on the Roman estate.

186

Plate 12c

Plate 12c

*Cassey Compton
near Withington:
the lane
that climbs
out of the Coln Valley
probably formed the
boundary between the
Roman villa estates of
Withington and
Chedworth*

Plate 12d

*Withington, with the
core of the settlement
centred around the
parish church*

Medieval Withington and its Open Fields

Withington is really made up of two villages. Upper Withington, the oldest site, clusters around the church, and it is likely that a settlement was in existence there in Roman times (Pl. 12*d*). Lower Withington or Brockhole End was probably first settled at some time in the early part of the eighth century. The proof of the making of a village at Brockhole End may be found in a comparison of the two earliest Anglo-Saxon charters about Withington. The first document dates from the last quarter of the seventh century A.D., while the second comes from a century later, dating to A.D. 774. The charters show that the amount of land owned by the Saxon monastery at Withington increased by one hide between the two dates. It is likely that this fresh land was added as a result of the clearing of forest on the east bank of the Coln facing the old village.

The building of the new farmsteads at Brockhole End early in the eighth century has left its mark on the modern map of Withington in the course of the parish boundary along the Coln Valley. If we trace the eastern boundary of the parish, we notice that for the most part it follows the line of the River Coln. But from a point close to Northfield Farm (031170) to the place where it rejoins the river at Cassey Compton, the parish boundary diverges to the east and climbs to the summit of the limestone plateau (0416). The earliest boundary of Withington, possibly dating back to Roman times and the villa estate, must have followed the River Coln for the whole way. The river would form a natural divide between the lands of the Roman villa at Withington and those of the Roman estate centred on the villa whose site has been uncovered in a wood at Compton Abdale (048163). The founding of Brockhole End brought about this drastic reshaping of Withington's parish boundary.

The system of open fields that survived in Withington until 1819 provides even more striking proof of the existence of two separate villages. Withington had four open fields, while most Costwold villages practised a two-field system of farming. The main village, Upper Withington, cultivated the land on the valley-floor to the north of the church and on the gentle western slopes of the Coln Valley (0216). This patchwork of arable strips was the North Field. The tract of land was so large that it was always worked as two separate fields; the North Field composed the

Plate 12e   The South Field of Brockhole End on the spur above Cassey Compton. It was enclosed in 1819 (138152).

Plate 12f Cassey Compton: on the slopes of a dry-valley tributary to the River Coln, the terraces of prehistoric farming become visible in the clear sunlight of a January day

two open fields of Upper Withington. Brockhole End's two fields occupied the top of the plateau and the spurs and gentle valleys to the east of the Coln (0415). The lane that climbs the hill from Withington on its way to Compton Abdale separated the two fields. The South Field of Brockhole End occupied the whole of the broad spur around which the river meanders from Withington to Cassey Compton (see Pl. 12e). On the steep slope behind the farms and cottages of Lower Withington you can recognise the rectangular enclosures of groups of strips that were once part of this open field (036152). The North Field of Brockhole End occupied the big embayment on the east side of the Coln above Withington (0316). Here the steepest slopes in the whole of the parish were put under the plough, and evidence of former strip cultivation can still be seen under the right conditions (Pl. 12f). When the land is freshly ploughed, darker and lighter bands show up in the rust-brown soil. The steepest slopes of all, lying just to the west of Ravens-well Farm (039163), form a rough pasture with scattered scrubby thorn trees. Here you may faintly discern the outlines of former strips running up the valley side from the rank, weed-infested meadows by the Coln.

Four open fields existed at Withington until the beginning of the nineteenth century and they provide the most striking clue to the evolution of this settlement as two separate villages. As far back as one can go in time with the help of records and documents about Withington, the fields to the east and west of the River Coln were always worked as separate units. The farmers of Upper Withington always held their strips in the two parts of the North Field and never in the fields of Brockhole End. Similarly the farmers of Lower Withington, the street-village, possessed all their arable land on the eastern bank of the Coln in the North Brockhole End Field and the South Brockhole End Field.

The most revolutionary transformation in the landscape of Withington took place at the start of the nineteenth century with the enclosure of the four open fields. The present pattern of fields, the hedges, and the low boundary walls built of thin slabs of Cotswold limestone, all date from the years about 1819. Perhaps the most dramatic change made by the Enclosure Act was the cutting of a new road northwards from the village to meet the main road from Gloucester to Stow-on-the-Wold. This runs in a dead straight line for two miles across the site of the former North Field. It could easily be mistaken for a Roman road; in truth it is only a century and a half old. At a stroke the communications of Withington were revolutionised. Previously the outside world had been reached by taking the lane that climbs westward from the centre of Withington to follow the ridge top (016154) northwards towards Cheltenham. Early in the seventeenth century this route was described as 'the market way from Withington to Cheltenham'. A survey of 1299 refers to the same road as 'the Ridgeway', and in an even earlier Anglo-Saxon document that describes the boundaries of Withington it appears as 'the old stone way'.

The oldest lanes of Withington date back into prehistory; the newest belongs to the replanning of the lands of the village at the beginning of the nineteenth century. Since 1819 the only important change in the communications of Withington was the building of the railway in 1891. This single-tracked line used the Coln Valley as a way across the Cotswolds between Cheltenham and Cirencester. Now it is closed. Bridges across the narrow lanes are broken down; embankments and cuttings begin to fade into the countryside. The railway age is over for Withington. Its effects on the landscape have been negligible, far less than those of Roman and Saxon village founders or of Frederick Phelps, Daniel Trinder and Joseph Large, who were the commissioners of the Enclosure Award and who came to write its terms into the landscape in 1819.

Further Reading

Finberg, H. P. R. *Roman and Saxon Withington – a Study in Continuity*, University of Leicester, Department of English Local History, Occasional Papers No. 8 (1955).

Fisher, D. A. *St Michael's Church, Withington, Gloucestershire* (1960).

Fox, G. E. 'The Roman Villa at Chedworth', *Archaeological Journal*, vol. XLIV (1887) pp. 322–36.

Richmond, I. A. 'The Roman Villa at Chedworth', *Transactions of the Bristol and Gloucester Archaeological Society*, vol. LXXVIII (1959) pp. 5–23.

Maps

O.S. 1-inch sheet 144 (Cheltenham and Evesham); O.S. 2½-inch sheet SP 01; Geological Survey 1-inch sheet 235 (Cirencester).

Suggested Itineraries

(*a*) A field study of Withington should begin with a visit to the earliest prehistoric site in the parish, the Neolithic long barrow in Withington Woods (031142). Next, the field that contains the Roman villa should be visited (031149); follow with an inspection of the excavated Roman villa and museum at Chedworth, little more than a mile away (054135).

A study of the geography of the village should begin at the centre of Upper Withington with a visit to St Michael's Church. This contains fine Norman work from the middle of the twelfth century and it probably stands on the site of the minster or monastic church founded in Withington towards the end of the eighth century. From the centre of Withington follow the footpath to the south of the parish church that crosses the wide valley floor of the Coln. Join and follow the lane to Ravenswell Farm (039164). This route presents excellent views of the meandering Coln Valley above Withington, the misfit stream of the present day, and the site of the former north fields of Upper Withington and Brockhole End. Return to Withington by the lane that leads from Ravenswell Farm to the Compton Abdale road. This plateau top, close to the parish boundary, was a common sheep pasture before the Enclosure Act. Note the shallow quarries, now abandoned, where stone was got for building (044162).

Follow the road to Withington and note the layout of farms, cottages, and small enclosures in Brockhole End, also the signs of strips in a former open field on the slopes above. Crossing the Coln back into Upper Withington, you see the site of

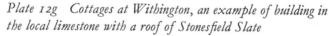

Plate 12g   Cottages at Withington, an example of building in the local limestone with a roof of Stonesfield Slate

the mill with its leat. This ground corn until late in the nineteenth century and it is almost certain that it stands in the same place as the mill mentioned in the Domesday Book's account of Withington.

(b) A longer excursion may be devised to study the roads of Withington, following the ancient ridgeway to the west, taking in the hamlet of Foxcote with its prehistoric associations, and returning by the post-enclosure road, noting Northfield Farm – an enclosure farm – and the site of Upcote, an early carving out of the open fields. Compare this with Cassey Compton that was likewise carved out of the South Brockhole End field at an early date.

Field Work

(a) During a visit to the villa at Chedworth make, in your field book, a sketch of the layout of a Roman villa. From the objects in the Chedworth museum make a page of sketches of things found on Roman villa sites.

(b) In your field book make a series of sketches of buildings and landscapes to show the various periods that have contributed to the making of Withington. A collection such as the following might be attempted:

  (i) the long barrow in Withington Woods
 (ii) a panorama sketch from a good viewpoint on the spurs to the east of the Coln showing the sites of the Roman villa, the main village of Withington, and the later street settlement of Brockhole End
(iii) Withington Church with details of late Norman architecture in the south porch
 (iv) the pattern of enclosure in the North Field seen from the lane to Ravenswell farm at 038162
  (v) Cotswold farm buildings in stone in Upper and Lower Withington.

Further Work

Use the 1-inch or 2½-inch maps of Withington to draw a large sketch-plan of the parish. Show the following features – the River Coln, the road network of the parish. Shade all land higher than 700 feet above sea level. Mark clearly following places and features of the landscape:

  (a) the sites of a Neolithic burial place and the Roman villa
  (b) a part of the parish boundary that may date back to Roman times
  (c) a place where a stone axe made in the Lake District was discovered
  (d) the site of the mill mentioned in Domesday Book
  (e) the site of North Brockhole End Field and the line of the boundary that separated it from the South Brockhole End Field
  (f) a piece of road that was made after the enclosure of Withington's open fields. Mark and name a farm that was built after the Parliamentary Act of Enclosure. What was the date of the enclosure of the four open fields?

Glossary

ADVECTION FOG   Formed when warm moist air is in contact with a cooler surface which reduces the temperature of the lower layers below dew point.

AIR MASS   A mass of considerable size with common characteristics of temperature and humidity originating from a specific source-area. The type of air mass depends on the nature·of its source and also any modifications which it might undergo on subsequent movement to another area.

ANGLO-SAXON PERIOD   Extends from the settlement of England by the Anglo-Saxons A.D. 450 until the Norman Conquest in the eleventh century.

ANTICLINE   An upfold of strata which dips outwards from a central axis often termed the crest.

ANTICYCLONE   An area of high pressure which often is associated with stable weather-conditions.

ARDEN SANDSTONE   A relatively thick sandstone occurring in the Keuper Marl beds of Worcestershire, Warwickshire and Gloucestershire but best seen in the Forest of Arden.

ASSART   A term that came into the English language after the Norman Conquest meaning to clear trees and bushes to make way for arable, hence 'a clearing in a forest'.

BASALT   A fine-grained, dark-coloured basic igneous rock which has cooled quickly as a result of extrusion at the surface.

BOULDER-CLAY   A heavy clay with an ill-assorted mass of rock fragments and boulders. It is a product of glacial activity and represents the debris carried by an ice sheet or glacier which subsequently deposited the clay.

BRECCIA   A rock composed of angular fragments cemented together in a finer matrix.

BRONZE AGE   A period of prehistory extending in the British Isles from 2000 B.C. to 500 B.C. and marked by the introduction of metal-working in bronze and copper.

BUNTER   The lower part of the Triassic system consisting mainly of sandstone and thick pebble-beds laid down under arid or semi-arid conditions about 200 million years ago.

BURGAGE   A plot of land or tenement in a borough that was held of the king or another lord for an annual money rent. Burgesses. the holders of burgage plots, were free from the usual services and rents in kind due to the lord of the manor.

BURGESS An inhabitant of a medieval borough who paid money rent in lieu of services and payments in kind to a manorial lord.

BURH Term applied to a type of settlement established in Wessex in the late ninth and tenth centuries, primarily for defensive purposes but with privileges that enabled some of them to evolve into towns.

CARTULARY A book in which the whole collection of records of a monastery is entered.

CHAMBERED TOMB A burial place, square or rectangular in shape, built of large stones and covered with a mound of earth and gravel. It is characteristic of the Neolithic period.

CHASE A hunting-ground that was unenclosed and defined only by recognisable topographical features. As opposed to a 'forest' – the property of the Crown – a 'chase' was held in medieval England by a subject.

CONGLOMERATE A rock composed of rounded pebbles cemented together in a matrix of finer material.

CONURBATION A continuously built-up area resulting from the coalescence of several expanding towns.

COOMBE A short, steep-sided valley with an abrupt head characteristic of chalk scenery but also encountered in other rock formations as in the Jurassic limestone along the face of the Cotswolds.

DIORITE A coarse-grained igneous rock which has been extensively quarried because of its value as a road metal.

DOBUNNI An Iron Age tribe of Roman Britain occupying the Cotswolds and the plain of the Severn below Gloucester.

DOLERITE A basic igneous rock, i.e. containing about 50 per cent silica, usually fine- or medium-grained and commonly occurring in dykes or sills.

DOMESDAY BOOK A survey of England ordered by William the Conqueror in 1086. It is contained in two volumes and the material, gathered by travelling commissioners, is arranged under counties and property owners.

DRIFT A term applied to the various materials – boulder clays, sands, pebbles – deposited by an ice sheet or glacier or meltwater issuing from them.

DRUMLIN A smooth elongated hummock of boulder clay varying in length from 100 feet to almost a mile. It has steep sides and the long profile is typically asymmetrical with a steeper slope facing the direction of ice movement. Drumlins often occur in groups forming what is termed 'basket-of-eggs' topography.

END-MORAINE A ridge formed of debris left behind at the margin of an ice sheet or at the snout of a glacier.

ERRATIC A rock or boulder transported by ice and deposited some distance from its original outcrop.

ESCARPMENT A continuous steep slope usually formed of resistant rock.

ESKER   A landform often in the form of a ridge or series of mounds consisting mainly of sands and gravels. The name is derived from the Irish *eiscir*. It is believed that the esker represents the material carried by sub-glacial streams.

ETRURIA MARL   Consists of purple, red or mottled clays found in the Upper Coal Measures. It has been extensively worked for the manufacture of Staffordshire blue bricks and pipes.

FELDON   A medieval regional name applied to south Warwickshire between the Avon Valley and the Middle Lias escarpment. In the Middle Ages this was dominantly an area of open-field settlements and an area strongly affected by the desertions of the fifteenth century.

FEUDAL AID   A tax levied by the king upon his vassals for a special purpose such as the raising of a ransom or the financing of a royal marriage.

FIRE-CLAY   A tough claystone which commonly underlies coal-seams. Originally it is considered to have been the soil which supported the coal-forming vegetation.

FOSSE WAY   A Roman road across the Midlands that connected Lincoln with Exeter via Leicester, Cirencester and Bath.

GEORGIAN   A period in English architecture that occupies most of the eighteenth century.

GIPPING GLACIATION   The second of the three main glacial episodes which affected the British Isles during the Pleistocene; equivalent terms are Chalky Boulder Clay Glaciation or Riss Glaciation.

GLEY SOIL   Formed as a result of water logged conditions and characterised by deoxidation which often gives a bluish grey colour.

GOTHIC   Term describing architectural styles between the twelfth and the sixteenth centuries. The Gothic Revival, a deliberate attempt to recreate the style and atmosphere of the Middle Ages, dominated English architecture in the middle of the nineteenth century.

GRANGE   A farm belonging to a monastery. The term was imported into England with the Norman Conquest.

HAMLET   A settlement containing only a few dwellings and too small to be called a village. It is often used to describe a subsidiary settlement in a parish remote from the main village and church.

HENGE MONUMENT   A circle of uprights in stone or wood of Bronze Age date.

HUNSTANTON GLACIATION   The last of the three glaciations which affected the British Isles during the Pleistocene. The ice only extended as far south as Hunstanton in Norfolk, hence the name for this glacial phase.

HURST   A copse or wood. The suffix 'hurst' is of late Anglo-Saxon date as a place name element and associated with areas of secondary settlement.

HWICCE   A people of early Saxon England whose territories lay between Mercia and Wessex, particularly in the northern Cotswolds and the Avon Valley.

HYDRAULIC LIMESTONE   A bed found in the Lower Lias which has been extensively worked for the making of lime and hydraulic cement around Rugby and other places in the Midlands.

ICE AGE   A period which began about a million years ago when true glacial conditions existed over large parts of Europe and North America. Between the main glacial episodes there were warmer interglacial phases.

IGNEOUS ROCK   Derived from the solidification of molten material or magma.

INFERIOR OOLITE   A bed in the Jurassic system characterised by thin, well-bedded limestones.

INLIER   An isolated part of a geological formation surrounded by younger beds.

IRON AGE   A period of British prehistory beginning about 500 B.C. and marked by the introduction of iron in the making of tools and weapons. It continues until the Roman occupation in the first century A.D., though the use of the term Romano-British Iron Age implies the extension of this period until the early fifth century A.D.

KAME   A hummocky deposit of sand and gravel laid down along or near the front of an ice sheet by meltwater streams.

KEUPER MARL   One of the major formations of the Trias consisting largely of a red clay but with occasional beds of sandstone.

KNICKPOINT   A distinct break in the longitudinal profile of a river marking the point of contact between an old valley floor upstream and a younger rejuvenated section downstream.

LACCOLITH   A solidified mass of igneous rock often in the form of a swelling like a blister.

LEAT   An artificial channel which is used to carry river water from a point upstream to a mill.

LEY   Old English place-name ending describing a clearing in woodlands associated with the later stages of the Anglo-Saxon settlement.

LEY   The name given to a tract of land under grass or clover within an arable rotation. *Short ley* is applied to land under grass for only a few years. With longer period of up to twenty years before reploughing the land is described as a *long ley*.

LIAS   A formation of the Lower Jurassic consisting largely of clays, though in the Midlands important limestone beds, like the White Lias, are to be found as well as sandy ironstones or marlstones. The name is based on a quarryman's term for a flat stone.

LOAM   A permeable friable soil with an admixture of clay and sand particles and a relatively high humus content.

LUDLOW SHALES   A formation within the Silurian characterised by grey shales and sandy mudstones with occasional thin beds of limestone. Being easily eroded, the outcrop usually gives rise to low ground.

MAGONSAETAN The name of people in early Anglo-Saxon England whose territory lay west of the Severn, largely in Herefordshire, and which was later absorbed by Mercia.

MARL A clay with an admixture of at least 15 per cent calcium carbonate.

MARLSTONE A bed within the lower Jurassic rocks of the Midlands consisting of an orange-brown sandstone but with important oolitic iron-ores at certain horizons.

MERCIA The Midland kingdom of Anglo-Saxon England with a capital at Tamworth. During the eighth century King Offa defined the western frontier of Mercia by the construction of a dike from the mouth of the Wye to the coast of North Wales near Prestatyn. In the tenth century and after the long period of Danish raids and invasions Mercia was absorbed by Wessex.

MERE A small circular lake formed either by the melting of a mass of dead ice or as a result of subsidence after the removal of underground salt deposits, as in Cheshire.

MILLSTONE GRIT A hard, coarse-grained massive sandstone occurring in the Carboniferous between the underlying Carboniferous Limestone and the overlying Coal Measures. Although predominantly a coarse sandstone, occasional shale beds and even thin seams of coal sometimes occur.

MORAINE A mass of glacial material, such as boulder clay, carried by ice. When the ice subsequently melts this debris may form a distinctive landscape feature, as a pronounced ridge, to which the term moraine is also applied.

NEOLITHIC PERIOD A major epoch of prehistory associated with the development of agriculture and the domestication of animals. In the British Isles it lasted from about 3000 B.C. until 1900 B.C.

NEW RED SANDSTONE A formation characterised by red sandstones and clays; part of the Trias.

OOLITIC LIMESTONE A Jurassic limestone characterised by small rounded grains or ooliths.

OPEN FIELD A large field communally farmed and composed of strips. Two or more such fields were characteristic of English villages before the enclosure movement.

OUTWASH FAN A landform feature composed of sand and gravel beds which have been deposited by streams issuing from glaciers or ice sheets.

OVERFLOW CHANNEL Formed by the escape of water from a glacial lake. If the lake level subsequently falls or if the lake disappears entirely the overflow channel may become completely dry.

OVERSAILING The projection of the first floor of a building above the ground floor, particularly in the Wealden type of house in south-eastern England and the Midlands.

PARLIAMENTARY ENCLOSURE ACT   The legal document by which common rights over a piece of land are extinguished and the land turned into 'ordinary freehold'.

PERIGLACIATION   A process typified by alternate freezing and thawing of the surface rock-layers particularly in areas marginal to an ice sheet.

PIPE ROLLS   One of the most important series of English documents. They record the affairs of the royal exchequer. The first surviving pipe roll dates back to 1130 and there is an unbroken series from 1156 to 1830.

PODSOL   A soil from which the base elements have been removed by leaching. It is commonly associated with heath or coniferous forest vegetation.

POLL-TAX RETURNS   Medieval lists of persons or 'heads' subject to a fixed tax. The first survey for what was a revolutionary system of taxation was made in 1377.

PRE-CAMBRIAN   The period of geological time before the beginning of the Palaeozoic epoch about 600 million years ago.

PRO-GLACIAL LAKE   Formed by the pounding back of water between an ice front and higher ground. With the melting of the ice the lake disappeared.

QUARTZITE   A rock formed almost entirely of pure quartz recemented by silica. It is usually hard and resistant to erosion and commonly occurs in veins.

QUATERNARY   The most recent of the geological systems which began with the onset of the Ice Age in Britain about 600,000 years ago

REJUVENATION   A process of renewed erosion caused by an alteration of the relative levels of land and sea.

RIVER TERRACE   The remains of a former flood plain of a river now raised to form a bench or shelf.

SCARP   See 'escarpment'.

SHALE   A rock formed from mud which has been compressed into thin layers that split easily.

SILT   Material laid down in water with particles intermediate in size between those of clay and sand.

SILURES   A British tribe in the Roman period who occupied part of south Wales and the southern Welsh Marches in Monmouthshire and the region of the Wye Valley.

SILURIAN   A major geological period of the Palaeozoic which began about 400 million years ago. The name is taken from the ancient tribe, the Silures.

SLITTING-MILL   A site where rolled iron plates were cut into long rods by means of a set of rollers with regularly spaced ridges. The rollers were driven by water-power. The rods were then used for making nails, etc.

SOLIFLUCTION   The movement of a wetted surface soil-layer over a frozen sub-surface, particularly under cold conditions during the Pleistocene.

SWAG   A depression in the ground caused by mining subsidence and in which water collects. In the Black Country the term is used in a more restricted sense to describe such a sheet of water.

TAXATIO ECCLESIASTICA   A valuation of church properties in England made in 1291 for Pope Nicholas IV to be used as a basis for papal taxation. It is the most precious survey of ecclesiastical estates made in the Middle Ages.

TOPSHOP   Industrial premises that form the upper storey of a dwelling-house, particularly used in the former silk-weaving quarters of Coventry and in the industrial villages of east Warwickshire.

TRIASSIC   The first of the geological periods of the Mesozoic lasting from about 225 to 180 million years ago. The rocks associated with it are principally sandstones and clays, predominantly red in colour, and they were formed under arid or semi-arid conditions.

TURNPIKE   A toll road of a kind widely constructed in Britain in the eighteenth century.

WELDON   A regional name applied to the forested parts of north Warwickshire during the Middle Ages.

WENLOCK LIMESTONE   A prominent bed in the Silurian which being relatively resistant to erosion gives rise to distinctive isolated hills such as the Wren's Nest near Dudley. It was formerly extensively quarried as a flux for the iron industry.

WICK   An Old English word from the Latin *vicus* meaning a dwelling-place or a farm. Most commonly it means a 'dairy farm' in English place-names.

WORTH   A term meaning 'enclosure' or 'homestead' associated with the late secondary colonisation of the Anglo-Saxons, and one which was actively used in the long period of settlement expansion after the Norman Conquest.

WREOCENSAETAN   A tribe of early Anglo-Saxon England whose territories lay in the Severn basin around the Wrekin. It was later absorbed by Mercia, the powerful Saxon kingdom centred on the Trent Valley and the Lichfield–Tamworth district.

Index